Corporate Foresight

T0312135

The world changes like the patterns in a kaleidoscope: trends expand, contract, break up, melt, disintegrate and disappear, while others are formed. Change – as opposed to stasis – is our normal condition, the only certainty in our lives, hence the need to create tools that provide organizations with the means to tackle change and navigate complexity. We must accept the reality of constant change and be prepared for a heavy shift in perspective: interconnection versus separation, acceleration versus linearity and discontinuity versus continuity.

Anticipating the future requires more than the traditional predictive models (*forecasting*) based on the forward projection of past experiences. Advanced methods use anticipation logic (*foresight*) and build probable scenarios taking into account weak signals, emerging trends, coexisting presents and potential paths of evolution.

Corporate foresight is fundamental to interpret and lead change. The two cornerstones of foresight are organization and management. As concerns organization, the authors advocate the separation of research (oriented to the market of tomorrow) from development (oriented to the market of today), the establishment of a foresight unit and the concentration of research activities mainly on the acquisition and recombination of external know-how. As regards management, after an overview of state-of-the-art literature on forecasting methods, the authors propose the implementation of a "future coverage" methodology, which enables companies to measure and verify the consistency between trends, strategic vision and offered products. These organizational and managing tools are then tested in a case study: the Italian company Eurotech SpA, a leader in the ICT sector.

Alberto F. De Toni is currently President of the Foundation CRUI (Conference of Italian University Rectors). Previously, he was Rector of the University of Udine and President of the Italian Association of Industrial Engineering and Management. He is member of the Academia Europaea and Professor of Operations Management and Management of Complex Systems.

Roberto Siagri is president and CEO of Eurotech SpA, of which he was a co-founder. He has a degree in Solid State Physics and has worked in the field of computer architectures. His current interests include human–machine interaction and the applicative scenarios of cloud computing.

Cinzia Battistella is associate professor of Polytechnic Department of Architecture and Engineering at the University of Udine. She has participated in foresight studies at the Area Science Park in Trieste and has explored future-related issues in the sectors of agrifood, telecommunications and e-governance.

Corporate Foresight
Anticipating the Future

Revised Edition

Alberto F. De Toni, Roberto Siagri and Cinzia Battistella

Translated from Italian
by Lidia Cremonese

Cover design by Gianluca Biotto

Volume printed with the contribution of
the University of Udine

Routledge
Taylor & Francis Group

LONDON AND NEW YORK

Revised edition published 2021
by Routledge
2 Park Square, Milton Park, Abingdon, Oxon, OX14 4RN

and by Routledge
52 Vanderbilt Avenue, New York, NY 10017

Routledge is an imprint of the Taylor & Francis Group, an informa business

First edition published by Routledge 2017

British Library Cataloguing-in-Publication Data
A catalogue record for this book is available from the British Library

Library of Congress Cataloging-in-Publication Data
Names: De Toni, Alberto F., author. | Siagri, Roberto, author. |
Battistella, Cinzia, author.
Title: Corporate foresight : anticipating the future / Alberto F. De Toni,
Roberto Siagri and Cinzia Battistella ; translated from the Italian by
Lidia Cremonese.
Description: Revised edition. | Abingdon, Oxon ; New York, NY : Routledge,
2021. | Includes bibliographical references and index.
Identifiers: LCCN 2020027310 (print) | LCCN 2020027311 (ebook) |
Subjects: LCSH: Forecasting. | Technological innovations. | Corporate
culture. | Organizational culture.
Classification: LCC CB158 .D437 2020 (print) | LCC CB158 (ebook) | DDC
303.49--dc23
LC record available at https://lccn.loc.gov/2020027310
LC ebook record available at https://lccn.loc.gov/2020027311

ISBN: 978-0-367-56746-0 (hbk)
ISBN: 978-1-003-09923-9 (ebk)

Typeset in Sabon
by KnowledgeWorks Global Ltd.

To the men and women
who have the future in their bones.

Contents

Figures

Tables

Contributors

Cinzia Battistella has a degree and PhD in Management Engineering. She is an associate professor at the Polytechnic Department of Architecture and Engineering of the University of Udine. She has discussed her PhD thesis on Corporate Foresight in the telecommunications sector, developing several case studies (Telecom Italia, Vodafone, Ericsson, Alcatel Lucent, Cisco, Tre, Wind). She has participated in foresight and technology roadmapping studies at the Area Science Park in Trieste, the largest science and technology park in Italy. She has explored future-related issues in other sectors, namely agrifood and e-governance. She is the author of several papers published in national and international journals, including *Technological Forecasting & Social Change*.

Alberto Felice De Toni has a Bachelor and Master degree in Chemical Engineering and a PhD in Science of Industrial Innovation from the University of Padua. He is currently President of the Foundation CRUI (Conference of Italian University Rectors). Previously, he was Rector of the University of Udine, President of the AiIG (Italian Association of Management Engineering), President of the MIUR (National Ministry of Education, University and Research) Committee for the Reorganization of Technical and Professional Education. He is member of the Strategic Steering Committee of European University Institute, member of the Academia Europaea and Professor of Operations Management and Management of Complex Systems. Among his many publications, he is the co-author of Open Facility Management (2009) and International Operations Management (2011).

Ugo Morelli teaches Psychology of Work and Organizations, and Clinical Psychology of Work and Institutions at the University of Bergamo. He is scientific director of the UNESCO World Natural Heritage Management Master, and of the Network of Education and Research UNESCO Dolomites. He is the author of several publications, including *Mente e bellezza. Arte, creatività e innovazione* (Allemandi, Torino 2010) and *Il conflitto generative* (Città Nuova Editrice, Roma 2013).

Renato Quaglia, project manager, coordinator of institutions and cultural projects, artistic director and organizational manager, is Professor of History of the Cultural Enterprise and Economics of Culture at the University *Suor Orsola Benincasa* of Naples. He is president of the CRT Foundation in Milan; coordinator of *Cluster,* a project for development and new employment in the Spanish Quarters of Naples; director of the Naples Theater Festival and general director of the Campania Festival Foundation from 2007 to 2011; organizational director of the Venice *Biennale* from 1998 to 2007. Advisor for development projects of *Regioni Obbiettivo 1,* he has collaborated with Studiare Sviluppo of MAE and with the DPS of the Ministry of Economic Development; he is *Chevalier de l'Ordre des Arts et des Lettres* of the French Republic.

Roberto Saracco has a degree in Mathematics from the University of Turin, and began his career in 1971 at CSELT. He is president and director of the Italian node of EIT (European Institute of Innovation & Technology) located in Trento. From 2001 to 2011 he was director of the Telecom Italia Future Centre in Venice. In 1996–1997 he chaired the Visionary Group to orient European research on the theme of Super Intelligent Networks. Recently he has been a member of the Internet 2020 Strategy Group and of the European Research Network (GEANT) Expert Group. He is the author of over one hundred publications, including six books. *The Disappearance of Telecommunications* (1998) has been published in the US by IEEE. He has been and is a professor at several Italian and foreign universities.

Roberto Siagri is president and CEO of Eurotech SpA, which he co-founded in 1992. The company is listed on the Milan stock exchange since 2005 and has branches in Europe, North America and Asia. He has a degree in Solid State Physics from the University of Trieste and has worked in the field of computer architectures. His current interests include man–machine interaction and the applicative scenarios of Cloud computing. He has been contract professor of Electronics of Digital Systems at the University of Udine. In the course of his career, he has received several prizes and awards, including the "Entrepreneur of the Year 2006" award for the finance category from *Ernst & Young Italy.*

Foreword

Roberto Saracco

I have spent most of my professional life either in research centers or in close contact with the world of research, which over the years, as a result of progressive demands for finalization, has turned into the world of research and development. Even today, as the head of one of the nodes of the European Institute for Technology and Innovation, I live in this environment and I am well aware of its tensions.

My long-standing experience, gained first in the field of telecommunications and later in the field of information technology, is certainly sectorial; therefore, I cannot claim that what I have observed firsthand is necessarily true for other sectors, such as medical research, agriculture and so on.

What I have witnessed in the area of what is now called Information and Communications Technology (ICT) is basically the failed attempt to bring together research and innovation. And, I think there is a very precise reason behind this failure.

Research is a tool that converts money into knowledge. You give money to researchers who devote time and passion to the achievement of a goal, who come up against seemingly impenetrable walls and who eventually "understand" and generate knowledge. Innovation, on the other hand, is a tool that uses knowledge to produce money, drawing on many different types of knowledge, not only on those resulting from "home-made" research.

Innovation and research are therefore very different activities that require different skills and different dispositions. People working in research are probably unsuited to develop innovation, and vice versa.

Unfortunately, the two roles have always been perceived as one and the same. In many companies, when funds began to shrink and market competition got tough, researchers were asked to "finalize", to bring their results to the market in order to generate cash: the research and development department was born, and it did not perform as expected.

Undoubtedly, innovation is connected to research because it stems from it, in the sense that innovation uses knowledge, which is the product of research. The mistake, I think, lies in the belief that research provides semi-finished results, which require some further refinement (industrialization?) to become products. But, it does not. Research produces knowledge, and it is by using this knowledge, integrated in a network of related factors and added to the knowledge independently produced by other researchers, that innovation is created.

Over time, many different approaches have been used, such as waterfall models where each step adds value to the previous one, complex models spiraling in a process of continuous refinement and network models based on the integration and aggregation of independent elements. Books have been written to prove their value and inevitability; in truth, none of these models has produced meaningful results.

In this book, I have been pleased to find that one of the main points is precisely the separation of research from development, together with a broad analysis of what innovation is. I have also appreciated the fact that many aspects independent from research, such as organization, processes, markets and disruptive events, are taken into account when addressing the problem of guiding a company through the process of evolution.

To some extent, I am skeptical about the existence of a general solution to the challenges posed to a company by the evolution of a recipe that could be applied to all. But, my skepticism is that of the elderly and must not curb the determination of young people to look for the right answers.

Disruptive events occur in many contexts, and most of the time, we do not notice them. Sometimes, however, we do notice them, but we are powerless, given the constraints in which we live.

Take for instance the change of the US policy towards Iran. Is it due to a finally enlightened president? Or, is it rather the result of a new technology, fracking, which suddenly makes so much gas available that the US have become independent from the Middle East, and can now afford to ignore the contrasts between Sunnis and Shiites and their impact on the availability and price of crude oil?

What will be the consequences of the change of regulations in telecommunications, almost certainly expected for 2015, when in Europe, operators will be allowed to sell their services in every country with no roaming fees? Italy will find itself with more than 160 Telecommunication operators, far too many for its market size (the same is true, of course, for any other European country). The Big Crunch is a certainty, but no one knows how it will happen, what shares will be allocated to private and public operators, how services and contents will be distributed among networks etc.

Companies will have more and more information, more and more "intelligence" at their disposal. But, in my opinion, this will not make it easier for them to steer a steady course and succeed in a market that for various reasons will be increasingly fluctuating and dynamic.

Regulations have had the great merit of creating a market (by imposing standards) and ensuring the stability that allowed long-term investments, such as those required by capital-intensive domains, such as telecommunication infrastructures. But, regulations have been effective, both in terms of network construction and implementation, because the actors were few and well known. Today, and even more tomorrow, as a result of the abatement of transaction costs and of the money amount required to start a business, the actors are, and will be, very numerous, in the tens of thousands or more. Applying to them the same rules that have worked for the past two centuries is simply unthinkable.

Value chains are being replaced by ecosystems, where the rules change every day and where the ability to adapt and reinvent oneself, to see changes as potential opportunities, is the key to success.

As the English say, "you can tame elephants, not cats", and our future will apparently be full of cats, taken as an example even in this book.

Therefore, if, on the one hand, I do not think we can give a recipe for navigating the rough seas of our times and of the future; I am nevertheless convinced that understanding what the relevant factors are can be helpful, and I believe this is one of the merits of this book.

We cannot direct the wind, but we can set the sails. I think that being aware of the wind, of the changing context, and knowing how to handle the tools of business management is the best possible starting point. Further on, the navigation will require skilled pilots and these cannot be invented, even if our schools can help to bring out the best.

And, here I close with a reflection.

I often meet bright young people, in Europe and the US, who devote themselves to research. When I meet a European, he begins by telling me, with sparkling eyes, how challenging and complex his research is. If I ask him how he is going to bring his results to the market, he shrugs and says it is not his job. When I meet an American, he begins by telling me, with sparkling eyes, how his research is going to make him a millionaire. And, if I ask him how he is going to bring his results to the market, he tells me he is going to create a start-up, which will be bought by a company with the means to get to the market.

The enthusiasm is the same, but the two approaches are radically different, and our schools are among the major causes of this abyssal difference. Later on, some of these young researchers will be hired by companies, the Europeans with a less entrepreneurial spirit than their American peers. Some will say that this is a good thing, because while US companies can leverage the entrepreneurial spirit of their employees, in Europe this is seldom the case, as employees tend to resist it instead.

But, then let us not complain if our capacity for innovation and our competitiveness cannot keep pace with the US.

Acknowledgements

"Thinking divides, feeling combines".
Ezra Pound

We would like to express our gratitude to everyone who helped and supported us throughout the research and writing process.

The idea of this book was born in 2006 during a meeting between two of the authors, Siagri and De Toni. The first, entrepreneur and CEO of Eurotech SpA, was pursuing with great passion his business idea, combining visionary innovation and efficiency. The second, academician and man of networking, perceived the "weak signal" of the meaningful experience gained by Eurotech in terms of anticipation of the future and R&D organization. As the subject was still little explored in the literature, a proposal arose for a degree thesis on foresight, followed by a PhD thesis by the third author.

First and foremost, we wish to thank Giampietro Tecchiolli – Chief Technology Officer at Eurotech – for the valuable information provided on ICT trends and for his support and assistance in our project of study and research and in the practical validation of results.

We acknowledge with much appreciation the crucial role of Andrea Barbaro – Investor Relations Manager & Strategic Planning Analyst at Eurotech – whose dedicated involvement and advice was essential to correlate trends, strategy and products.

Our deep gratitude goes to Roberto Pillon – New Ventures Development Advisor at the Innovation Factory of the Area Science Park in Trieste – for his precious assistance in examining the subject from the perspective of technology roadmapping, of which he is an expert.

We express our deep appreciation to Roberto Saracco – president of the Italian node of the European Institute of Innovation and Technology – author of the Foreword. Roberto is a pioneer of futures studies in Italy. After thirty years of future technology studies in Telecom Italia, he now devotes his time and experience to the economic aspects of innovation at the European level.

We are sincerely grateful to Renato Quaglia – former director of the Venice *Biennale,* today director of the Friuli Future Forum promoted by Giovanni Da Pozzo, the visionary president of the Chamber of Commerce of Udine – author of an Afterword, who surprised us for his ability to connect the future with the history of music.

We would also like to thank Giuseppe Zollo – professor of Management Engineering at the University "Federico II" of Naples – a creative and wise teacher who gave us the idea of using art to unveil the future.

A warm thank-you to Gianluca Biotto – post-doc at the University Ca' Foscari of Venice – for the design and creation of the original front cover, and to Lidia Cremonese, for her hard and precious work of translation.

Finally, Cinzia Battistella wishes to dedicate this book to her love Fabio and her sons Bianca and Pietro.

Book structure

> "It belongs to the great order that there should be some small disorder".
> Gottfried Leibniz

This book is structured in four parts. The first part deals with anticipating the future in an ever-changing environment. Chapter 1 introduces the reader to a future which is increasingly unpredictable, near and singular, shaped by interconnection, acceleration and discontinuity. Chapter 2 presents innovation in its various forms and aspects. Chapter 3 identifies the attitudes (flexibility, promptness and resilience) and the foresight responses (detecting weak signals, studying trends and building scenarios) best suited to cope with change. Chapter 4 explains how to anticipate the future by responding proactively to change, and advocates a transition from a logic of prediction to a logic of anticipation (from *forecasting* to *foresight*).

The second part is devoted to the anticipation of the future in business companies. Chapter 5 focuses on the corporate level, proposing a foresight based on the two pillars, namely, organization and management. Chapter 6 discusses organization: the authors distinguish between the market of today and the market of tomorrow; they propose the separation of research (oriented to the market of tomorrow) from development (oriented to the market of today); they suggest the establishment of a foresight unit operating internally in close association with strategy and research and externally in association with scouting; finally, they propose to organize research activities mainly as the connection and recombination of internal with external knowledge. Chapter 7 investigates management: the authors describe the foresight process. In Chapter 8, the authors propose their methodology, which tests the consistency between trends, strategic vision and products offered on the market. This methodology, called "future coverage approach", measures how effectively the corporate strategy matches future trends.

The third part presents the case study of Eurotech, an Italian company in the ICT sector. Chapter 9 identifies the study background, namely,

ICT megatrends, and more specifically, the trend of man-machine symbiosis. Chapters 10 and 11 describe how the organizational and managing tools described in Part II are developed and tested within the company, which has distinguished itself for its outstanding ability to predict the future of ICT.

The fourth part closes the book by recalling the importance of imagination.

Introduction

"If you do not think about the future, you cannot have one".
John Galsworthy

People have always tried to imagine their future. As far back as 424 BC, Herodotus stressed the importance of looking to the future, arguing that nothing stays the same, and that whoever does not want to grow will soon be overtaken by those who do. For men, it has always been essential to plan for the future in an effective way.

This urge, this desire to know where we are going has not changed, nor have the eternal questions of man. Change – as opposed to stasis – is our normal condition, a constant in our lives. The verb "to change" comes from the Greek kàmbein or kàmptein, which means to bend, to fold, to turn something around. Figuratively, it seems to indicate a path that is linear up to a given point, and then suddenly opens up to the possibility of a breakthrough.

But today, the context is no longer the same. Our world keeps changing like the patterns in a kaleidoscope: trends expand, contract, break up, melt, disintegrate and disappear, while others are formed. Nothing stays the same. Global trends know no borders and affect every aspect of the society: they have the potential to profoundly change the way the world will function tomorrow, and may impact more quickly than one might think. Hence, the need to create tools that provides organizations with the means to prepare for change, tools that can tackle complexity and reduce uncertainty.

Faced with change, we can decide either to resist (uselessly), to adapt (reactively) or to act in advance (proactively). Anticipating the future requires more than the traditional predictive models (*forecasting*) based on the forward projection of past experiences. Advanced methods use anticipation logic (*foresight*) and build scenarios that detect weak signals and emerging trends in external sources, taking into account the multiplicity of presents and the possible paths of evolution. We believe that this innovative approach is the only way to respond to a change that is increasingly interconnected, accelerated and discontinuous, the only way to deal effectively with the complexity of reality.

The purpose of this book is to provide support to organizations faced with interconnected, accelerated and discontinuous change. The case study describes Eurotech SpA, an innovative and future-oriented Italian ICT company based in Amaro (Udine), as an example of how it is possible to undertake a journey into the complexity of the future.

Corporate foresight has a strategic value in that it enables organizations to innovate, to identify opportunities and to respond to the latent vulnerabilities of the environment. It is a powerful tool, still not much explored, which can help companies to get ready for a future which is increasingly unpredictable, near and singular. But, to be effective, this approach has to be supported at all corporate levels, from internal organization to management:

- for the organization, we advocate: a) the separation of research from development, because the first is oriented to the market of tomorrow and the second to the market of today; b) the establishment of a foresight unit, operating internally in accordance with strategy and research, and externally through scouting; c) the concentration of research activities on the identification, acquisition and recombination of external know-how, rather than on the internal generation of knowledge;
- for the management, we propose the implementation of a methodology called "future coverage approach", which should enable companies to measure and verify the consistency of trends, strategic vision and offered products.

Organization and management are the two pillars of foresight. But, as always, it is our vision of the future that leads change in the first place, and this vision must break free from the paradigms of the past. Innovation creates the future through new ideas, challenges dominant notions and always requires a certain amount of disobedience to former rules. But, when unsuccessful, innovation is at best a clever attempt, a disobedience which does not result in real benefits. True innovators not only break consolidated mindsets and open up new perspectives, but are also able to draw fruit from these discontinuities. In other words, innovation is a successful disobedience. Furthermore, innovation is always born at the periphery, far from the dominant design which always occupies the center.

Dream, vision and myth are the real drivers of change, because they are respectively the imagination of individuals, groups and society. They are engines fueled by the power of imagination. The Italian writer and poet Leopardi tells us what imagination can give us: "Imagination is the primary source of human happiness". Einstein says where imagination can take us: "Logic will get you from A to B. Imagination will take you everywhere". For Kant, "Imagination is a necessary ingredient of perception itself": through imagination, it is possible to transform experience, the world of reality, doomed to mutability and change.

For the American writer Carl Sandburg, "Nothing happens unless first a dream", and Martin Luther King once said: "I have a dream" (he did not say: "I have a five-year plan"!). From the ancient myth of the Promised Land to the more recent one of the American frontier, myths have always guided and accompanied great social changes. And, on a smaller scale, visions lead change within organizations.

In the impetuous river of change, if we think, we are in a large steamer and we can resist the current, we are deceiving ourselves. In truth, we are in a frail canoe dragged along by tumultuous waters. If we carefully observe the water flow, believing we are part of it, knowing that it is changing constantly and that it is constantly leading to new complexities, every now and then we may be able to plunge an oar into the water and steer clear of eddies.

Notwithstanding the difficulties, living with change opens up an infinite horizon because, in the words of Schopenhauer, "Change alone is eternal, perpetual, immortal". Paraphrasing Charles Snow, the challenge of today is to be men who "have the future in their bones". In other words, the future belongs to those who can imagine it.

Part I
Anticipating the future

1 The future is increasingly unpredictable, near and singular

"Now, here, you see, it takes all the running you can do, to keep in the same place.
If you want to get somewhere else, you must run at least twice as fast as that!"
Lewis Carroll

1.1 All is not as it seems

Do you know the story of the king's chessboard? A courtier presented the Persian king with a wonderful handmade chessboard. Praising the beauty of the object, the king asked him what he wanted in return for his gift. He was very surprised when the courtier said he would like some rice, but according to the following rule: starting from one grain on the first square of the chessboard, the number of grains had to be doubled on each subsequent square. The king thought it was a ridiculous request, but he readily agreed and ordered his servants to bring forth the rice. But how much rice did the king need in order to meet his courtier's demand?

At first all went well: one grain on the first square, two grains on the second, four on the third and so on. But in the second half of the chessboard, the demand for grains became increasingly impossible to meet: the 21st square required over one million grains, the 41st more than a quadrillion! In the end the king had to hand over his entire kingdom, because there was not enough rice on Earth to fill the last squares and honor the pact.[1]

How is this possible? Mathematically a chessboard is an 8*8 square with 64 cells. If you double the amount on each subsequent cell and sum up all the results, you obtain the following series: each cell contains 2n-1 grains, where n is the cell's progressive number.

$$T_{64} = 1 + 2 + 4 + \ldots + 2^{63}$$
$$= 2^0 + 2^1 + 2^2 + \ldots + 2^{63}$$
$$= \sum_{(\text{for i going from 0 to 63})} 2^i = 2^{64} - 1$$
$$= 18.446.744.073.709.551.615$$
$$= \text{over 18 billion billion grains.}$$

This number is about 80 times larger than one year's harvest of all the arable land on the planet. Why didn't the king guess as much? Because men's minds are accustomed to thinking in linear terms.

Let's make another example. Take a sheet of paper, fold it in two, and then again in two for as many times as possible. Obviously there is a physical limit due to the thickness of the paper sheet, which is about 12 folds.[2] But in theory (see Figure 1.1), if you could fold a sheet of paper 51 times, it would reach a height of over 225 million kilometers, far greater than the distance between the Earth and the Sun![3]

These simple examples show how difficult it can be, for men and organizations alike, to think "exponentially" (Figure 1.2), accustomed as they are to think in linear terms. This lack of familiarity with exponential thinking has an important consequence: when the exponential curve meets the socalled knee (where the tangent-chord angle is over 45 degrees) and starts to grow vertically, both men and companies are unable to respond effectively, because the sudden pace change catches them by surprise. Change can be exponential: it is of the utmost importance to find new ways to imagine it and act accordingly.

People, products and ideas are starting to move faster and faster in every direction, and society is facing unprecedented challenges. The knowledge

N° OF FOLDS	HEIGHT (in km)	N° OF FOLDS	HEIGHT (in km)
1	0,0002	27	13.422
2	0,0004	28	26.844
3	0,0008	29	53.687
4	0,0016	30	107.374
5	0,0032	31	214.748
6	0,0064	32	429.497
7	0,0128	33	858.993
8	0,0256	34	1.717.987
9	0,0512	35	3.435.974
10	0,1024	36	6.871.948
11	0,2048	37	13.743.895
12	0,4096	38	27.487.791
13	0,8192	39	54.975.581
14	1,638	40	109.951.163
15	3,277	41	219.902.326
16	6,554	42	439.804.651
17	13,11	43	879.609.302
18	26,21	44	1.759.218.604
19	52,43	45	3.518.437.209
20	104,9	46	7.036.874.418
21	209,7	47	14.073.748.836
22	419,4	48	28.147.497.671
23	838,9	49	56.294.995.342
24	1.678	50	112.589.990.684
25	3.355	51	225.179.981.369
26	6.711	52	450.359.962.737

Figure 1.1 Number of folds and corresponding heights.

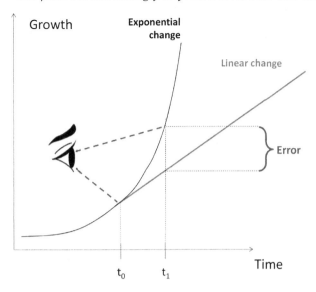

Figure 1.2 Things aren't always as they seem.

society, the emerging technologies and the globalized economy force men and organizations to cope with rapid change, complexity, uncertainty, chaos and paradoxes. Like Berger (1957, in Gordon 2009), we can say that the acceleration of history compels men to predict their actions differently, because tomorrow can never be the same as yesterday.

Sometimes the turbulence is of mild intensity. Other times it is stronger, like in 2008 when the global financial crisis left us dumbfounded as markets recorded huge losses. Theories based on the assumption that change proceeds at a constant or linear rate, or that change is cyclical, no longer explain what is going on today. Acceleration is apparently a sign of our times. Those theories can still be applied in contexts of limited turbulence, but if the rate of change keeps accelerating, there will be unexpected consequences for men and organizations.

In order to deal effectively with the future, we must absolutely learn how to manage two equally inevitable conditions: uncertainty and risk. Some trends are clear, like the strong decline in telecommunication costs and the aging of the population in many Western European countries. But even if they are not particularly difficult to identify, it can be extremely hard to understand exactly when and how they will begin to impact in the medium term.

Other trends are very difficult to foresee. Among them, a number of unpredictable events with devastating impact commonly called *wild cards*: the September 11 attack on the Twin Towers, the Indian Ocean tsunami of 2004, the rise of Hitler and the war that followed, the rapid fall of the USSR, the spread of the Internet, the collapse of Wall Street, the success of Google, Facebook, WhatsApp and so on. As Nassim Taleb explains in his book *The*

Black Swan (2008), these are single events which invalidate a conviction supported by unfailing evidence, just as black swans surprised European explorers when, upon landing on the shores of Australia, they saw them for the first time. For men as well as organizations, black swans are a significant part of today's world and developing effective coping strategies is essential.

1.2 Complex events cannot be predicted

Whenever we look back in time, we inevitably find a rich collection of wrong predictions (see Box 1.1).

In truth, however, the central question is not whether the prediction is correct or not, but rather which actions and consequences result from it.

Box 1.1 Wrong predictions: some examples

Thomas Watson, head of IBM (1943): "I think there is a world market for about five computers".

Bill Gates (1981): "640K ought to be enough for anybody".

Popular Mechanics magazine, on the relentless march of science (1949): "Computers in the future may weigh no more than 1.5 tons".

An engineer at the Advanced Computing Systems Division of IBM, commenting on the microchip (1968): "But what…is it good for?"

Ken Olson, founder and president of Digital Equipment Corporation (1977): "There is no reason anyone would want a computer in their home".

But wrong predictions are not limited to computer science. In 1876, US President Rutherford B. Hayes said to Alexander Graham Bell when he patented the telephone (invented by Antonio Meucci): "It's a great invention, but who would ever want to use one?"

And a Western Union internal memo (1876): "This 'telephone' has too many shortcomings to be seriously considered as a means of communication. The device is inherently of no value to us".

David Sarnoff's associates, in response to a request for investment in the radio (1920): "The wireless music box has no imaginable commercial value. Who would pay for a message sent to nobody in particular?"

Dr. Pierre Pachet, Professor of physiology in Toulouse (1872): "Louis Pasteur's theory of germs is ridiculous fiction".

A president of the Michigan Savings Bank, talking to Henry Ford (1908): "The horse is here to stay, but the automobile is a novelty – a fad".

Lord Kelvin, President of the Royal Society (1895): "No balloon and no aeroplane will ever be practically successful. Heavier-than-air flying machines are impossible".

Charles H. Duell, commissioner of the US Patent and Trademark Office (1899): "Everything that can be invented has been invented".

Forecasts are crucial even when they are contradicted by facts, because they affect decisions and contribute to strategic change in development policies.

According to Bishop (1980): "People often ask me how often I find I have-been right, when I look back and think about the forecasts I made in the past … but they are asking the wrong question. What we really ask of futures studies is how useful a forecast is. A forecast can be disproved and maintain its usefulness, especially if it is a negative forecast which outlines possible problems or even disasters. If the prediction is taken seriously, someone will work to prevent and avoid the problem. The forecast itself will therefore be 'wrong', but it will have contributed to the creation of a better future. In futures studies, the most useful forecasts do not necessarily give an accurate and faithful image of what will happen. Rather, they provide an understand-ing of the dynamics of change, of how certain events might occur, given spe-cific circumstances; their aim is therefore to offer tools which enable people to choose their own future, and to start creating it" (*Our translation, N.d.T.*).

Most events, in their complexity, are not predictable (as Niels Bohr said, "Prediction is very difficult, especially if it's about the future"), but if we are generally unable to predict the future state of a complex system, we can predict its *possible* future states, in other words, its structure. Lindberg and Herzog (1998) quote the mathematician Ben Geoertzel, who distin-guishes between prediction of state and prediction of structure: the state of a chaotic system is unpredictable (i.e., a specific weather condition), but the structure, the sum of its possible states, can be easily inferred (i.e., the climate of a specific region).

Complexity generates bewilderment since it makes it increasingly diffi-cult to take decisions. To decide, you have to come to terms with the uncer-tainty and the impossibility of prediction, "because you can never know for sure how other choices would have turned out" (Jaques, 1991:108).

The future is not written, but remains to be done. It is multiple, indeter-minate and open to a wide array of possibilities. The actions we take mold the future into what we expect it to be. As Charles Handy (1996) writes, we need to learn new ways of "handling" the future: "the past might not be the best guide to the future, […] we must, however, be wary that the future needs to be rooted in the past if it is to be real".

The path is certainly fraught with obstacles. Nothing stays still. Complexity is the space of possibilities, the future is a combination of changing situations, and we must learn to accept uncertainty: in our envi-ronment, in our organizations, in every decision we make.

Because of our increasingly unstable and discontinuous context, and of the ever greater impact it has on our lives, we believe that the 21st century will bring about a big change in perspective for men and organizations alike. We just learned it the hard way with the financial crisis of 2008, which lasts to the present day.

The word "crisis" recalls the adjective "critical": men and organizations live in a complex world, in a network made of diverse and manifold players, in a system where dynamism, uncertainty and acceleration are essential features. How can men and organizations manage the unpredictable? What is the most suitable approach to the future? What are we doing to prepare for the future today? If we wish to navigate the network of the present and the labyrinth of the future, we need to understand the complex forces that induce change. And to adopt the most suitable forms of organization and the right methodologies.

The good thing is that opportunities also increase exponentially. Indeed, "everything is possible, but, perhaps, nothing will be achieved. Conversely, anything can be. Perhaps it is about the immeasurable reserves of Being, the inexhaustible supply of forces not deployed. Forces that no dream forbids us to use tomorrow" (Neher, 1977, in De Toni and Comello, 2005) (*our translation, N.d.T.*). There are countless possible futures, and men and companies must be ready to seize upon every hint of opportunity. As Vicari (1998:61) argues: "Complexity can be a great opportunity, as long as we are able to convince ourselves that unpredictability is not a hindrance, not a problem, not a malfunction. On these premises, complexity can open new spaces for creativity, innovation, change" (*our translation, N.d.T.*).

For men and organizations alike, it is a bad idea to stop and wait for events to follow their course, or to simply bet on the future. But if they make an effort and try to act proactively, to grasp weak signals ahead of time, sometimes (and this is especially true for larger companies, or for those which are keystone in their field) they will be able to create their own future. The right attitude is to accept the complexity and uncertainty of reality, and be ready to handle the unpredictable and to become agents of change. For Wheatley (1994:25): "Reality emerges from our process of observation, from decisions we the observers make about what we will see. It does not exist independent of those activities".

The task of a leader is precisely to promote the creation of productive futures as yet unforeseeable (Marion and Uhl-Bien, 2001), always keeping in mind that the path cannot be optimal or even linear, and that its many bifurcations do not necessarily lead to the best, but to the possible. Stacey (1992) calls the activity of creating the future "open change": we begin by learning something, but our initial knowledge gets constantly modified, namely, each time we encounter a critical situation. The art of learning, the art of guessing a future criticality is a difficult exercise.

"What events or innovations are going to remain without consequence, and which are likely to have global impact and irreversibly determine the outcome of civilization? Furthermore, what are the zones of choice and the zones of stability?" (Prigogine and Stengers, 1990, in Godet et al., 2009).

1.3 Systems are increasingly interdependent

It is not just a matter of change happening faster and faster, it is a matter of impact, of the influence change has on the network of individuals and organizations. The consequences of change impact at a deeper and deeper level. Besides, change itself becomes nonlinear, because it is constantly modified by many factors which operate at different levels, with different objectives, and which are furthermore strongly interconnected.

Due to the increasing technological complexity and dynamism of the market, today's businesses coevolve with their environment, in an ongoing dialogue with other entities sharing the same environment. Hence the need for models that can explain economic phenomena marked by nonlinear dynamics, instability, multiple balance points and unexpected events.

As Wilson (1999, in De Toni and Comello, 2005) writes: "Complexity of change is increased by the growing interdependence of our world. [...] Nations, institutions and individuals are now so inextricably interrelated by so many webs of communications, economics, cultures and ideas, that it is difficult to predict how a tug on one thread in the pattern will affect other parts of the design".

Let us give an example. Take, for instance, the near-extinction of bald eagles, the awesome birds of prey which are the symbol of the United States. Scientists have discovered that the dramatic decline in bald eagle population in Alaska is due to the extensive practice of whaling off the coast of Japan. The causal link is quite surprising, as whales and eagles belong to two originally independent food chains, those of Alaska (Figure 1.3) and

Alaskan food chain

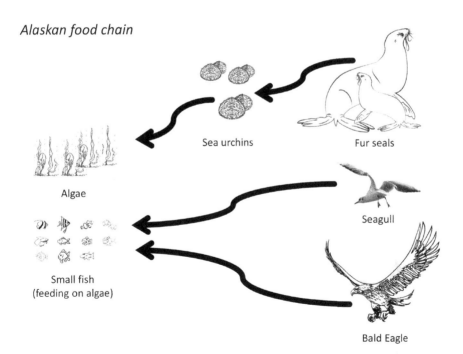

Figure 1.3 Alaskan food chain.

Japanese food chain

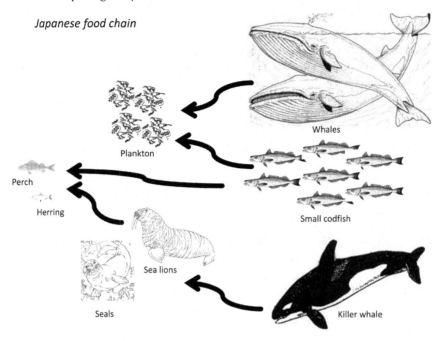

Figure 1.4 Japanese food chain.

Japan (Figure 1.4). The unexpected connection between the two is a good example of interdependency.

Figure 1.5 explains how the two food chains become interconnected: due to extensive whaling off the Japanese coast, an imbalance results in the Alaskan food chain and – after a long series of causal links – leads to the near extinction of bald eagles (Rasetti, 2007):

1 Japanese whalers bring to near-extinction a variety of whales that feed on plankton.
2 The amount of plankton increases.
3 As more plankton is now available, Alaskan codfish proliferate.
4 As the codfish population grows, the preys it feeds on (namely herring and perch) diminish.
5 Seals and sea lions also feed on herring and perch, but now they have less food available. The number of seals and sea lions decreases.
6 Killer whales typically eat seals and sea lions, but given their declining number, they begin to turn to fur seals. The fur seal population decreases. This is where the connection between the two food chains takes place.
7 Fur seals feed on sea urchings. As fur seals diminish, they eat less urchings. The urching population explodes.
8 Urchins feed on algae. As they multiply, the seaweed forests covering the bottom of the ocean are increasingly affected.

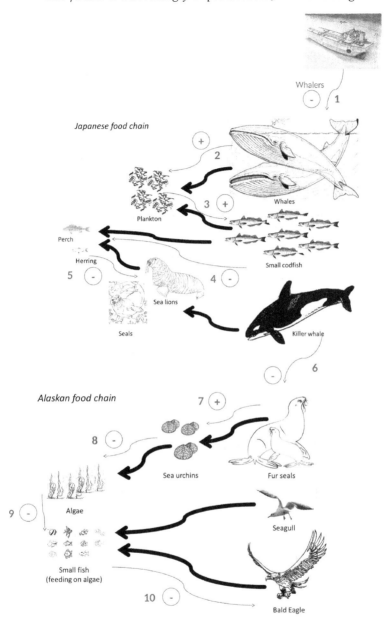

Figure 1.5 Interconnection of two formerly independent food chains.

9 The seaweed forests are home to small fish, which now decrease in number.

10 Small fish are eaten by seagulls and eagles. But while seagulls can find food elsewhere, bald eagles cannot, and thus end up in serious trouble.

1.4 We live in exponential times

This is undoubtedly a truth that we experience directly, day after day. It is true of biology, of technology, of society in general.

It is also true of philosophy. According to Laing (in Olson and Eoyang, 2001:xiii): "We live in a time in history where change is so speeded up that we begin to see the present only when it is already disappearing". Paul Virilio (1999) attempts an explanation: "Ours is a world of absolute acceleration. In ancient societies acceleration was relative, it meant using four horses instead of two, adding more sails to a ship and so on. Starting with the invention of the steam engine, and then aviation, high-speed trains, supersonic jets..., reality itself has accelerated. Not only our history, but our historical reality as a whole has accelerated. How so? Because we have gone from the local and relative speed of transportation to the global and absolute speed of transmission, in other words, we now use the speed of light in our actions and perceptions" (*our translation, N.d.T.*).

For instance, microorganisms in a culture grow exponentially after the appearance of the first one. Even viruses (SARS, West Nile, smallpox) with sufficient infectiousness spread exponentially if no vaccine is available, and every infected person can infect many others. Logarithmic patterns can also be detected in the way living beings respond to stimuli.[4] This is equally true of human perception: sound pitch and frequency are perceived logarithmically by the human ear. In physics many phenomena, like the nuclear chain reaction or the breakdown of dielectric material, follow an exponential law.

In the technology field, futurist and inventor Ray Kurzweil (2006) describes how and how quickly the world is going to change thanks to technology and to nanotechnology. Based on his "law of accelerating returns", Kurzweil affirms that the acceleration rate of technological progress doubles every decade, and that the 21st century will see the equivalent of 20.000 years of progress, when compared to the progress made in the last century, and that in 2029 the power of a $1.000 computer will equal the power of the human brain. "The power (price-performance, speed, capacity, and bandwidth) of information technologies is growing exponentially at an even faster pace, now doubling about every year" and "indeed, the economy kept growing exponentially, thereby more than overcoming a very high deflation rate ... There are a great many examples of the exponential growth implied by the law of accelerating returns, in areas as varied as electronics of all kinds, DNA sequencing, communications, brain scanning, brain reverse engineering, the size and scope of human knowledge, and the rapidly shrinking size of technology" (Kurzweil, 2006).

The processing power of computers and the growth of online traffic also follow an exponential law. Just think about the spread of the

Internet, its growing capacity to act as a catalyst, and how it is changing our world – with outcomes that are sometimes asymmetrical, and not entirely expected: in 2008 in Italy Facebook has grown exponentially, with a 961% increase of users over the previous year. The last survey of August 2013 shows further growth: active users for the month amount to 24 million, of which 17 million are connected daily. Another 15 million connect from mobile on a monthly basis, and 10 million on a daily basis. Because of its physical nature, the Internet binds and promotes the transfer of information in a more than exponential way, by expanding active nodes that keep multi-plying: Internet devices were about one thousand in 1984, one million in 1992 and one billion in 2008. What is more, estimates say that 4 exabytes (10^{19}) of new information will be generated this year, more than have been produced in the past 5,000 years.

The same accelerated pattern can be found in the business world, in the race between competitors. Hamel and Prahalad (1994) give the example of Sony: in a time span of 13 years (1979–1992), Sony has developed 227 Walkman models, roughly one every three weeks. Extending this reasoning, it is estimated that Sony is launching a new product every 20 minutes, and Disney every 3 minutes. Competition is increasingly fast and multiform, acceleration seems irreversible. As they say at Hewlett-Packard (Pascale, 1999): "The biggest single threat to our business today is staying with a previously successful business model one year too long".

Just think of the labor market: the US Department of Labor has estimated that young people who are now at the university will prospectively change 12 jobs before they are 38 years old, and that one worker in four has worked with his current employer for less than a year, and one in two for less than 5 years. Acceleration rates also affect many other fields. Patents registered in the US are up from 132,000 in 1986 to 211,000 in 1996, to 452,000 in 2006 and to 930,000 in 2013; always in the US, mergers and acquisitions have resulted in shifts in capital for 173 billion dollars in 1986, 469 billion in 1996, 1,484 billion in 2006 and 2,133 billion in 2013, again showing a steady growth rate.

Even the history of technological progress proves that, contrary to common sense, change is not linear but exponential. It took ten thousand years for the first technological innovations – the Levallois points[5], the fire, the wheel – to be used worldwide, and this means that human communities did not see any significant improvement even in one thousand years. Much later, in the Middle Ages (around 1000 AD), progress was faster and a paradigm shift required only one century or two. In the 19th century, we have witnessed more technological change than in the nine previous centuries. The first 20 years of the 20th century have seen more progress than the entire 19th century. Now paradigm shifts occur in the space of some years. Just think of the World Wide Web: only a few years ago it did not exist as we know it, and before 1991 it did not exist at all. Time is increasingly compressed, like a movie, and images are projected so fast that we are unable to perceive single frames.

In all these examples the key concept is clearly acceleration, and speed is the core feature which best summarizes the transformations of contemporary digital society. Speed of travel, speed of communication, speed of learning, speed of perception, speed of thought – these are the things we are living with on a daily basis. Everything has indeed become super fast, not only trips around the world, but more importantly the flow of data, the exchange of information and of knowledge. Besides, a new trend is emerging everywhere: global competition shifts focus from a local dimension to a much wider scale. Notwithstanding the rise of global GDP, social and economic problems now have a much greater impact, while local uncertainties remain.

The speed increase has become a fact of everyday experience, the normal transformation law of the world. The situations people find themselves in are therefore constantly new. The effects of a decision will materialize in a completely different world from the one where the decision was taken. Thus, "the future is ahead of ideas" (Berger, 1957) (*our translation, N.d.T.*).

1.5 The future comes like a cat

We are living in exponential times. Often the things that can happen – happen sooner than expected! One problem, as we said before, is that our perception is linear rather than exponential. Another one is that we do not pay attention to weak signals.

The future does not only come accelerating, it also comes by surprise. We could say that the future comes like a cat: it strolls casually at first, then it slowly gets nearer, waiting for the right moment – and all of a sudden, it jumps unexpectedly and here it is! Approach – ambush – jump (Figure 1.6). All quiet at first, aggressive soon afterwards, the future is quick and sudden. As Peters writes: "Things are moving too fast for us to sort out logically what's going on" (1992:525).

Think about the moon landing: in 1865 Jules Verne writes *From the Earth to the Moon*, in 1902 Georges Méliès films *A Trip to the Moon*, in 1960 Neil Armstrong lands on the moon. After less than 100 years, what had been science fiction has become reality.

Same thing for the human genome: in 1975 Jane Bottenstein of CIT&MIT declared that will take more than 100 years before we can decode the entire human genome. In 1992 Matt Ridley, biologist and science journalist, said it will take another 30 or 40 years to decode the human genome. In June 2000, Craig Venter and Francis Collins, of the Human Genome Project, complete the decoding. What should have taken 100 years took only 25!

Figure 1.6 The future comes like a cat.

1.6 In every field, responses are greatly amplified

In today's world, not only do things happen faster and faster, the consequences of change are also very dramatic. During the last three recessions, for instance,

- 60% of organizations survived despite the downturn – the remaining 40% were put out of business;
- 90–95% of survivors totally focused on preservation: they cut costs dramatically, they gave up on growth, they saved resources for better times; and
- only 5–10% did not merely survive but managed to turn the recession into an incredible opportunity to grow and to overtake competitors.

When facing a fork in the road, we do not know what to do. For every decision we make, consequences could be much more serious than expected, or even totally unimaginable. Often, we are unable to identify the actual trends that run below the surface.

Men have always tried to imagine the future, often making mistakes. Figures 1.7, 1.8 and 1.9 show how people in 1856 envisioned the year 3000: the ferry and public highway are simply projections of familiar things, and the same can be said of fashion. These mistakes come from the tendency to project the current world too far ahead, failing to take into account

THE BOMB-FERRY.

Figure 1.7 The ferry in the year 3000 [Source: *Harper's Magazine*, 1856].

THE PUBLIC HIGHWAY.

Figure 1.8 The highway in the year 3000 [Source: *Harper's Magazine*, 1856].

A MAN OF FASHION IN THE THIRTY-FIRST CENTURY.

A LADY OF FASHION A.D. 3000.

Figure 1.9 Fashion in the year 3000 [Source: *Harper's Magazine*, 1856].

innovations that we are unable to imagine. The reason this kind of projection does not work is that, somewhere down the road, there is an exponential growth, a wild card, a paradigm shift.

Sometimes the trend is correctly identified, and imagination does not stray too far from reality. In Figure 1.10 we can see a drawing by Geoff about the history of computing: as early as 1990, the author was able to

Figure 1.10 The future of portable computing as imagined in 1990.

imagine a possible future. Among other things, it is interesting to note that he spotted the dawning trend of miniaturization, probably because the historical moment was right: the early '90s were the turning point, and the first signs of change were beginning to show.

1.7 Bifurcation and the butterfly effect

Bifurcation takes place when something branches out, duplicates, splits into multiple sub-elements. Mathematically, a bifurcation occurs when a small change in the parameters which regulate a system in "normal" (stable) conditions causes a sudden change in the system, so that the points of equilibrium are no longer the same in terms of quantity and/or quality. The values for which these phase transitions occur are called "critical values".

Passage through a bifurcation point is due to amplified fluctuations which cause a system to shift out of equilibrium. A breaking of the symmetry occurs, a phase transition that may either tend towards a new state of equilibrium or of nonequilibrium. No prediction is possible.

When the reference parameter (λ) reaches the critical value λ_c, the behavior of the system (described by the variable x) begins to follow a nonlinear trend. The concept of bifurcation is related to the so-called butterfly effect, a common expression which illustrates the more technical notion of sensitive dependence on the initial conditions, present in chaos theory. The idea is that small changes in the initial conditions produce major variations in the long-term behavior of a system.

The term "butterfly effect" seems to have been inspired by one of the most famous science fiction short stories by Ray Bradbury, *A Sound of Thunder* (1952), where the author imagines that in the future, thanks to a time machine, tourists can go back in time for guided safaris. In remote prehistoric times, a hiker of the future treads on a butterfly, and this small event has amazing consequences for all human history. The butterfly metaphor means that a single action may unpredictably determine the future, just as the tiny movement of air molecules generated by the flapping of a butterfly's wings can end up triggering a hurricane.

The practical consequence of the butterfly effect is that the behavior of complex systems becomes very difficult to predict in good time. To simulate the system, a finite model has to approximate, eliminating some of the information on the initial conditions (when simulating the weather, you cannot include the air moved around by each butterfly). In the simulation of a chaotic system, approximation errors tend to increase over time, until the residual error becomes greater than the result itself.

Edward Lorenz was the first to analyze the butterfly effect in a paper written in 1963 for the New York Academy of Sciences. According to this document, "one meteorologist remarked that if the theory were correct, one flap of a seagull's wings would be enough to alter the course of the weather forever". In subsequent speeches and writings, Lorenz used the more poetic butterfly, perhaps because the diagram generated by the Lorenz attractors looks exactly like the insect. "Does the flap of a butterfly's wings in Brazil set off a tornado in Texas?" is the title of a lecture given by Lorenz in 1972.

The butterfly metaphor is hugely evocative. It influences the way scientists look at the world, and has become a familiar concept for many of us.

In Spielberg's movie *Jurassic Park*, the mathematician Ian Malcolm explains the characteristics of chaos and unpredictability, illustrating the behavior of a drop of water running down the skin of the leading actress. A reference to the butterfly effect can also be found in the movie *The Oxford Murders*, where the plot deals with the possible consequences of a number of small factors.

A whole set of possible futures spread out at bifurcation points. It is therefore impossible to attempt a prediction without taking them into account, and without using scenario thinking. Evolution proceeds by consecutive bifurcations; in this sense it has a historical dimension which is usually referred to as "path dependence".

Examples of bifurcation can be found in biology. From unicellular organisms, a new property emerges at the bifurcation point: multicellular life. The individual units, instead of dying because of food shortage, respond to the new environmental conditions by coevolving structurally in a process of self-organization.

According to Ervin Laszlo (1996), even history proceeds by consecutive bifurcations. The evolutionary models of human societies follow the dynamic patterns of complex systems in a way that depends on the conditions laid down by peoples and their specific values, beliefs, customs and habits. In this sense, history can be represented as a journey through countless bifurcations. Periods of stability are followed by periods of crisis and transformation, and with each discontinuity new structures arise and changes occur.

Typical forecasting mistakes include:

- projecting the present too far ahead, forgetting that progress is not linear but exponential;
- ignoring innovations and technological advances which are likely to cause an acceleration and a paradigm shift over time; and
- underestimating the amplification effect of the Internet.

The problem is that we do in fact identify megatrends (service-based society, aging of the population, dematerialization etc.), but the interpretative tools we use continue to be rooted in the present. Besides, we are unable to translate our knowledge of megatrends into a concrete advantage, namely, into research and operativity inside companies and organizations.

Mathematically, we use the tangent to simplify in the short term (because the trend is a prosecution of the past), and the asymptote to simplify in the long term (because the trend has become vertical). The difficulty lies in the middle, because in the medium term we do not know how to interpret the curve, how to identify a potential bifurcation, how to spot the moment when everything will change. This is why we need effective tools that help us understand when exactly a megatrend is starting to become meaningful, and above all how we can take advantage of it in the medium term.

1.8 Change is interconnected, accelerated and discontinuous

Change is a process that involves every area of our lives, both as individuals and as a community, and concerns groups, companies and institutions at every level.

More often than not, humans want to preserve their daily routine. Being able to tell what will almost certainly happen tomorrow, expecting a specific behavior, activating an automatic response to a stimulus are operations that minimize the strain of interacting with the surrounding environment; they are, in other words, the easy way out. New things, even if they may appear attractive to our curious mind, often imply the idea of exertion, because they require the effort of discovery, selection, adaptation and reconfiguration. Conventional wisdom does not seem to support the idea that change is mainly positive. "Better the devil you know than the devil you don't know" is a saying that somehow calls for caution, for the preservation of the status quo which gives us an anchor in the safe haven of habit.

But change – not stagnation – is our normal condition, a permanent feature in our lives. Over the centuries we have learned that the entire universe is in perpetual, irreversible change. Change is intrinsic to our existence. The word "change" comes from the Greek *kàmbein* or *kàmptei* which means "to bend", "to fold", "to turn something around". Figuratively, it seems to indicate a path that is linear up to a given point, and then suddenly opens up to the possibility of a breakthrough. Thus, change transforms the present, leads to a new future and alters the way we look at the past.

We must accept constant change and be prepared for a heavy shift in perspective: interconnection versus separation, acceleration versus linearity, discontinuity versus continuity. Interconnection, acceleration and discontinuity are the three ingredients of change (see Figure 1.11).

Change is interconnected. Change is increasingly interconnected because we live in systems that are more and more interdependent. We live multiple presents: every one of us belongs to several networks simultaneously: a cultural network, a social network, an economic network and so on. Moreover, our many presents intersect each other on many levels: on an individual level, on a group level, on a social level. Of all these presents, we do not know which one will prevail. The future seems more unpredictable, more unexpected than ever, whereas if we look back, the paths leading up to these many presents appear strongly intertwined.

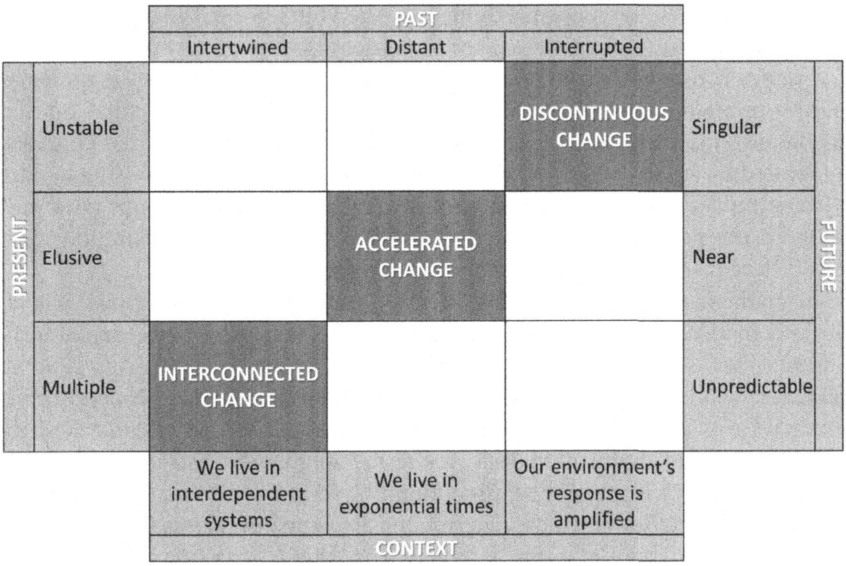

PAST		
Intertwined	Distant	Interrupted

<table>
<tr><td rowspan="2">PRESENT</td><td>Unstable</td><td></td><td></td><td>DISCONTINUOUS CHANGE</td><td>Singular</td><td rowspan="3">FUTURE</td></tr>
<tr><td>Elusive</td><td></td><td>ACCELERATED CHANGE</td><td></td><td>Near</td></tr>
<tr><td></td><td>Multiple</td><td>INTERCONNECTED CHANGE</td><td></td><td></td><td>Unpredictable</td></tr>
</table>

We live in interdependent systems	We live in exponential times	Our environment's response is amplified
	CONTEXT	

Figure 1.11 The characteristics of change.

The Italian writer Italo Calvino explores the nature of interconnection in the short fantasy novel *The Castle of Crossed Destinies* (1969). Calvino's book is an example of combinatory literature: the characters tell their story in images, slowly placing tarot cards on the table, and since each character can take part in many stories, all stories – as the author writes in the presentation – stem from "a finite number of elements whose combinations are multiplied to billions of billions" and find "a place in the network of the other stories".

Change is accelerated. Change is accelerating at such a pace that it has become impossible to respond to everything quickly enough. We are living in exponential times. In 1970 the world population was around 3.5 billion, today it exceeds 7 billion. The first text message was sent in December 1992; today the number of text messages sent and received every day is higher than the number of humans on the planet. It took 38 years for the radio to reach an audience of 50 million people, television made it in 13 years, the Internet in 4 years, the iPod in 3 years, Facebook in 2 years. The users connected to the Internet were one thousand in 1984, one million in 1992, they are more than 2 billion in 2014.

When you live in exponential times, your present is elusive: the moment you begin to understand it, it has already disappeared! Because of acceleration, the past seems increasingly distant and the future gets closer and closer, as it were, "squeezed" on the present. In the words of our dear friend, the late Ernesto Illy: "When life flowed slowly like a lazy river, complexity existed but was not perceived. Today we all feel it in our bones, because the pace has become tight, like the course of a swirling torrent" (*our translation, N.d.T.*).

Change is discontinuous. As the response of our environment is increasingly amplified (think of the consequences a local financial crisis has on the whole system), the present becomes very unstable, exposed to great changes generated by small causes, according to the logic of the butterfly effect. The discontinuity of change and the nonlinearity of responses disrupt continuity with the past and announce a singular future. The term "singularity" has different meanings, depending on context.

In mathematics, the term "singularity" generally indicates a point where a mathematical entity (like for instance the function of a curve or surface) "degenerates", namely, loses some of the properties it has in the other generic points, which by contrast are called "regular". In a singularity, a function and its derivatives can be undefined, and in its neighborhood, they can "tend to infinity". In mathematical analysis, the term "singularity" is sometimes used interchangeably with "point of discontinuity". In linear algebra we say that a matrix is "singular" when it has determinant zero and is therefore not invertible.

In physics, a singular point is where a mathematical singularity of the field equations occurs, for example due to a geometrical discontinuity of the domain. Although singular solutions of field equations are very useful to describe physical behavior outside the singularity, they lose their physical meaning in proximity of the singular point. Basically, the physical behavior in such neighborhoods can be described only by more complex physical theories where the singularity does not occur. In the Theory of Relativity, a gravitational singularity is a point in the neighborhood of which the gravitational pull tends to infinity (as in the Big Bang and in blacks holes). When approaching these points, it would be necessary to use a quantum theory of gravity instead of Einstein's relativity.

In the context of futures studies, a singularity is a moment in time when progress suddenly speeds up and takes on a completely new character. At the bifurcation point, three things happen simultaneously: the straight line of the past stops, the present becomes unstable (because the microdisruptions nearing the bifurcation point increase in intensity as the discontinuity approaches), and the future unfolds on the two possible hyperbolic branches. The future is therefore singular, no longer in line with the past.

In his book *The Garden of Forking Paths* (1941), the Argentine writer and poet Jorge Luis Borges depicts a metaphor of complexity and in particular of discontinuity, analysing concepts like ramification of times and bifurcations. A sentence by one of the characters is famous: "I leave to several futures (not to all) my garden of forking paths". In the essay "An Examination of the Work of Herbert Quain" (1944), Borges shows how the ramification of several possible timelines allows multiple potential pasts to converge on a single future.

We are not helpless in the face of complexity. In Chapter 2 we will talk about the models, methods and tools that can help men and organizations to prepare for a change that is interconnected, accelerated and discontinuous.

Notes

1 Source: Meadows et al. (1972:29).
2 12 folds at the utmost. See the so-called folding problem of Britney Gallivan (2002).
3 The average distance between the Earth and the Sun is 149.6 million kilometers: this value is called Astronomical Unit (AU), and is used to measure distances within the solar system. However, as the Earth's orbit is elliptical and not circular, this value oscillates between a minimum of 147 million kilometers (perihelion in January) to a maximum of 152 million kilometers (aphelion in July).
4 Mathematically, a logarithmic curve is the inverse of an exponential curve.
5 The Levallois technique is associated with the Neanderthal industries of the middle Palaeolithic. It was used to obtain sharp stone flakes with a distinctive profile from a prepared core.

2 Innovation shapes the future

"Disobedience, in the eyes of any one who has read history, is man's
original virtue.
It is through disobedience that progress has been made".
Oscar Wilde

2.1 The dominant design

Light creates shadows. A bright lamp aimed at one thing hides many others. In this regard, Maurice Allais (1992) denounces "the tyranny of dominant ideas". Just as the majority of people only listen to information that confirms their thoughts, organizations will only take into account what is in line with their corporate culture and with familiar, sometimes even trite, issues. This can induce many forms of silence (Morel, 2006).

One of the main challenges of anticipation is precisely to break the "organizational silence" (Morrison and Milliken, 2000) which limits the expression of "deviant" ideas (i.e., ideas which diverge from the dominant design), and hides not only disagreements, but also weak signals and warnings.

In order to innovate, we must think outside the box, rejecting the accepted paradigm. This view is endorsed by great epistemologists like Kuhn and Popper. For Thomas Kuhn (1962), science does not gradually move forward towards the truth, but is instead prone to periodic revolutions: the so-called paradigm shifts. Paradigm shifts originate from anomalies in "normal science", in other words, from events that fail to confirm the paradigm. If the contradiction is particularly persistent or evident, the anomaly can become strong enough to question established beliefs and techniques within the paradigm, thus opening a crisis. As a result of this crisis, a different paradigm is then created. It is important to note that these new paradigms do not arise from the previous theory, but from the rejection of well-established beliefs within the dominant paradigm.

While for Kuhn these "revolutions" are extremely rare, Popper (1934) argues that science should be in a state of continuous transformation. In the field of epistemology, "permanent revolution" is Popper's motto: every scientist should always strive to undermine accepted notions, trying to disprove them and then improve them, in asymptotic approximation to the truth. For Popper, a critical attitude is at the heart of any scientific endeavor.

Ties must be severed and all certainty must be left behind. In the words of St. John of the Cross (1542–1591): "To reach a place unknown, you must travel the path unknown" (*our translation, N.d.T.*).

If we observe technology from a historical point of view, we clearly see how paradigm shifts work. As an example, let us take the history of the bicycle, which clearly illustrates the impact of dominant technologies on product design and development. Table 2.1 shows an overview of bike models over time, namely, from the end of the 17th to the end of the 19th century.

Table 2.1 The bicycle over time.

	BICYCLE	YEAR		BICYCLE	YEAR
	Doctor Richard's four-wheeler	1696		Baron von Drais's running-machine	1818
	Tricycle by bauer	1820		Gompertz's bicycle	1821
	McMillan's bicycle	1839		A quadricycle by sawyer	1845
	Fisher's bicycle	1853		A paris tricycle for ladies	1863
	Guilmet's bicycle	1869		The michauline	1869
	Ariel by J. Starley	1870		Coventry racer	1877

(*continued*)

Table 2.1 The bicycle over time. (*continued*)

BICYCLE		YEAR	BICYCLE		YEAR
	"Devon" symmetrical tricycle	1878		The singer "xtraordinary", a "high wheel safety"	1879
	Lawson's "bicyclette"	1879		A sociable tricycle	1880
	Bsa "dwarf safety"	1884		The "kangaroo", a "high wheel safety"	1884
	Humber "dwarf safety"	1885		A cripper tricycle leading in a race	1885
	The "rover ill", a "safety" bicycle by J. K. Starley	1885		The ordinary as sporting machine	1885
	Spring frame	1885		The Hillclimber – a tricycle safety	1886
	Young Dunlop's tricycle with pneumatic tyres	1887		Asymmetrical tricycle by Starley	1887
	"Psycho" by J. K. Starley	1887		Bicycle	1892
	End of the ordinary	1892		Tricycle	1900

Source: Van Nierop et al., 1997, with permission of Oxford University Press and the authors.

The bicycle has evolved through a complex nonlinear pattern, at times diverging, at times converging, so much so that it is hard to find some logic in the variety of solutions that have been designed and proposed. Actually, as we shall see, bicycle models have been developed along three main lines.

Van Nierop et al. (1997) interpret the bicycle as a complex adaptive system (CAS) that co-evolves with society in a kind of bicycle-society system. They show how the modern bicycle stems from innovations that were equally applied to three- and four-wheel vehicles.

Baron von Drais's 1818 machine is often considered the forerunner of the modern bicycle (see Figure 2.4) and indeed, it shares the main features of today's bikes: two small aligned wheels and a rider sitting upright between the wheels, with his feet touching the ground. But in other models, we find a wide variety of solutions concerning propulsion, stability and rider comfort.

Before the positive establishment of a dominant idea, technology or product, it is impossible to know for sure what this idea, technology or product will be. In other words, no one can say how things will turn out, because different ideas are contending for dominance and the various technologies overlap. This is what we call the turmoil stage. Turmoil persists until one idea, technology or product gains a clear victory over the others, and the time of dominance begins. But with dominance, tyranny also begins. Only a discontinuity, a change, can set things in motion again with a new period of turmoil.

For the bicycle, the turmoil stage took place between the late 1600s and early 1900s, and the battle was fought over two main features: the type of transmission and the number of wheels. Based on the different directions taken by manufacturers, three groups of dominant products were born: three- and four-wheelers with indirect transmission (Figure 2.1),

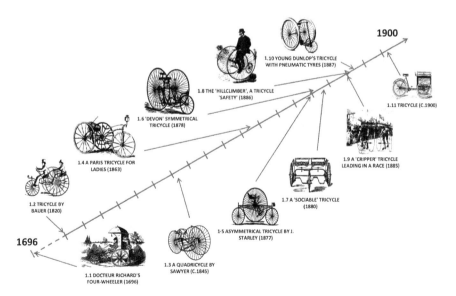

Figure 2.1 Three- and four-wheelers with indirect transmission. (With permission of Oxford University Press and the authors.)

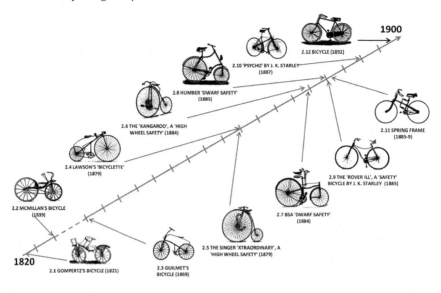

Figure 2.2 Two-wheelers with indirect transmission. (With permission of Oxford University Press and the authors.)

two-wheelers with indirect transmission (Figure 2.2) and two-wheelers with direct transmission (Figure 2.3).

Of course the current dominant design (the two-wheeler with indirect transmission) has benefited from the innovations and failures of the other two, because a designer's creation always stems from the original

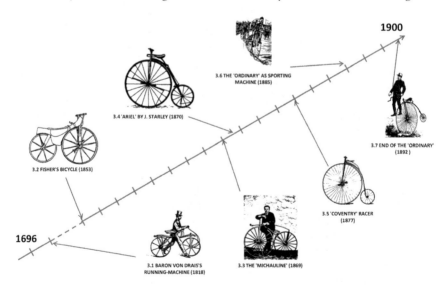

Figure 2.3 Two-wheelers with direct transmission. (With permission of Oxford University Press and the authors.)

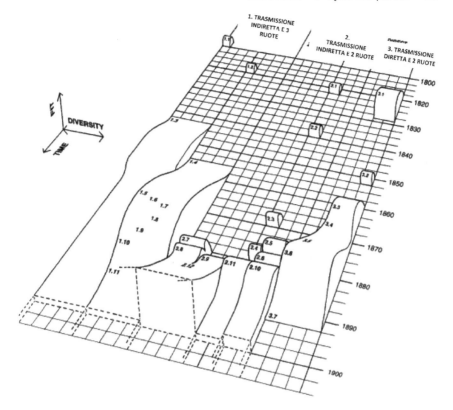

Figure 2.4 Evolution landscape of bicycle design.

combination of separate elements and ideas. At first there is a rather unde-fined search for dominance, with a sequence of failures and successes. Later, when an acceptable level has been reached, a "local search" for excellence takes place. The landscape of Figure 2.4 shows how models appear and dis-appear, and at what moments the differences and competition are greater. As we can see, the bicycle-society system has evolved along the edge of chaos.

Figure 2.4 is a qualitative description of the evolution of bicycle over time. On the x-axis, we have the three groups of dominant products (three- and four-wheelers with indirect transmission, two-wheelers with indirect transmission, two-wheelers with direct transmission). The y-axis repre-sents time. On the z-axis, the height of each curve shows the success rate of each model, based on the sales volume and on the number of models available at a given time. The landscape changes with time: there are eight different solutions between 1800 and 1860 (60 years), then as many as 22 solutions between 1860 and 1890 (only 30 years), and finally only one solution (the affirmation of the dominant design) at the end of the century.

To adapt to a changing environment change is obviously necessary, but because of selection, only one or two changes will be appropriate and successful. Of course, bicycle evolution did not end back in 1902. The journey of adaptation still continues: recent examples are the folding bike (Urban Street Bike Concept – Design: Gregor Dauth – 2007), the uni/bicycle (a bicycle which converts to unicycle, like the Rotation model designed by Yirong Yang), bicycles with new kinematics (Design: Bradford Waugh – 2006) or innovative forks (Alberto Del Biondi – Industry of Design – 2007). In any case, the dominant design is never "safe": we even find revivals of long-forgotten models, like the new quadricycle (GBO Design – 2007).

2.2 Innovation is born at the periphery

Radical innovation is critical to the long-term success of a company. It can dramatically change the company's competitive position, weaken or even destroy large corporations, encourage new entries and create new market leaders. A recent case is Kodak, the photography giant which went bankrupt after the appearance of the digital camera.

The typewriter, the abacus, the slide rule, the traditional camera have all been dominant products, and all of them are now virtually extinct. They have been replaced by radical innovations: word processors, electronic calculators, digital photographic machines. Interestingly, all these new products have been brought to market by small companies and start-ups (Utterback, 1994).

This David and Goliath scenario is of great interest to managers. But is size really so important?

In his seminal work on the concept of "creative destruction", Joseph Schumpeter (1912; 1942) argues that large companies innovate more than small businesses. Later, the effects of size on innovation have been studied and measured (Cohen and Levinthal, 1990), with diverse and contradictory results. Some authors affirm that large companies benefit from economies of scale (especially in R&D), better risk distribution and easier access to financial resources (Galbraith, 1952; Arrow, 1962). Others argue that large companies are hindered by too much bureaucracy, are slower to react and less likely to take risks (Mitchell and Singh, 1993; Tornatzky and Fleischer, 1990).

Anecdotal evidence suggests that all companies, either large or small, can be radical innovators. For example, the first cellulose nitrate roll was sold by Kodak, which was a small company at the time. The air conditioner was brought to market by Buffalo Forge, a medium-size company. The first microwave oven was produced by Raytheon when it already was a big company. So the next question is, why are some companies better than others at radical innovation?

Radical innovation has the potential to destroy the value of expertise and specialization. For a company, the value of investments is strongly linked to a particular product technology. Investments involve both tangible assets (equipment and instruments) and intangible assets (culture, knowledge, experience, access to distribution channels and so on). Specialization is therefore strongly linked to the dominant culture, to the internal organization, to the management strategy and to the used technologies. No wonder that companies are reluctant to accept, let alone to encourage, radical innovation in their markets.

Companies that innovate are companies that disobey, that choose to push innovation even if doing so means challenging the dominant design and cannibalizing specialization. Very large market-leader companies are not likely to do so; they are much less inclined to disobey because they occupy a central position in the dominant culture, they are deeply rooted into it, and furthermore they are bound by earlier investments (both tangible and intangible). Disobedience is much easier at the periphery, where specialization is still irrelevant and there is openness and willingness to innovate.

Kijkuit and van den Ende (2007) have studied the different stages of creativity in relation to a company's dynamics and level of connection. The generation of new ideas is favored at the periphery, where there are lots of knowledge, but the company's connections are few and weak. Later, at the stage of development and evaluation, cohesion needs to be higher and relationships stronger, with a greater involvement of decision makers. This is why creation thrives at the periphery, and development dwells at the center.

However, we cannot ignore that some central and dominant companies, like for instance Google, are undoubtedly also radical innovators. This is because internally they promote a culture of disobedience, which of course is far from easy. Chandy and Tellis (1998) suggest that core companies may overcome their natural tendency to obedience through three specific behaviors:

- Being active in domestic markets, granting a high degree of autonomy to the managers of the various business units and allowing competition among the business units themselves
- Valuing champions, promoting the work of highly creative employees
- Focusing on future markets, cultivating customers who are interested in some new technology and who might become more and more relevant in the future

Hargadon (2003) shares the same view: he argues that innovation, and in particular creativity within organizations, is a function of the creativity of its members. Innovation is also greatly influenced by context, specifically, by the readiness to accept errors as a normal part of the innovation process, by the fostering of internal entrepreneurship (so-called intrapreneurship) and by the commitment to focus not only on current, but also on future customers.

As Proust has said, "The real voyage of discovery consists not in seeking new landscapes, but in having new eyes". Innovation involves openness, a correct perception of problems, flexible thinking, the ability to form and to redefine original associations, tolerance for ambiguity and diversity. That is why "open innovation" (Chesbrough, 2003) suggests a shift from research

& development to connection & development, where the know-how coming from the periphery is recognized, internalized and recombined.

To innovate means above all to borrow meaningful contributions from a large number of players and put them together, connecting external and internal knowledge. In order to configure the connection & development model, internal teams need to activate two fundamental processes.

The first is the acquisition of knowledge from outside the company: research centers like universities and specialized institutes, "traditional" players (suppliers, consultants, test & measurement laboratories, certification agencies, companies from different sectors, consortia, customers, communities of practice, communities of interest, competitors etc.) and less "traditional" players (as technology gets more and more pervasive, relevant knowledge can often be found in different and unfamiliar sectors). The acquisition of knowledge can either be regulated by contracts and cooperation agreements, or be the result of simple interactions.

The second fundamental process is the connection of internal and external knowledge, in a recombination as much as possible unique and discontinuous. In this sense, the researcher becomes more and more of a "knowledge broker" whose main target is to increase the value of distributed knowledge.

2.3 Innovation is a successful disobedience

Innovation takes place when a change is successful. In the context of economy and management, this change can involve a number of different aspects: products, services, production processes, organizational routines, business models and so on.

The technological improvement of a product or process is known by the term "invention". The concept of innovation is broader than the concept of invention. Many inventions do not have a real economic impact because they are not applied extensively. Only inventions that assert themselves in actual practice, contributing to technological, economic and social progress, can be said to be true innovations. In other words, only an invention that finds concrete application is an innovation in its own right. Conversely, any innovation in product or process technology is a successful invention.

Similarly, changes in the organization, in the management strategy, in the business model and so on can be considered real innovations only if they are successful.

The rise of a new idea, the challenge to a dominant design, the ambition to make improvements, the assumption that it is possible to change the reality so far observed, may be considered in our opinion as a real "disobedience" to former rules. But, as we have seen before, for us to speak of true innovation the change must be a successful one. In other words, innovation is a successful disobedience.

A striking example of disobedience to existing paradigms is the Copernican theory of heliocentrism, as opposed to Ptolemaic geocentrism.

The Greek astronomer Ptolemy (AD 100–175) is the author of important scientific works, the largest of which is the astronomical treatise known as the Almagest (i.e., the Great). In this work, which is one of the most influential scientific endeavors of all antiquity, Ptolemy gathered all the astronomical knowledge of the Greek world, largely based on the studies on geocentricism made three centuries before by Hipparchus. Ptolemy formulated a geocentric model in which only the Sun and the Moon, considered as planets, had their epicycle (i.e., the circumference along which they moved) centered directly on the Earth. This model of the solar system, named the "Ptolemaic system" in honor of its creator, was a stable reference for the whole Western world (but also for the Arab world) for centuries, until it was replaced by the heliocentric model proposed by the Polish astronomer Nicolaus Copernicus.

The theory formulated by Copernicus incorporates the heliocentrism of the Greek scholar Aristarchus of Samos. Aristarchus put the Sun at the center of all the orbits of the planets of the solar system, and gave a theoretical demonstration of his model using Pythagorean mathematics.

The core of Copernicus's theory, which puts the Sun at the center of the solar system, was published in the essay *De Revolutionibus Orbium Coelestium* (On the Revolutions of the Heavenly Spheres) in 1543, the year of his death. This work is the starting point of a doctrinal conversion from the geocentric to the heliocentric theory and it contains all the main elements of modern astronomy, including a correct ordering of the planets, the revolution of the Earth around its axis, and the precession of the equinoxes.[1] This work is Copernicus's act of disobedience.

The Copernican theory impressed great scientists like Galileo and Kepler, who slowly improved his model with corrections and extensions. To gather evidence supporting the Copernican theory, meticulous observations were necessary, and the telescope had just been invented. Galileo improved and potentiated it, and in 1606 he undertook scrupulous astronomical observations, acquiring more precise information on the mountains of the Moon and on the composition of the Milky Way, and discovering the four largest satellites of Jupiter. The new findings were published on March 12, 1610, in *Sidereus Nuncius* (the Starry Messenger).

Galileo's observations of the phases of Venus provided the first empirical evidence of Copernicus's insights. Copernicus had an intuition, Galileo proved its validity. We can say that Galileo made Copernicus's disobedience successful. Thanks to the telescope, the entire Ptolemaic system was finally shattered.

But changing a paradigm can be risky, even when the new paradigm is validated, as Galileo discovered at his own expense. The tutelary orders of the scientific and theological culture (Jesuits and Dominicans) were determined opponents of Galileo, and denounced the danger of his theories for the traditional teachings of the Church. Following a request by the Holy Office, theologians unanimously declared that the statement: "the Sun is the center of the world and is absolutely devoid of local motion", was "foolish and absurd in philosophy, and formally heretical" (*our translation, N.d.T*) since it contradicted many passages of the Holy Scriptures and the beliefs of the Fathers of the Church. The pope ordered Galileo to be summoned and admonished to abandon his opinion and abstain from defending it. The dominant culture was resisting: the Church accused Galileo of heresy and of attempting to subvert the natural philosophy of Aristotle and the Scriptures. Galileo was then tried and condemned by the Holy Office, and forced, on June 22, 1633, to disown his astronomical theory.

Galileo claimed to have reread his Dialogue "almost as it had been a new writing by another author" (*our translation, N.d.T*) and admitted that a reader unfamiliar with the author might have gathered the impression that he had intended to validate the Copernican theory (Figure 2.5). Apologizing to the inquisitor for "an error so averse to my intention", he offered to "re-examine the arguments presented in support of that false and damned opinion, and to confutate them in the most effective way, as the blessed Lord will direct me to do" (*our translation, N.d.T*). Confronted with the dominant culture, Galileo did not ask for permission, he begged (after the trial) for forgiveness. But the Church could not stop the unstoppable advance of the heliocentric theory, and the 17th century is now called *the century of discoveries* for the great progress that took place in every field of knowledge, thanks to the scientific method introduced by Galileo.

COPERNICUS' INTUITION
(1473 – 1543)

GALILEO'S PROOF
(1564 – 1642)

De Revolutionibus Orbium Coelestium
Astronomical Treaty, Nurnberg, 1543

Sidereus Nuncius
first astronomical observations
with a telescope, 1610

Figure 2.5 Copernicus's intuition, Galileo's proof.

Obedience is no longer a virtue. This is the title of a famous 1965 essay by Father Lorenzo Milani, an Italian priest who challenged the stance of military chaplains on conscientious objection. Against these priests, who had always followed the troops at war and had declared themselves against the possibility of refusing military service for moral reasons, Father Milani argued that to obey was no longer a virtue, because the army's purpose should have been to "defend the Fatherland along with the lofty values this concept contains: the sovereignty of the people, freedom, justice" (*translation by G. Blaylock*).

Innovation is a successful disobedience. Behind every act of disobedience to the dominant system, a new opportunity may be hidden. Within organizations, we need to implement good practices to promote and control creative disobedience. These practices will be discussed in Chapters 6, 7 and 8.

2.4 Innovation is coevolution: *The Barbarians*

Innovation infiltrates a consolidated system and starts to undermine the existing order. Innovation overturns former rules and dictates a change of perspective. It unleashes competition between a steady internal force and an ambitious external force. Innovation is also necessary to transform the dominant culture into something new, to open the way for a future re-assembly and a new "triumph", according to a "challenge and response" dynamic. In the words of the historian Chester Starr: "Every so often civilization seems to work itself into a corner from which further progress is virtually impossible along the lines then apparent; yet if new ideas are to have a chance the old systems must be so severely shaken that they lose their dominance".

Innovation is often seen as something negative, because it subverts the rules. But precisely for this reason, innovation can lead to something unusual, different and maybe positive. In his essay *The Barbarians* (2006), the Italian writer Alessandro Baricco uses the metaphor of the barbarians to explain change and mutation. He writes: "And every time someone rises up to decry the misery of every transformation, exempting himself from his duty to understand it, the wall is raised, and our blindness multiplies in the idolatry of a boundary that doesn't exist, but which we pride ourselves on defending. There is no boundary, believe me; there is no civilization on one side, no barbarians on the other. There's simply the forwardmost edge of the mutation advancing inside us. [...] We each stand where everyone stands, in the only spot there is, within the current of mutation, where we call what is known to us *civilization*, and what does not yet have a name *barbarism*. Unlike others, I think it's a fabulous place".

So, when the barbarians come and we have to confront them, what are we going to do?

Many will cling desperately to what they know, trying to protect themselves, to resist. But they will be overwhelmed. In the epilogue, Baricco presents the Great Wall of China as a symbol of how civilizations react to the nightmare of an invasion. In his opinion, the Great Wall teaches us that any civilization, in the fight against barbarians, "always ends up choosing not the best strategy for winning, but the one best suited to confirming its own identity". According to Baricco, the Great Wall was built not so much as a defense against invaders, but rather as a boundary, a way of delimiting civilization; it "didn't protect against barbarians: it invented them. It didn't defend civilization: it defined it".

For Baricco, change can be handled only by letting go of the old paradigm of the clash of civilizations, and by accepting the idea that a mutation is in progress. We need the courage to expose ourselves to change, adapting to each other. What is really important is not to build walls on a border that does not exist, but to decide what we want to save of the old world, and to bring it into the new: "It's a difficult task, because it cannot ever mean bringing things to safety away from the mutation, but only within the mutation. Because what we do salvage will never be what we have kept sheltered from time, but what we have allowed to mutate, so that it might become itself again, in a new time". We cannot preserve the "old world" and transfer it to the "new world" in its entirety, but if we learn to adapt, we can take at least a part of it with us. We must learn to co-evolve, because the answer lies precisely here, in coevolution: the joint evolution of different species belonging to the same environment, which influence each other in a symbiotic relationship.

Similarly, in management and business, innovation is nothing more than a series of barbaric acts which are gradually assimilated and finally accepted as normality. A company always begins with product innovation, then it starts innovating the production process, then it modifies the business model. And for each of these aspects, it must be able to assimilate changes without losing efficiency.

2.5   Innovation is exaptation: The panda's thumb and the spandrels of St. Mark's Basilica

The concept of exaptation was introduced by paleontologists Stephen J. Gould and Elisabeth S. Vrba in 1982, but it dates back to Charles Darwin's concept of pre-adaptation. The term "pre-adaptation" was first used by Darwin in 1872, to indicate the possibility that in nature the relationship between organs and functions could be redundant; in other words, that an organ developed for a specific adaptive reason could be "co-opted" or converted to an entirely different function. This functional co-optation, which complements, but does not in any way replace, the gradual adaptation fostered by natural selection, was called by Gould and Vrba "exaptation", to indicate how organisms often take advantage of already available structures, in an opportunistic fashion, re-adapting them to new functions.

The concept of exaptation is a particularly interesting one, in that it involves both the structure-function relationship and the concept of redundancy. It is by accident that an old structure is given a new function.

As Gould writes in *The Panda's Thumb: More Reflections in Natural History* (1982): "The majority of organisms and ecosystems can not be the result of an optimal design. [...] Imperfections are the primary evidence of evolution, since optimal designs erase history milestones".

A classic example of exaptation is the panda's thumb. The panda (*Ailuropoda melanoleuca*) is a strange animal: it is a member of the bear family and belongs to the order Carnivora. So, the panda is formally a carnivore, but its diet consists exclusively of bamboo. It is therefore a herbivore in the order of carnivores (it is not alone, the common bear for instance is an omnivore in the order of carnivores, but the panda in particular has developed a very specific food preference).

The panda is marked by its history: it has the structure of a carnivore, designed to hunt prey. In the course of evolution, its legs have adapted to running, hitting, clawing, scratching, slaughtering – certainly not to eating bamboo! If we observe a panda, we can see that it uses its paws very skilfully. But how can it hold bamboo canes, and clean bamboo leaves, with paws? Simple (Figure 2.6): the panda has thumbs!

The thumb is a sign of evolution of the human race, derived from primates. Some mammals have sacrificed their thumbs in favor of paws more adapted to running faster, hitting or scratching, but some do have a thumb, like the panda.

From an anatomical point of view, the panda's thumb is a "false" thumb: it is not a finger at all, it is a kind of bulge at some distance from the five clawed fingers, that is used as an opposable thumb. The "thumb"

Figure 2.6 Exaptation in nature: the panda's thumb.

protuberance has grown from a bone called the radial sesamoid, which in other animals is a small part of the wrist. In the panda, the sesamoid is very enlarged and elongated, almost as big as the real fingers. The radial sesamoid is located under one of the fleshy pads of the foreleg, while the five fingers form the structure of the palmar pad. Between the two pads is a shallow groove, which is perfect to hold bamboo canes!

The panda's thumb is also equipped with muscles for agility. These muscles are anatomical parts remodeled for a different purpose. The adductor muscle of the radial sesamoid (which distances the thumb from the other fingers) is not directly connected to the thumb as in other carnivores, but to two shorter muscles. The change in the sesamoid has been co-opted; later, the hypertrophism of the sesamoid has been retained, because of the usefulness of the opposable thumb.

The panda's thumb is therefore a complex device that re-adapts the normal components of carnivores' paws for a different purpose. It is an imperfect adaptation, somewhat impractical if compared for example to a real opposable thumb with dedicated joints and muscles, like the human thumb. But in the history of evolution, there are constraints that cannot always be overcome. As Gould writes in his essay: "The panda's true thumb is committed to another role, too specialized for a different function to become an opposable, manipulating digit. So the panda must use parts on hand and settle for an enlarged wrist bone and a somewhat clumsy, but quite workable, solution".

This particular type of "rough evolution" (in this case, the elongated sesamoid bone and the associated muscles) is an exaptation, an unexpected way of assembling a limited set of available components. It is a derivative adaptation, in that it is the result of a long sequence of functional adaptations which take advantage of useful characters (i.e., characters that increase the chances for survival), even if those characters have not been originally shaped by natural selection for their present role.

The spandrels of St. Mark's basilica in Venice (Figure 2.7) provide another interesting example of exaptation. One of the most prominent elements of St. Mark's architectural design is the central hemispherical dome. On the dome's interior, beautiful mosaics represent a detailed iconography of the Christian faith.

From a structural point of view, the dome had to be supported by four architectural elements called spandrels. More specifically, a spandrel is an elongated triangular space formed by the intersection of two adjoining arches. Its presence is inevitable when a dome is supported by rounded arches. In St. Mark's, the spandrels were later decorated with mosaics which adapted the represented scenes to the irregular space.

These mosaics are one of the most beautiful works of art in the Venetian basilica. The design is so elaborate, so balanced and so harmonious that it almost looks as if the spandrels were given a triangular shape to accommodate the mosaics!

Figure 2.7 Exaptation in architecture: the spandrels of St. Mark's basilica.

Of course, nothing could be farther from the truth – the four spandrels had originally been an architectural limitation, something that could not be avoided. But their irregular shape inspired mosaic artists to produce something extraordinary. This is a clear example of exaptation: by pure accident, a structural limitation resulted in a great masterpiece.

Note

1 Copernicus's theory was not devoid of errors; namely, he believed that the orbits of planets and the epicycles were not elliptical but circular.

3 Responding to complexity

"If one takes care of the means, the end will take care of itself".

Mahatma Gandhi

3.1 The foresight approach

Many experts of corporate strategy and innovation management focus on building systems that make it possible to run businesses under discontinuous conditions.

In his 1970 book *The Age of Discontinuity*, Peter Drucker (1992) was among the first to call attention to a changing reality, and to the subsequent inadequacy of traditional paradigms for sustaining competitive advantage. "In turbulent times, an enterprise has to be managed both to withstand sudden blows and to avail itself of sudden unexpected opportunities. This means that in turbulent times the fundamentals have to be managed, and managed well". In his book *Only the Paranoid Survive* (1996), the former chairman and co-founder of Intel Andy Grove affirmed that "strategic inflection points occur in all businesses as a direct result of specific forces affecting particular businesses". Alan Greenspan (2007) in *The Age of Turbulence* and Clayton Christensen (1997) in *The Innovator's Dilemma* make similar considerations.

How do companies successfully become "future-oriented"? What skills, what processes, what organizational structures need companies implement to ensure sustainability and long-term success? These are key questions, and they must be answered.

D'Aveni (1994) introduces the concept of hyper-competition: the extremely rapid evolution of many sectors means that competitive advantage can no longer be sustained in the long term using traditional paradigms. This happens because competitive advantage is constantly being created, eroded, destroyed and re-created as a result of the strategic maneuvers of companies that disrupt markets, sometimes cutting across entry barriers. Hyper-competition occurs because technologies and products are so new and different that standards and rules no longer apply. With rules constantly changing, a competitive advantage acquired in the past becomes utterly ineffective.

Men and organizations are not helpless in front of complexity. According to Godet (1985) there are three possible attitudes:

- Being subjected to change: passivity
- Taking action in an emergency: responsiveness
- Preparing for change and trying to orient it in a favorable direction: proactivity

Responsiveness is not an end in itself; while desirable in the short term, it does not lead anywhere if it is not oriented towards the company's long-term goals. Being responsive means detecting change when it is already under way. But having a forecasting attitude is something quite different: it does not mean waiting for change to happen, and then react to it! It means taking action, either to steer an expected change, or to bring about a desired change. This is true proactivity. In this sense, a company will greatly benefit from trying to perceive trends and future changes in advance, so that it can plan its strategy in time.

Given the impossibility of prediction, business competition shifts to the level of anticipation and perception. It now relies on corporate imagination (Hamel and Prahalad, 1995). Companies need to acquire more knowledge on expected trends and discontinuities than their competitors. They need to identify, earlier than anyone else, risks and future opportunities. Furthermore, they need to translate this knowledge into concrete innovation, into advantages for their customers, and they also need to know how to transfer these advantages and how to find new competitive spaces. Today, the pace is tight like a swirling torrent and companies need to be more "liquid": aware of being part of an open ecosystem, able to cultivate knowledge, able to identify and impact invisible networks, ready to find new approaches and to reorient themselves.

More specifically, to imagine the future and to prepare for change, companies can avail themselves of three very effective foresight methodologies (see Figure 3.1): detecting weak signals, understanding trends and building scenarios. To implement them successfully, companies need to develop three very specific qualities: strategic flexibility, promptness and resilience. The present chapter will explore these approaches thoroughly.

At the strategic and organizational level, the company must be able to react quickly to unexpected problems and opportunities (Lane and Maxfield, 1997). It must adapt for survival and reorient itself towards radical change (Nystrom, 1990). Most works on company longevity (*The Living Company* by Arie de Geus, 1997; *Built To Last* by Jim Collins and Jerry Porras 2012, *Enduring Success* by Christian Stadler, 2011) examine the problem from a different point of view: while studies on anticipation try to

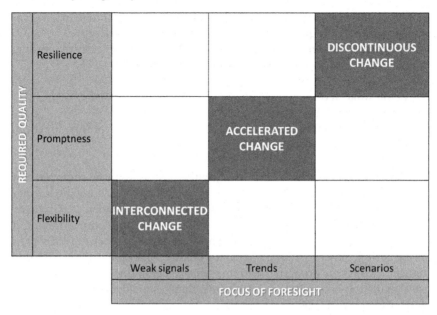

Figure 3.1 The foresight approach to change.

understand how companies can anticipate change in the environment and select the right strategy to protect their competitive advantage, longevity literature focuses on the characteristics that allow companies to survive for more than 100 years. Not surprisingly, the features that emerge from these studies are precisely flexibility, promptness and resilience, which in turn lead to business diversification, adaptable mentality, openness to cultural change etc.

Needless to say, the simultaneous presence of these three features increases the odds of company success, because each one of them sustains and improves the others.

In order to respond to interconnected change, a company must be able to steer its course in a tangle of cause-and-effect connections that it cannot fully understand. This is not easy, but it can be done if the company is able to identify weak signals as "harbingers" of the future, to encourage fertilization from different knowledge sources and to be flexible on its strategic plan, with a number of options always available. On the other hand, an understanding of the trend is required to respond to accelerated change in a timely manner. Finally, the key asset for tackling discontinuous change is resilience, or the ability to find new stability after a big shift from physiological balance.

In challenging times, the ability to imagine future scenarios leads the company to take into account potentially new contexts, both favorable and hostile, in which it might have to operate, and to implement alternative

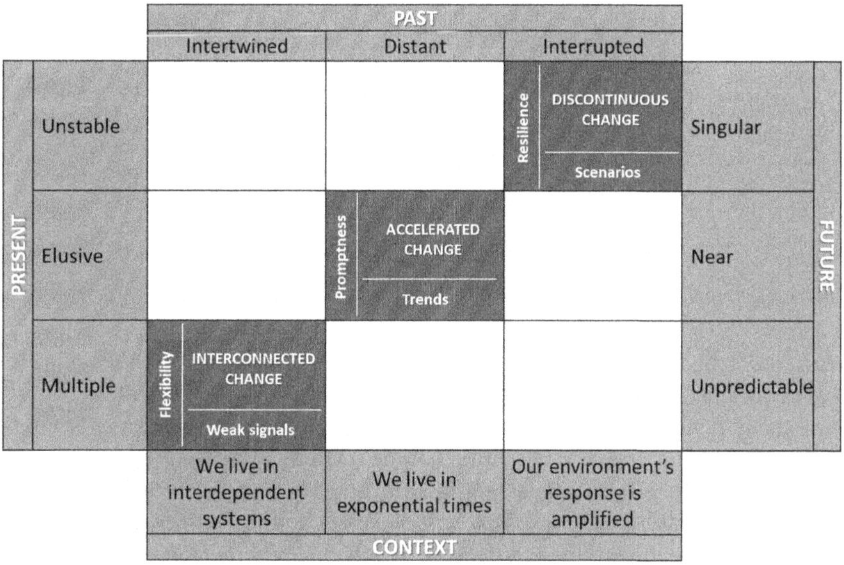

	PAST			
	Intertwined	Distant	Interrupted	
Unstable			DISCONTINUOUS CHANGE / Scenarios (Resilience)	Singular
Elusive		ACCELERATED CHANGE / Trends (Promptness)		Near
Multiple	INTERCONNECTED CHANGE / Weak signals (Flexibility)			Unpredictable
	We live in interdependent systems	We live in exponential times	Our environment's response is amplified	

(PRESENT — left axis; FUTURE — right axis; CONTEXT — bottom)

Figure 3.2 The characteristics of change.

strategies (for instance devising different business models, ready to be implemented according to the situation, or securing minority interests in other companies, preferably young and small, to keep a foot in other businesses).

Figure 3.2 recalls the three types of change discussed in Chapter 1 (Figure 1.11) and adds the related features.

3.2 Flexibility

Any living being which is not flexible enough, which is incapable of quick adaptation to changing conditions in its environment, will be unable to survive. For organizations, the concept is similar.

Complex and rapidly changing environments require open and flexible structures to allow for reorientation and radical change (Nystrom, 1990: 9), and sometimes just to allow mere survival. In a complex environment, companies absolutely need strategic flexibility (Figure 3.3):

- the ability to quickly modify competitive priorities,
- the ability to quickly move from one business to another,
- the availability of viable strategic options and
- the availability of potentially scalable businesses.

A flexible company must necessarily implement organizational structures and processes suited to a scenario which is increasingly turbulent, uncertain, unstable and unpredictable, a scenario where it becomes difficult to

	OBJECT OF THE VARIATION	
	Competitive priorities	Businesses
Rapidity of the variation	Strategic flexibility as the speed of variation of competitive priorities within a business (Hayes and Pisano, 1994)	Strategic flexibility as the rapidity of movement from one business to another (Stalk, Evans and Shulman, 1992)
Scope of the variation	Strategic flexibility as the scope of the strategic options within a business (Clark, 1996)	Strategic flexibility as the variety of the possible new businesses (Upton, 1994)

Figure 3.3 Types of strategic flexibility.

Source: De Toni and Tonchia, 2005.

plan and schedule in the medium and long term (Dioguardi, 1995). Nature leaves very little room for what is stiff and hard to change. Just like complex biological systems that constantly transform to adapt to the external environment and sometimes to create it, organizations are called upon to seize the moment and identify weak signals in time: this is why preserving flexibility is crucial. O'Reilly and Tuschman (2004) define *ambidexterity* as the ability of organizations to stay flexible by allocating attention and resources part to sustaining activities, part to radical innovation, so as to be ready to react to turbulence. Such a system is also called a *poised organization*.

Assuming that the environment is both continuous (for long periods) and discontinuous (for short but intense periods), only an ambidextrous organization has the means to find the organizational and managerial solutions required to survive turbulence and remain successful.

In the medium to long term, the only fixed elements in a company are vision, mission and values, while the business model keeps evolving all the time. The ability to grow thanks to a new product or technology is often related to the ability to develop a set of activities that can take the business into the new scenario. This shift can be performed quickly only if the company is ambidextrous: while the right hand focuses on current products and technologies, the left works on new areas. This attitude is fundamental to be able to adapt to an environment which is always in dynamic equilibrium.

According to Christensen's definition (1997), it is essential to combine two kinds of innovation: sustaining or incremental innovation on one side, and disruptive or radical innovation on the other. Incremental innovation is essential in the short term, but insufficient to support growth; on the other hand, too much radical innovation can lead to instability. Ambidextrous organizations are able to juggle both kinds, for instance finding a balance between exploration and exploitation, or implementing organizational solutions like spin-offs, separating or integrating specific business functions, building an external knowledge network etc.

All these elements are necessary to create a multi-option strategy, different from traditional strategic approaches such as planning, balancing, positioning, or controlling resources. The multi-option strategy is based on the management of many new business models simultaneously.

Strategic flexibility as the ability to quickly move from one business to another, and strategic flexibility as the availability of potentially new businesses are clearly linked to the innovation of the business model. Often the entire business model has to be changed in order to "follow" an innovation.

A business model is a set of organizational and strategic solutions through which the company acquires a competitive advantage. In other words, it is the logic according to which an organization creates, delivers and captures value.

Not all innovations have the same impact. Independent research by IBM and Boston Consulting Group has clearly proved that companies that innovate their business model have a large competitive advantage – measured against profits – compared to those making only product/service innovation: namely +8.5% in a period of three years, +6.1% over five years and +2.7% over ten years. But why is business model innovation so important? A major reason is that while product innovation is easily replicated by competitors (think of any software or smartphone model), innovation in business departments and functions is not, and this is what accounts for such a big difference.

The pressure to innovate the business model does not only come from inside, but is also due to other factors, like different environmental conditions, interactions with customers, changes in the management, new opportunities to stand out and to compete in many different industrial sectors.

Let's take an example: women's gyms. Thanks to hydraulic machines (an innovation by Curves, the well-known fitness-center chain for women only), women are now offered the highest standards of service and outstanding fitness results, with affordable monthly subscriptions. Besides, mindful of its clients' need to reconcile family, work and leisure, Curves proposes 30-minute workouts. With this innovative approach, Curves has become the franchising with the fastest opening rate on the planet.

3.3 Promptness

The well-known saying "time is money" is undisputed in competitive systems, especially in Western countries, but the first scientific studies on the importance of time in competitive environments are quite recent. The first two important articles on the subject date back to 1988: "Time – The Next Source of Competitive Advantage" by Stalk, published in the *Harvard Business Review*, and "The Merit of Making Things Fast" by Schmenner, published in the *Sloan Management Review*.

In this era of acceleration of change, time is undoubtedly a critical factor. Promptness and rapidity of reaction can be evaluated by measuring the average reaction time, and they are crucial, along with timeliness and reliability, to respond quickly to the challenges of an exponential context. Change is less and less linear and more and more exponential, and companies need to adopt the right tools and routines to facilitate promptness of response.

3.4 Resilience

In engineering, resilience is the capacity of a material to absorb impulsive stress. In biology and ecology resilience is the ability of an ecosystem, be it a single organism or an entire city, to self-repair after damage. It is defined as the capacity to return to a global equilibrium following a perturbation. Similarly, resilient companies have the capacity to absorb disturbances caused by sudden "impacts" or unexpected events in the business environment.

Resilience is not so much sturdiness as elasticity, the ability to resist adversity by seizing whatever opportunities arise and to survive stressful situations by developing new skills, all the while preserving one's identity. The ability of an organization to be resilient depends on two main factors: on one side, the knowledge, skills and abilities of the individuals, on the other, the routines and procedures implemented to cope with the potentially destructive consequences of a sudden shock. The relationship between individual resilience and organizational resilience implies a "system-subsystem" interaction. The organization's skills do not amount to a simple sum of individual skills, because the interactions among individuals create a complex social network which helps to develop a capacity for resilience in the whole organization.

High reliability organizations (HROs) are resilient organizations par excellence, which routinely operate in turbulent environments and are, by nature, ready to face the unexpected. They are nuclear power plants, air traffic control centers, hospital emergency departments, hostage negotiation teams etc. HROs stand out for their effective management of high-risk technologies through the organizational control of risks and probabilities (Rochlin, 1993:14).

Counterintuitively, the key to HROs' performance is that they react to weak signals with a strong response. High reliability is grounded in processes of collective mindfulness; in other words, HROs focus on increasing the quality of attention across the organization and on establishing a set of processes and practices which contribute to the system's culture of safety.

According to Weick and Sutcliffe (2001), there are five characteristics of HROs that keep them working well when facing unexpected situations:

- Preoccupation with failure
- Reluctance to simplify interpretations
- Sensitivity to operations
- Commitment to resilience
- Deference to expertise

These characteristics can be translated into managerial attitudes for business companies (see Figure 3.4).

CHARACTERISTICS		MANAGERIAL ATTITUDES
Preoccupation with failure	→	Monitoring and peripheral vision Detecting errors as possible weak signals
Reluctance to simplify interpretations	→	Scenario building
Sensitivity to operations	→	Monitoring and peripheral vision Detecting weak signals
Commitment to resilience	→	Openness to anticipation
Deference to expertise	→	Openness to the outside environment Technological brokering

Figure 3.4 Managerial attitudes derived from high reliability organizations.

HROs endlessly reinvent themselves, completely restructuring their response according to circumstances. They are learning organizations, so flexible and resilient that they are able to manage unexpected events that by definition cannot be planned for. This concept has been developed by Doz and Kosonen (2008), who propose the idea of "strategic agility". Strategic agility is the ability to continuously adjust and adapt the strategic direction in the core business, as a function of strategic ambitions and changing circumstances, and create not just new products and services, but also new business models and innovative ways to create value for the company. The key enabling capabilities are as follows:

1 Strategic Sensitivity: sharpness of perception and intensity of awareness and attention
2 Resource Fluidity: internal capability to reconfigure business systems and to rapidly redeploy resources
3 Collective Commitment: the ability of the top team to make bold decisions, and to make them fast, without getting involved in "win-lose" politics

3.5 Detecting weak signals

Foresight is clearly connected to change and risk. Change mainly occurs in three forms: trend and/or cycle shifts, weak signals and wild cards. As regards strategic planning, innovation and foresight, the management should ask the following questions: "Which are the most important trends for our organization? Are there cycles? What are the most important emerging issues? Which wild cards could completely change our business? Can we anticipate them? What actions can we take?" Executives must be able to observe and identify the factors of change, and to put a correct strategy in place to deal with them. Of course, by asking these questions managers are in fact initiating a process of foresight.

Companies often face demographic changes, new competitors, new technologies, new regulations and other environmental changes that suddenly appear, apparently for no reason (Day and Schoemaker, 2005). To describe weak signals, Wack (1985) uses the rabbit metaphor: "As any adult knows, a magician cannot produce a rabbit unless it is already in (or very near to) his hat. In the same way, surprises in the business environment almost never emerge without a warning". These warnings are *weak signals*. They are weak in the sense that they are hard to detect, but their potential impact can be devastating. Like the rabbit which is already in the magician's hat before we see it, the future is already here even if we can't see it clearly. And we can't see it clearly because in the beginning the future reveals itself only through weak signals.

It is essential to detect weak signals because, as we said before, the future comes like a cat. Like all felines, a cat approaches on padded feet, making almost imperceptible noises (the weak signals). Then, for a brief moment, all noise actually stops, everything is still – but all of a sudden, the cat jumps and here it is! The future comes upon us before we even realize it.

Ansoff (1965) was a pioneer in the field. He defined weak signals as warnings, warnings that are too incomplete to permit an accurate estimation of their impact, and/or to determine a complete response. Mendonça et al. (2004) define weak signals as the ideas or trends (technological, competitive, social, political etc.) that will affect the business or the business environment. Weak signals may be a new and surprising opportunity, but also a threat to the organization. They are often difficult to detect at an early stage, for many reasons: they are unfamiliar and therefore easily ignored, they are difficult to track down because of background noise and mixed signals, and they are often underestimated by experts in the field (Godet, 1985; Mendonça et al., 2004).

According to Harris and Zeisler (2002), weak signals are most likely found at the edge of chaos, in the rich environment between continuity and discontinuity.

By detecting weak signals, companies can see what risks and opportunities lay ahead. This attitude has been key to many success stories, like that of Virgin Group. In the words of Harris and Zeisler (2002): "Entrepreneur Richard Branson's forays to find and develop the diverse businesses that make up the Virgin Group, detecting in many cases a weak signal ignored by incumbents with a 'sense of fun', distinguish his business ventures in what many consider staid or impenetrable markets".

Another example could be Nintendo, which understood early the need for closer physical interaction with the game and the latent need for socialization in the video game market, and created the Wii. Or the Italian eye-wear company Luxottica, which understood in advance that glasses were no longer a mere corrective tool, but an element of style and fashion.

To implement radical innovations, the starting point is not today's market, where needs are already met and where innovation demand is mainly incremental, but tomorrow's market – what Bob Galvin, the former chairman of Motorola, liked to term the "total imaginable market" – the market for products that do not yet exist in the customers' minds. In the words of Akio Morita, the co-founder of Sony: "We don't ask consumers what they want. They do not know. Instead we apply our brain power to what they need, and will want, and make sure we're there, ready". To navigate the fog of uncertainty and manage the unexpected, it is necessary to develop the ability to perceive today what will be needed tomorrow.

In global research conducted in 2002 by the Fuld-Gilad-Herring Academy of Competitive Intelligence, more than two-thirds of the 140 business managers involved in the survey admitted that their organization had been taken by surprise by more than three disruptive events in the previous five years. Moreover, the vast majority, about 97%, stated that the company did not have "anticipatory intelligence", that is, an early warning system able to collect and analyze strategic information, and to identify weak signals at an early stage. In all this, the most surprising thing was that almost all of them admitted to having been aware of the importance of detecting weak signals prior to the disruptive events. Clearly, it is not enough to know that the external environment is full of warning signs; we must also have the right tools and above all the right abilities. One of the most effective ones is *peripheral vision* (Day and Schoemaker, 2005; Fink et al., 2004; Rohrbeck, 2010).

In complex and rapidly changing environments, companies need to develop a good peripheral vision. However, if the environment is relatively stable, too much peripheral vision can cause a company to become "neurotic" and waste resources by focusing on irrelevant signals. We can say that all companies need this ability, but with the appropriate degree of intensity (Day and Schoemaker, 2005). First of all, detecting weak signals requires an *active monitoring system*. Secondly, to help support internal monitoring and research, it requires a network of external relations with potential innovators, in the form of collaborations, conventions, agreements etc., namely, a *safeguard network* which monitors the sites of potential innovation in order to increase the degree of fertilization and to improve the ability to conceive original ideas.

Perceiving weak signals is important because it minimizes reaction time, not only to threats but also to opportunities. As the available reaction time decreases, both the external environment and the organization itself increase in complexity. When the environment is complex, the organization is forced to respond earlier and earlier to the new state of knowledge (Ansoff, 1979; Ilmola and Kuusi, 2006).

3.6 Understanding trends

In order to find one's way in the maze of the future, it is necessary to understand the complex forces that lead to change, the emerging trends, the potential dislocations, the alternative scenarios, the political, social and economic context. Potential new technologies, competitive dynamics, future customers must also be taken into account. In meteorology for instance, the continuous monitoring of complex and interrelated sets of forces allows us to infer how these forces will impact in terms of the weather. Similarly, visionary organizations have to implement a monitoring process to detect the key trends that can potentially impact on their business.

The challenge for companies is therefore to be alert and aware of the surrounding environment. Monitoring technological and market trends is important to understand in which direction the industry sector and the business are moving. This is done mainly by retracing the state of the art of the technological landscape (expertise areas where technologies develop, new technologies, interdependencies among different sectors and technologies etc.). Monitoring the market through the constant use of available information sources allows to identify opportunities, to understand possible criticalities in the application of technological innovations to the company reality, and to define programs and strategies.

The first focus of foresight is on *trends*. To anticipate means not only to identify hidden signals, but also to spot and follow trends that are already clear in the here and now, but could evolve in different directions and affect the company's business in different ways. The real value of trend analysis is precisely to understand the implications of a trend for one's business, and to consider the reciprocal influences between trends. An isolated trend will not say much about what can or will happen, because it will probably be influenced by other trends that will affect it in turn. The hard part is to connect trends so that it becomes possible to identify patterns of change and emerging opportunities. For example, the trend of video-game technology development, if taken alone, does not suggest interesting future opportunities; however, if combined with the trend of a rapidly growing middle class in developing countries (China, India and Brazil), and with the trend of mobile phone penetration in these same countries, a scenario appears of excellent opportunities for handheld video-game devices (Daheim and Uerz, 2008).

In addition to trends, part of the literature on foresight stresses the importance of considering technological *cycles* in order to anticipate the possible development of different technologies in the future. According to some authors, besides the evolution from past to future, other recurring paths of development can be found in technologies.

To effectively capture trends, it is critical to observe not only markets up and down the value chain, but also markets at the periphery of the sector (Foster and Kaplan, 2001). A study of 60 German companies interested in futures studies (Daheim, 2004) shows that 70% of them have a broad horizon of study that goes beyond the reference business and focuses on three main areas: core business, contiguous businesses and "white spaces". It is important to note that changes and opportunities often come from outside the company's sector; it is therefore critical not to look only "at one's own garden", but to keep a broad focus on the emerging trends of adjoining sectors (Hines, 2006). And this is not all: it is also necessary to consider the so-called white spaces, new areas of influence unrelated to the business and often to the whole sector, but linked to innovations coming from totally different places (Rohrbeck, 2008; Reger, 2006). Effective monitoring requires a balanced mix of all these areas, together with the awareness of the social and political environment, of competitors and of consumers.

Wild cards (Mendonça et al., 2004; Burmeister et al., 2004; Cuhls and Johnston, 2006) refer to incidents with perceived low probability of occurrence but with potentially high impacts for an organization and a society. Events like September 11th are such wild cards. These sudden and unique incidents can constitute turning points in the evolution of a certain trend or system. Wild cards can become plausible at any time and are one of the most unpredictable and potentially damaging triggers of change. If a strategy is formulated in advance to deal with a specific wild card or discontinuous event, the time devoted to the crisis resolution is reduced and incorrect responses, typically made when under pressure, are avoided. (Mendonça et al., 2004).

As shown in Figure 3.5, wild cards are completely unexpected and surprising events, trends are strong signals that any monitoring activity can easily identify, and weak signals are prospective changes in the business environment which are hard to detect or unclearly perceived by the company.

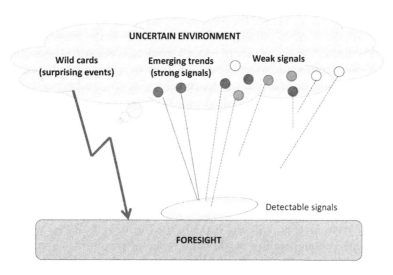

Figure 3.5 Monitoring the environment to identify weak signals and trends.

3.7 Building scenarios

To innovate and to build a strategy for the future, it is necessary to imagine scenarios that are different from the present reality, in a 360-degree environmental scanning. A company which does not find the time to think about the future and to plan for it, which only focuses on immediate concerns, implicitly surrenders a major, maybe decisive, share of its competitive advantage. Hence the importance and the difficulty of navigating the complexity of the future, of monitoring and exploring emerging trends in order to develop scenarios that represent opportunities for possible future businesses.

Amid complexity and turbulence, the future consists of a combination of a number of factors. "The discontinuity and turbulence which characterize complexity render the prediction modes known to date utterly ineffective" (Sinatra, 1989:22) (*our translation, N.d.T.*). We cannot compress or simplify the future into a forecast delusion, we can only try to imagine it through scenarios, so that it does not find us completely unprepared.

At the stage of conceptualization (i.e., innovation and strategy), the company tries to imagine future events and how it could respond to them, and it can only do this by construing alternatives and by building scenarios (Scifo, 2002). A scenario contains the description of a future situation and the sequence of events that lead from the present to the imagined situation. Alternative scenarios can be built and different responses can be devised using a *what-if* logic.

As Godet (1985) notes, the term scenario comes from the theater, but in futures studies it takes on a different meaning. In ordinary usage, a scenario is the plot outline of a dramatic work, detailing the scenes, characters and situations as they will take place on stage. It is therefore something already defined, a given future. In futures studies, a scenario is an imagined or projected sequence of events, especially any of several detailed plans or possibilities. For each imagined situation, scenarios can be multiple, the result of several outcomes unfolding simultaneously.

A metaphor of infinite possibilities is perfectly represented in "The Library of Babel" (1941) by the Argentine writer Jorge Luis Borges. The short story describes a fantastic library consisting of an enormous expanse of adjacent hexagonal rooms. In each room, four walls of shelves disorderly contain all possible books, written with every possible character combination. In the library imagined by Borges it is possible to find, amidst an enormous amount of useless nonsense, all the books that have been written in the past, all that will be written in the future and all that will never be written, although falling within the range of possibility. Some books are extremely boring, they contain for instance only the letter *A*, or all-white pages. Some, not yet written, contain the biography of each of us, in very precise terms or with countless variations. Others are translations of every book in every other language; others describe, in detail, the battles of Cannae or Waterloo, or future wars or wars that will never be fought; still others describe the theory of relativity, its bogus variants, and theories that will be discovered only in AD 15000. Because the letters can, by accident, compose meaningful sentences, weary men keep exploring the labyrinthine library, in search of the Book that contains the Truth. *The Library of Babel* is a sum of infinite possibilities, only some of which will become reality.

Just like in a complex tapestry, where pulling a thread moves many others, scenario planning helps to understand how the options may change if a variable changes. There are very specific techniques to process this, such as for example morphological analysis, cross-impact analysis and trend impact analysis.

Beside trends, scenario planning focuses on uncertainties, things that we are unable to determine about the future. In the words of Olson and Eoyang (2001:52): "To achieve results, the agents of change must develop a level of comfort with uncertainty". Scenario planning blends the known and the unknown (trends, weak signals and uncertainties) into a limited number of alternative views of the future that span a large range of possibilities.

Scenarios do not predict the future, but they help us think about it and elaborate a consistent framework for our decisions. According to Sifonis and Goldberg (1996), companies should be aware that a complex environment requires complex, unpredictable, creative, innovative answers. But scenarios also teach us other things. Given a specific situation, scenarios raise our awareness of the multiplicity of possible futures. They also force us to take into account the interdependence of the elements that make up the studied system. Finally, they may induce the management to accept constructive but unpleasant hypotheses, and promote the recognition of problems, relationships or issues ignored or deliberately left out as controversial.

The impossibility of prediction should not engender stillness and passive behavior; a proactive attitude is essential, together with risk acceptance. It is important to realize that a company is always in unstable equilibrium, at the edge between predictability and unpredictability, but not helpless in front of the forking paths of the future. Just as Borges's library contains infinite possibilities, only some of which will come into existence, a successful company envisions multiple future paths and prepares strategically for possible outcomes.

The best known example of the use of scenario planning is Royal Dutch/ Shell, which has used it since the '70s to generate and evaluate its strategic options. Another example, told by Godet, is Volkswagen. Scenario development at Volkswagen is based on a 15-year-long experience. In the company's view, the knowledge of basic trends in customers' needs and values is essential for the design and production of successful models. Scenarios are built by interdisciplinary teams from the marketing and production of the four brands VW, Audi, Seat and Skoda. An example from the past is the Golf GTI model, a sporty compact car conceived in the '70s, which seemed weird at the time. An analysis of the potential market would have suggested inadequate sales volumes, but Volkswagen bet on the scenario of a car as a symbol of a very specific way of life. In turn, the model itself boosted the growth of this new style: in the early '90s, the Golf GTI sales exceeded one million units.

4 Anticipating the future

"By striving to do the impossible, man has always achieved what is
possible".
Michail Bakunin

4.1 From forecasting to foresight

Not only is it impossible to predict what will happen, but also it is necessary to be extremely fast in adapting to opportunities and threats. Facing
the unexpected requires alertness and flexibility.

Predicting the future is impossible, but it is possible to get ready for an
uncertain future and a complex and dynamic environment, by remaining
vigilant and attentive to the signals that can be seen in the present. Hence
the importance and difficulty, but also the appeal, of this challenge for
companies willing to follow this path – actively monitoring and exploring
emerging trends and developing alternative scenarios for business opportunities five or ten years in advance.

As Tom Peters (2006) says, *Distinct or extinct!* Creating and sustaining
growth is a major challenge that requires alertness in front of the future, a
great capacity for adaptation, an ability, as it were, to "feel" the market. In
this sense, men and organizations must change their perspective, no longer
looking to the future with the traditional linear approach, but with a more
complex approach of feedback and anticipation, standing ready to grasp
the weak signals coming from the market and actively monitoring trends.
In other words, since there can be no real prediction, competition shifts to
the level of *perception*.

The business universe is opening up to a new competitive space, referred
to as "blue ocean" by Kim Chan and Mauborgne (2002), as opposed to the
"red ocean" of the market space as we know it today.

Since the dawn of the industrial age, companies have waged a relentless
battle to gain an advantage in the bloody red ocean of competition, full of
rivals fighting for ever shrinking profits. From Ford's Model T to Apple's

iPod, they have identified principles and tools in order to outperform competitors and to create uncontested market spaces, with the limitless possibilities of a blue ocean.

In red oceans, industry boundaries are defined and accepted, prices tend to go down and the rules of the game are well understood. As the space gets more and more crowded, prospects for profits and growth are reduced. In blue oceans, the approach is the opposite: demand is created rather than fought over, companies give themselves new rules, capable of opening unknown market space, untainted by competition, where there is ample opportunity for growth. In red oceans, companies seek customers in the existing market. In blue oceans, they look to non-customers. In red oceans, companies try to understand how customers choose between different competitors in the same sector. In blue oceans, they know that customers make their choice looking beyond sector boundaries. In red oceans, companies create niche markets, segmenting customers. In blue oceans, they look for commonalities among all customers, in order to create mass demand and collect huge profits.

To be countered with the appropriate response, changes in the outside environment must be detected in time. With a still inadequate sense of urgency, a lot of companies still have not implemented processes and organizational routines that enable them to scan the surroundings carefully enough and to transform signals and information into specific actions for change. The well-known Kodak case is a good example of the consequences of such attitude.

Companies compete to gain knowledge about trends and discontinuities in the PEEST[1] environment. This knowledge is used to create new technologies, to answer completely new customers' needs and to perceive future opportunities. All this is subsequently transformed into action in the processes of innovation and strategy, by figuring out new products and services and new business models that can create new competitive spaces and modify sector boundaries.

The problem is overcoming the trade-off between invention and innovation, because, unfortunately, there are always more ideas in search of solutions than solutions to concrete problems. In other words, the question is not so much to have good new ideas, as to channel them into solutions that are feasible and acceptable for the market. Often the technologies are already present: all that is needed is an innovator, not an inventor, to actualize them.

Moreover, companies must learn to explore new business models even while they are still using the old ones, the models that gave them success; companies that have this ability to explore the new while exploiting the old are also called *ambidextrous*. They are generally the most long-lived, because they know how to adapt to technological change and to the market. Companies must also learn to invest in dynamic capabilities, making use of old resources and absorbing new ones, thus equipping themselves with the required skills to compete at all times in a dynamic environment.

4.2 We need new abilities to find the right answers

For men and organizations, the environment becomes increasingly complex and dynamic, mutations are more frequent and unexpected, business becomes more risky and difficult. But what can be done? The new context of the 21st century, characterized by complexity, turbulence and acceleration, very strongly requires on the part of people and companies the capacity to address change. Accelerated change and turbulence on the rise demand a constant 360-degree scan of the surroundings, an unrelenting search for ways and methods to anticipate the future. In a world where complexity and uncertainty seem to be the norm, organizations are in dire need of gathering global knowledge from internal and external sources.

The evolution of a complex system is unpredictable, the more so when it is positioned at a bifurcation point, at the edge of chaos. The effects of the many interactions mean that any action carried out by a company, or by its autonomous components, will lead to an unforeseeable variation of its future state. From a managerial point of view, understanding a network of this type implies accepting the fact that unknowable events cannot be planned. This state of uncertainty and helplessness can be overcome only by holding a general view of the connections in the network and by practicing observation of its proactive behavior. However, only specific criteria or, better still, heuristic models, allow to identify the "best" behavior among the many alternatives present at every moment. These models act as orienting vectors towards specific attractors.

This approach, while allowing a formulation that we can still call "strategic", assuming a set of orienting heuristics, does not correspond to strategic planning as proposed by classical economical doctrine. Finally, for long-time sustainability, the company must adapt dynamically to all interactions with all the external and internal agents in the set of stakeholders, and to the entire economical and physical environment.

Therefore, men and organizations need to adopt a new set of critical skills, methods and processes to identify and define responses for the future, in particular:

- System perspective and pattern recognition: the ability to visualize the whole system rather than its isolated components, and the ability to see the general course instead of the single factors.
- Acceptance of complexity: systems are not deterministic and closed, but unpredictable and open.

- Consideration of the future: the competence to understand the direction suggested by trends, weak signals and wild cards, to determine their impact and effect on the system, and to respond quickly and appropriately.

In this context, classical methods (prediction or extrapolation) are not enough, since they are mainly based on experience, that is to say, on the past.

These methods are retrospective and no longer suitable by themselves. Anticipation based on the past, even when done in its most quantitative and scientific form (data extrapolation, or linearization of past curves), determines what will happen if the observed phenomenon stays still, out of time. It is only in conditions of very low complexity that methodological solutions based on the idea that companies are deterministic and closed systems can provide a somewhat effective approximation.

At the strategic level, a forward-looking approach is vital because it allows to deal with future challenges proactively: it is necessary to develop management tools that increase the ability to master both internal and external complexity. Prediction is risky, all we can do is pay attention to weak signals and proceed by trial and error. For some time now, traditional *forecasting* models – based on the forward projection of past experiences – have been insufficient to predict the future. More advanced methods use the logic of anticipation instead, also called *foresight*, which strives to detect weak signals, emerging trends and wild cards from external sources. Foresight is an approach based on three fundamental assumptions (Amara, 1981):

- The future is not predictable.
- The future is not predetermined.
- Future outcomes can be influenced by choices made in the present (in a way, the present already carries the future).

The difference between the two approaches has been highlighted by Cuhls (2003), who compares forecasting and foresight. The first difference can be found in the definition of objectives: while in forecasting questions must be clear and precise from the start, in foresight they are always open, and are themselves a part of the foresight process. Forecasting is based on historical data, a known basis which is then projected forward, and is therefore precise. On the contrary, foresight takes a leap into the future and then comes back to the present; it is much less accurate, it looks at things from a "system" perspective, it takes into account many arguments and many points of view, on the assumption that everything is interconnected.

Another important difference concerns the nature of the applied techniques: while forecasting is based on numerical and quantitative approaches (econometrics or modeling, which derive a future behavior from past data), foresight uses qualitative techniques, looking for signs of change in science and technology, in politics and economics, in society, culture and in the competitive environment (May et al., 2000), while relying in part also on quantitative techniques.

Besides, foresight does not only aim at obtaining results, like forecasting, but also at sharing results, by creating an environment of participation and communication. Shared results will then be used to take meaningful decisions that contain implications for the future and for the present.

4.3 Different presents, multiple paths, possible scenarios

The term "foresight" was used by Irvine and Martin, in 1984, to describe forecasting processes promoted at the national level (Cattell, 2002). Later the term has shifted, as mentioned above, from the level of world/continent/country (country foresight) to the level of sector (industry foresight) and company (corporate foresight).

At the level of corporate foresight, which is the focus of this book, the first question we have to ask ourselves is the following: what difference is there between classical forecasting, typically used in the past, and the more recent process of foresight or anticipation?

In the previous paragraph, several differences have already been identified:

- Clear and precise questions against open questions dictated by the process itself
- Linear perspective against systemic perspective
- Numerical and quantitative techniques versus qualitative techniques
- Consensus on possible results against consensus on results sought after

But there are still other meaningful differences. First of all, the initial input. A forecasting process makes use of historical data to extrapolate the future. A foresight process focuses on trends and weak signals.

Besides, forecasting assumes the existence of one given present, which is unique and can be clearly described. On the contrary, foresight assumes that many presents coexist simultaneously, each one contradicting the others, each one competing with the others, and that only some of them will materialize in the future.

Another difference is that in forecasting, the future is one and is determined by the extrapolation which describes its path; in foresight there are many possible futures, described by different scenarios, and each of them can be reached through different paths.

Finally, foresight takes into account the occurrence of wild cards possibly impacting both the different presents and the different paths.

In summary (see Figures 4.1 and 4.2), forecasting starts from one perceived present (*one present*), elaborates historical data (*single path*), and identifies one possible future (*one future*). Foresight starts from coexisting

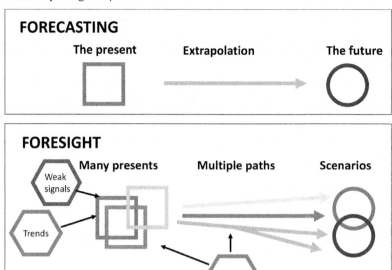

Figure 4.1 Differences between forecasting and foresight.

presents (*many presents*), builds various possible routes (*multiple paths*) based on trends and weak signals, and identifies different possible scenarios (*many futures*), with strategic surprises impacting both the presents and the paths.

A scenario is "a story of what happened in the future". Scenarios describe different situations that may occur in the future. They help us

	CORPORATE FORECASTING	CORPORATE FORESIGHT
Questions	Clear and precise	Open and part of the process
Perspective	Linear	Systemic
Methodologies	Quantitative	Qualitative
Input	Historical data	Weak signals Trends
Present	One	Many
Path	Single	Multiple (path dependence)
Wild cards	Not considered	Considered
Future	One, determined by extrapolation	Many, based on scenarios
Consensus on results	Possible	Sought after

Figure 4.2 Features of forecasting and foresight compared.

understand and represent the ways in which future events may unfold. They are used to challenge mental models and to offset people's perceptions on the probability of specific events. In this sense, each scenario is a different possible future. Even in the course of action, various events and situations can occur.

A specific scenario is not reached by following a specific path because, also depending on the past and present (because of path dependence), the same future can be reached by different paths.

It is important to stress that possible futures depend on one's point of view: the expected future is "what I think will happen", the preferred future is "what I wish would happen" and alternative futures are "what could happen instead".

4.4 The history of foresight

The origin of futures studies can be traced back to the dawn of time, when we first began to ask ourselves questions on the future. But it was only in the Enlightenment period, during the 17th century, that we started thinking about the future as such, through utopian writing and logical reasoning. Mercier (1771) was the first to write a book on the year 2440, in which, with typical Enlightenment optimism, he outlined the scenario of a society made perfect by the application of scientific principles. This interest in the future will later be found in the science fiction works of 19th-century authors like Jules Verne and Herbert George Wells. A good example is Edward Bellamy's novel *Looking Backward: 2000–1887*, an important treatise on social perfectibility (Bellamy, 1888).

The first scientific approaches to the study of the future date back to the first half of the 20th century. They are national studies performed by the US government, closely connected with issues of security and military strategy (Mietzner and Reger, 2005). In that period, the US began to systematically examine trends and indicators of change, with the purpose of anticipating events (McHale, 1978; Clarke, 1979; Cornish, 2004; Masini, 2006).

The most important of these early studies on the future were conducted by the US Army during World War II and greatly developed in later years, under the looming threat of a catastrophic nuclear conflict. These studies were indicated with the term "forecasting". The US Department of Defense appointed the Rand Corporation, an influential think tank including great futurists like Ted Gordon, to imagine likely scenarios and predict possible futures.

The sixties were a time of great social change and tension, and many kept their eyes on the future. The first futurology courses were offered at Yale University and Virginia Polytechnic, and during the late '60s and early '70s associations were born such as the World Future Society and the World Futures Studies Federation. During those same years, Houston-Clear Lake

University activated a course of futures studies. In order to anticipate and counter the possible Cold War threats, a large number of methodologies (such as scenario planning and Delphi analysis) were developed to assist the military and aerospace. Since then, many countries (especially the US, Japan and the UK) have invested in research on the future to help them select and direct their investments.

At the corporate level, in 1970 Shell was one of the first companies to successfully use scenario planning as a method to support the strategic planning process and to deal with uncertainty in the business environment (Ansoff, 1980; Van der Heijden, 2004). Its success was emblematic, and fostered a change in the way of studying the future that would bring governments and companies to embrace the new approach of foresight.

Ever since, futures studies have been used in companies and other organizations. At the beginning, these studies were mostly based on forecasting and made heavy use of quantitative and econometric techniques, targeting specific issues and based on past data. However, it was soon evident that this approach was inadequate and too restrictive: it was aimed at making a precise and unambiguous prediction of the future, and it did not take into account alternative scenarios. The future is indeed unpredictable: relying on one single alternative is clearly limiting, and exposes companies to the risk of unexpected events and emerging phenomena.

In the '70s and the '80s, foresight techniques spread through the corporate world, partly due to the very success of Shell. A survey of US companies made in 1981 revealed that if before the oil crisis of 1973 there had been a limited use of foresight, in the early '80s almost half of the 1000 industrial companies actively involved in the survey were using forecasting techniques in their planning processes. They were mostly large companies, with major investments in equipment and machinery (capital intensive), which planned on the very long term (over 10 years) and came from the chemical, oil and aerospace sectors (Linneman and Klein, 1983). In Europe the spread of foresight was similar. After an initial test-and-trial period in the early '70s, foresight was increasingly used in the '80s, especially by corporations with a long-term planning horizon like automobile makers and electricity suppliers.

At the end of the '80s, there was a confused period in which scenario analysis (the most prevalent method at the time) was in turn applied and rejected. But in the '90s, when governments became more interested in futures studies, foresight had a revival in the corporate world, especially as large companies such as Philips, Lucent Technologies, Siemens, DaimlerChrysler and Shell already had their own prediction systems. Since then, foresight has been increasingly used by all companies (Cuhls and Johnston, 2006).

A well-known definition of foresight was given by UNIDO (1995): "Technology foresight is regarded as the most upstream element of the technology development process. It provides inputs for the formulation of technology policies and strategies that guide the development of the

	AUTHOR				
	Martin (1995)	Coates (1985)	Georghiou (1996)	Slaughter (1996a)	Horton (1999)
WHAT FORESIGHT DOES — Expands the boundaries of perception				x	
Analyzes possible future developments	x	x	x	x	x
Identifies emerging situations	x	x	x	x	
Supports decisions		x			x

Figure 4.3 What foresight does.

technological infrastructure. In addition, technology foresight provides support to innovation, and incentives and assistance to enterprises in the domain of technology management and technology transfer, leading to enhanced competitiveness and growth".

For Martin (1995), foresight is "the process involved in systematically attempting to look into the longer-term future of science, technology, the economy and society with the aim of identifying the areas of strategic research and the emerging generic technologies likely to yield the greatest economic and social benefits". Coates (1985) defines foresight as a process for a deeper understanding of the factors that drive the design of the long-term future. In the activity of governance, foresight is not intended to define policy, but it can help to figure out when choices are more appropriate, more flexible and more robust in their implementation, in the moment when certain circumstances change. Foresight is therefore one of the steps in planning.

For Georghiou (1996), foresight is "a systematic means of assessing those scientific and technological developments which could have a strong impact on industrial competitiveness, wealth creation and quality of life". Slaughter (1996a) sees it as "quintessentially a directed process which broadens the boundaries of perception through careful scanning of possible futures and the clarification of emerging situations". Horton (1999) asserts that foresight is "a process of developing views on possible ways in which the future can be built: by understanding that present actions will contribute to the future's best scenario". Figure 4.3 resumes the main features of foresight according to different authors.

4.5 Foresight for countries, for sectors, for companies

Foresight was born at the national level, and has traditionally been linked to technology. Technology foresight is the natural prosecution of technology forecasting, and we can find it at three different levels: country foresight, which deals with areas of investigation ranging from regions to nations to

	ACTORS	AREAS OF INVESTIGATION	OBJECTIVES	MAIN AUTHORS
COUNTRY FORESIGHT	Governments and institutions	• Politics • Economy • Society	Directing national investments	Miles, 1999; Keenan, 2005
INDUSTRY FORESIGHT	Research centers and institutes	• Sectors • Technology • Design	Identifying sector trends	Hamel and Prahalad, 1994; Anderson, 1997
CORPORATE FORESIGHT	Companies	• Business • Technology • Design • Products	• Providing input for strategy • Orienting and nurturing research	Becker, 2002; Ruff, 2006; Rohrbeck, 2011

Figure 4.4 Foresight classes and levels.

continents to the entire world, and studies topics such as politics, economy and society; industry foresight, which concerns whole technological sectors and investigates market segments; and corporate foresight, which studies future developments related to businesses and their environment (Figure 4.4).

Country foresight is carried out by governments, organizations and national and international institutions. Depending on the actors who promote it, it is defined in slightly different ways: for nations we talk about national foresight or policy foresight, for narrower geographical areas we speak of regional foresight. Its use is fairly widespread in the world, more specifically: United Kingdom (Keenan, 2005), Portugal, Japan (Martin, 1995), Germany (Martin, 1995; Heraud and Cuhls, 1999), Spain (Heraud and Cuhls, 1999), France (Heraud and Cuhls, 1999), the US, the Netherlands, Australia, New Zealand and Great Britain (Martin, 1995) and Switzerland (Wiek et al., 2006). At the level of national and regional programs, foresight is mainly used to direct investments with regard to research and innovation. Governments really need to understand which sectors might become the most important in terms of future economic impact and which areas have the best prospects of development, especially in science and technology, in the following 5 or 10 years or more (Breiner et al., 1994). This is why Germany, for instance, has decided to concentrate its efforts and investments on the chemical sector. From the use of foresight, governments expect higher returns on their economical and social investments (Blind et al., 1999).

Other secondary, although not negligible, objectives are to build consensus on national priorities, to form new partnerships with other nations, and to encourage networking between universities, companies and government agencies within the nation itself (Anderson, 1997). In this sense, foresight can also be seen as a catalyst of multidisciplinary relationships between the actors of the so-called triple helix – government, business and universities – as a means to foster dialogue and to build a shared vision on long-term challenges. This type of foresight exercises is based on the participation of stakeholders from different backgrounds, on the emergence of temporary and hybrid organizations involving the actors of the triple helix, on the exchange of formal roles etc.

Industry foresight is mainly promoted by research centers and institutes, and focuses on a specific industry sector, identifying its trends. The results of these studies may be of interest to industrial clusters and districts, and to single companies operating in the field of study, to help them monitor trends of international significance. Examples of industry foresight are the analyses of the nanotechnology sector in Denmark (Andersen et al., 2005) and of the electricity distribution sector in Finland (Bergman et al., 2006).

Finally, corporate foresight is applied at the company level. It is considered a valuable tool to support decision-making activities, both at the strategic level and at the level of innovation and research. It has a strong impact on key decisions within the organization. For companies, the objectives of corporate foresight are the identification of technological discontinuities and of global changes in the economy and in society, the impact assessment of technological insights on new research fields, and the analysis of new ideas to renew and expand the current business (Bürgel et al., 2005). The ultimate goal is therefore strategic: ensuring future competitiveness, identifying threats and opportunities, supporting the most feasible R&D projects.

Corporate foresight has benefited from two important contributions, directly derived from country foresight.

The first contribution is a set of forecasting and foresight tools and methods. Many methodologies have in fact been created and developed at the national level, like the Delphi analysis and trend extrapolation (Breiner et al., 1994; Martin, 1995; Grupp and Linstone, 1999).

The second contribution is the evolution of "national" approaches to foresight, which in the '70s were mainly based on mathematical modeling and trend extrapolation. Later on, as it became clear that a too-technical approach made it difficult to identify new technologies and discontinuous changes, expert opinions began to be added to the equation (Grupp and Linstone, 1999; Cuhls, 2003; Kameoka et al., 2004). As we shall see, today foresight projects are geared towards the exploration of possible developments (McMaster, 1999) and include a greater number of qualitative methods (Grupp and Linstone, 1999; Miles, 1999). Another important element is participation: the stakeholders are involved in the study at an early stage, in order to ensure that foresight will be followed by concrete actions.

Note

1   PEEST: Political, Environmental, Economical, Sociological, Technological.

Part II
Organizing and managing corporate foresight

5 Corporate foresight

"What is the future? I don't know. It intrigues me because it is
strongly, highly, gloriously improbable, inventive".
Michel Serres

5.1 Foresight for companies

The philosopher Gaston Berger is considered the father of forecasting, on
which he wrote a seminal paper in 1957. Berger himself was a student of
Maurice Blondel, who envisioned the future as a field to be constructed
using materials from the past: "the future is not forecasted, it is prepared",
he said. Berger went even further, arguing that "the future is the *raison
d'être* of the present" and that most of our actions can be explained by the
projects which justify them.

Truth be told, these ideas are not new and can already be found in Aristotle,
who distinguished efficient cause, which provokes an effect, from final cause,
which justifies our actions through a project. The idea of having a project
and an action plan to reach a goal is not new either: Seneca's statement res-
onates across the centuries: "There is no good wind for he who knows not
where he is headed".[1] Even Herodotus, as far back as 424 BC, stressed the
importance of planning for the future: "Nothing stays the same, and those
who do not want to grow, will soon be overtaken by those who do! If we do
not plan for the future in a realistic way, the alternative looks terribly bleak".

As stated in Chapter 4, foresight studies conducted within companies are
called *corporate foresight* (CF): this term is mostly used by companies to
describe their research activity on the future.[2]

There are different definitions of CF in the literature. One of the most evocative is "*the art of the long view*" (Schwarz, 1991). The primary goal of the CF
approach is in fact to increase predictive capacity in the medium to long term.
Many authors emphasize its great effectiveness in anticipating trends, whether
scientific, technological, economic or social, and turning them to advantage
(Martin, 1995; Slaughter, 1996; Reger, 2001; Blackman and Henderson,
2004; Tsoukas and Shepherd, 2004), or in identifying threats before they

become real crises (Day and Schoemaker, 2004b). Not surprisingly. Rohrbeck (2010) has recently defined foresight as "organizational future orientation".

Consequently, other CF objectives are to support strategy and research, to attract and create innovation, and ultimately to encourage lifelong learning. Many authors, like McMaster (1999), Slaughter (1999) and Alsan (2008), emphasize its inherently strategic nature, considering CF not as an alternative to strategic planning but as an enrichment of the same. In this sense, CF is defined as the ability to orient vision in a manner consistent with trends and functional to the organization.

CF concerns the medium to long-term analysis of business environments, of markets and new technologies, and of their implications for corporate strategies and for innovation (Ruff, 2006). CF is a participatory and systematic (Becker, 2002; Burmeister et al., 2004) process (Becker, 2002) which looks at the future with a medium to long-term vision (Daheim and Uerz, 2008) identifying threats and opportunities (Cuhls, 2003) in political, sociocultural, competitive and technological environments (Rohrbeck, 2010) in order to support decision-making, to nurture the innovation process (Burmeister et al., 2004), to identify new business models and to build scenarios for communication (Daheim and Uerz, 2008).

CF therefore scans both the company's business environment and the macro-environment surrounding it, assessing technological trends, exploring future developments in the behavior of competitors and customers, evaluating the development of political, economic and legislative trends. The obtained results aim to reduce the uncertainty of decisions and to allow a more effective management of complexity.

5.2 The roots of corporate foresight

The literature on CF is indeed recent, but it is based on solid grounds. The debate among researchers in the management field stems from different literatures, but all scholars agree that the key to a company's success is the capacity for future orientation. There are three main lines of research in CF:

1 Strategic management
2 Innovation management
3 Futures studies

In the literature, the two branches of strategic management and innovation management are mainly focused on building systems that allow to operate businesses under changing conditions. They are clearly connected to the third branch, more closely related to futures studies, in that they assist businesses in understanding the complex forces that drive change, and in managing strategy and innovation in contexts of turbulence and uncertainty (Burmeister et al., 2004; Kaivo-oja and Marttinen, 2006; Van der Duin, 2006; Von der Gracht et al., 2010; Vecchiato and Roveda, 2010). The key

	MAIN FEATURES	DESCRIPTION	MAIN AUTHORS
STRATEGIC MANAGEMENT	EXTERNAL CHANGE/DISCONTINUOUS AND RADICAL CHANGE	When facing external change, companies must alter their strategy and their organization. Change can be either slow and incremental or discontinuous and radical.	Ansoff, 1976; Shrivastava and Grant, 1985
			Whitehead, 1933; Tuschman *et al.*, 1985; Brown and Eisenhardt, 1997
	ENVIRONMENTAL SCANNING/COMPETITIVE INTELLIGENCE/TECHNOLOGY INTELLIGENCE/BUSINESS INTELLIGENCE	These processes produce relevant and updated knowledge on the direction and strength of the emerging external change (at the competitor, technology and business levels).	Jain, 1984; May *et al.*, 2000; Day and Schoemaker, 2004b
	SENSEMAKING	The ability of a company to perceive change and to give it meaning, acquiring the necessary skills.	Weick, 1979
	ORGANIZATIONAL AMBIDEXTERITY	The ability to apply simultaneously exploitation and exploration, thereby adapting both to incremental and to radical change.	Tuschman and O'Reilly, 1996; Andriopoulos and Lewis, 2009; Raisch *et al.*, 2009
	RESILIENCE	The ability to remain flexible and handle crises, avoiding disaster in high-risk environments.	Weick and Sutcliffe, 2001
	DECISION-MAKING	The process of making strategic decisions.	Mintzberg, 1979

Figure 5.1 Corporate foresight in strategic management literature.

question behind CF is how companies can become future-oriented, thus ensuring their own long-term survival and success.

As in Rohrbeck (2010), Figures 5.1, 5.2 and 5.3 summarize the main notions of the three lines of research on CF, related to how organizations can anticipate discontinuous change and manage it successfully.

	MAIN FEATURES	DESCRIPTION	MAIN AUTHORS
INNOVATION MANAGEMENT	DISRUPTIVE INNOVATION	Innovation which totally disrupts previous patterns.	Christensen, 1997
	RADICAL INNOVATION	Acquiring new technologies.	Lambe and Spekman, 1997
		Connecting emerging technologies with customers' needs.	Dushnitsky and Lenox, 2005
		Launching new R&D projects using the opportunity created by discontinuous change.	Arnold, 2003
		Promoting specific personality traits in radical innovation teams.	Stevens and Burley, 2003
		Identifying the promoters and champions of radical innovation.	Gemünden *et al.*, 2007
		Separating radical innovation teams from incremental innovation teams.	O'Connor and De Martino, 2007
	ABSORPTIVE CAPACITY	Ability to acquire know-how and to use it to create a competitive advantage.	Cohen and Levinthal, 1990; Zahra and George, 2002; Lichtenthaler, 2009
	NETWORKING CAPACITY	Development and exploitation of innovation networks from the focal firm perspective.	Pittaway *et al.*, 2004
	OPEN INNOVATION	Innovation that is shared between the various actors in an open exchange system.	Chesbrough, 2003; Lichtenthaler, 2008

Figure 5.2 Corporate foresight in innovation management literature.

MAIN FEATURES	DESCRIPTION	MAIN AUTHORS
WEAK SIGNALS	Non-obvious signals of possible trends or events.	Ansoff, 1976
WILD CARDS	High-impact unexpected events.	Ayres, 2000; Van Notten *et al.*, 2005; Saffo, 2007
FORECASTING	Future developments are forecast using S curves, mathematical modeling and Delphi analysis.	Cuhls, 2003; Phillips *et al.*, 2006;
POSSIBLE FUTURES	Identification of possible, probable, plausible and preferable futures.	McMaster, 1999; Cuhls, 2003
SCENARIO PLANNING	Strategic analysis used to envision different possible outcomes.	Kahn, 1967; Van der Heijden, 2004
NATIONAL FORESIGHT PROGRAMS	Programs which identify technologies leading to the greatest economic and social benefit.	Martin, 1995; Blind *et al.*, 1999; Grupp and Linstone, 1999; Cuhls, 2003; Porter *et al.*, 2004

(Rows grouped under the vertical heading: FUTURE STUDIES)

Figure 5.3 Corporate foresight in future studies literature.

5.3 The objectives of corporate foresight

The value of CF is not so much in predicting the future, but in preparing the organization to recognize and respond to future changes in advance. The broader goal of CF is to create awareness of the external environment and ability to react to change (Patton, 2005). It is aimed at identifying discontinuities, technology trends, emerging technologies, future business opportunities and the most promising areas of research (Ashton and Stacey, 1995; Martin, 1995; Reger, 2001; Patton, 2005; Reger, 2004). A further objective is to provide timely warnings about potential opportunities and threats, in order to support planning and to shape strategy (Blackman and Henderson, 2004; Coates, 1985; Slaughter, 1998).

CF helps companies build a vision that will help them understand the complex forces that drive change, take the right decisions and orient strategy and R&D. The role of CF is essentially to handle complexity and to prepare the company for an uncertain future. Its main objectives (see Figure 5.4) are the following:

- Anticipatory intelligence: reducing uncertainty by identifying trends and weak signals (Rohrbeck, 2010)
- Support to decision-making: laying a steady base for strategic decisions in three steps: defining directions, prioritization and strategy formulation (Hines, 2006)
- Learning: building a knowledge base in terms of an increasing awareness of complexity among employees (Fink et al., 2004)
- Acting as innovation catalyst: stimulating and supporting the innovation process (Day and Schoemaker, 2005)
- Creation of new business models: identifying possible business areas or new markets for future development (Daheim and Uerz, 2008)

OBJECTIVES		Becker, 2002	Cuhls, 2003	Cuhls and Johnston, 2006	Daheim, 2004	Daheim and Uerz, 2008	Day and Schoemaker, 2005	Fink et al., 2005	Hines, 2006	Rohrbeck, 2011	Rohrbeck, 2008	Schwarz, 2008
Anticipatory intelligence	• Detecting weak signals and emerging trends • Developing peripheral vision • Trend analysis	X				X	X			X	X	
Support to decision-making	• Defining orientations • Defining priorities • Formulating the strategy	X		X	X	X		X	X	X	X	X
Learning	• Ongoing feedback		X			X		X		X		X
Innovation catalyst	• Incentives to the innovation process • Collaborations	X		X	X	X	X	X		X		
Creation of new business models	• Redefining the current business model • Identifying new areas of potential business	X		X	X	X	X	X		X		
Promotion/ Communication	• Futuristic company • Social engagement			X		X						

Figure 5.4 Corporate foresight objectives in the literature.

- Promotion/communication: creating an orientation to future developments and tying the company's brand to the idea of future and innovation (Daheim, 2004; Cuhls and Johnston, 2006)

For some (very large and very powerful) companies, the aim is also to "invent" the future, to shape it. For example, Klaus Weyrich of Siemens AG says: "For companies, one of the most promising survival strategies is to become a trendsetter that doesn't merely react to changes in the market, but instead shapes that market". In Siemens, foresight is used to quantify future markets, identify new technologies with ample growth potential, anticipate upcoming customer requests, create new business opportunities as well as a unified vision of the technological future of Siemens itself.

CF can contribute to value creation in several ways:

- Identifying relevant changes by monitoring trends in the PEEST context
- Supporting responsiveness to change, for example by suggesting the creation of new business models or products/services

- Fostering the development of innovation by providing insights on the future such as information on emerging technologies
- Supporting research, development and acquisition of strategic resources through knowledge networks
- Contributing to the decision-making process through the creation, absorption and diffusion of knowledge and through the dialogue and participation of internal stakeholders
- Overcoming dominant mental models and putting new ones to the test, evaluating whether they effectively work to the company's advantage

5.4 Resistance to corporate foresight

"It has nothing to do with our business", "We don't have time for these fantasies" and "It's just a fad of the moment" are the most common statements against CF. Although some of them are based on misguided perceptions, their frequency and persistence hides a major problem: for many companies, the reasons why foresight may be relevant are still unclear.

Although many companies declare themselves satisfied with their foresight activities, there are still critical issues requiring some improvement, mostly at the level of practical implementation. In the surveys of Müller (2006) and Daheim and Uerz (2008), 70% of participating companies said that the relevance of foresight within their company had increased in the previous 5 years, and 60% found that in general the relevance of foresight for the business community had increased.

If we observe the collected data, it becomes apparent that the field of CF is very heterogeneous, albeit with some common dominant trends that show a growing importance of CF in companies (such as a greater technical understanding of CF, an increase in its perceived usefulness, an increased budget, a more frequent use of trend and scenario analysis etc.).

CF operates with a high variety of approaches, organizational forms and tools as well as with different objectives and different outputs. However, the problems that need to be tackled turn out to be the same in almost all situations. These common problems are for example a lack of clarity on which tools are most appropriate to reach a specific objective, or difficulties in communicating the results and in linking them to the decision-making process of the company. In the survey, the participants stated that the reluctance to take part in the foresight process was mainly due to very long-term orientation, high costs, inapplicable results and lack of time. The challenges of CF are therefore:

- organizational barriers,
- insufficient validation, and
- high perceived costs.

These problems can be divided into three main areas (for an overview see Figure 5.5): strategic and cultural issues, organizational problems, managerial-methodological problems. The most relevant appear to be related

PROBLEMS OF CORPORATE FORESIGHT*	AUTHOR
STRATEGIC ISSUES	
Lack of sufficient commitment.	Becker, 2002; Burmeister *et al.*, 2004
Lack of a bridge between the foresight process and subsequent actions; foresight is not a process in itself but must be connected with strategy and innovation.	Becker, 2002; Daheim and Uerz, 2008
Foresight does not generate relevant information; it should be more problem-oriented and produce concrete results and real products.	Becker, 2002
Foresight activities are not separated between those that lead to a specific product development and those that support strategy in general.	Becker, 2002
Shareholder's mentality of the top management, too much short-term thinking.	Becker, 2002
Budget constraints.	Müller, 2006
Lack of support by the company.	Müller, 2006
Difficulty in finding really important themes and trends; insecurity on contents and processes.	Burmeister *et al.*, 2004; Müller, 2006
ORGANIZATIONAL ISSUES	
Difficulty in exporting foresight results to the relevant target groups (e.g., R&D employees).	Becker, 2002
Lack of ways to tie foresight to strategy: foresight trends and results should be translated into options supporting management decisions.	Becker, 2002; Burmeister *et al.*, 2004; Müller, 2006; Daheim and Uerz, 2008
Excessive fragmentation (no centralized offices and departments) and segmentation (activities are very specialized and fail to see the big picture).	Becker, 2002
Lack of a foresight culture: foresight should be repositioned inside the company through monitoring systems, workshops on the future etc.	Becker, 2002
Difficulty in assessing the real contribution of foresight activities to the business. Tools should be developed to measure the benefits of foresight and facilitate its promotion.	Becker, 2002
Knowledge management problems: lack of tools for the scanning of appropriate sources and the systematic collection of data.	Daheim and Uerz, 2008
Lack of a network of foresight professionals.	Becker, 2002
MANAGERIAL AND METHODOLOGICAL ISSUES	
Lack of a consolidated methodology to ensure accuracy of results.	Becker, 2002; Müller, 2006
Skepticism towards qualitative methods.	Müller, 2006
Unawareness of which methods are available and whether they can be applied to specific objectives or answer specific questions.	Müller, 2006; Daheim and Uerz, 2008
Lack of feedback from recipients: feedback is important to get precious information and make more accurate and customer-oriented predictions.	Becker, 2002; Burmeister *et al.*, 2004
Lack of continuity.	Burmeister *et al.*, 2004; Müller, 2006
Too many redundant activities and inefficient reuse of previous work; "wheel re-invention" syndrome.	Becker, 2002; Daheim and Uerz, 2008
Insufficient commitment to integrate the results of foresight at the macro level.	Becker, 2002

* The survey was conducted in 18 European companies (Becker, 2000), 26 German companies (Burmeister et al., 2004) and 40 European companies (Müller, 2006; Daheim and Uerz, 2008).

Figure 5.5 Problems of corporate foresight.

to "soft factors" and to the organization itself, such as difficulties in communicating and in implementing consequent actions. The main obstacles to CF do not in fact concern the weakness of results, but the uncertainty about how to connect these results to the decision-making process and to meaningful business players. A strong handicap is also the lack of a methodological bridge between CF and the subsequent steps.

5.5 How to overcome resistance

One reason for the persistence of CF problems is a lack of clarity about its objectives and performances. In another survey (Burmeister et al., 2004), about three quarters of the participants (30 companies) did have explicit targets for their foresight process, but some did not even have explicit goals or indicators of implicit success (15%). Only 37% of companies were monitoring the implementation of the foresight process either formally or informally. In addition, only a third of companies (37%) were regularly improving the process, while 79% did it occasionally. These surveys reveal the need to set clear goals, to connect foresight more closely to leadership activities, and to revise, adapt and improve the process on an ongoing basis. Besides, an attentive analysis of the questionnaire reveals some contradictions, for instance, only 10% saw CF as involving participation and communication, but participation was indicated as the third most critical factor for success.

Critical factors all point in the same direction: quality of results, strategic importance, participation, communication, corporate culture and commitment. The most relevant factors for the success and impact of CF activities appear to be clear results providing useful answers to strategic problems, a high level of participation and involvement, appropriate communication of the process and its results, a supporting corporate culture and a strong commitment.

Based on these considerations, we suggest three guidelines for improvement:

- Raising awareness of foresight
- Supporting organizational and management development
- Tying foresight with strategy, increasing the strategic importance of foresight for the company

The problem with CF is its distance from daily goals and the fact that positive effects cannot be seen in the short term.

Several studies point to a variety of issues and challenges that arise in the implementation and institutionalization of CF. Steinle et al. (2000) identify problems such as lack of validation, bottlenecks in the organization or shortcomings and problems related to people's skills. Burmeister et al. (2004) identify a criticality in the discrepancy between potential and expected benefits, and Van der Heijden (2004) suggests that the motivations of the key players should be included in CF planning and implementation.

Clearly CF is called upon to meet many different needs, and for this reason it is first and foremost necessary to deal with corporate mentality and culture.

Several mistakes must be avoided. The first is to give complete authority to the experts, forgetting that any change requires both general consensus and a strong commitment on the part of the management. The second is to snub the experts and their competence and to heed only low level employees, forgetting that without sharing and validation on the part of the management, participatory anticipation idles and spins round and round on the present.

It is important to create a sense of the value that CF can bring to the company, mostly by communicating better its use and its utility, or by explaining its benefits with examples and case studies.

Research has often kept its focus on the strictly structural aspect of the organization, that is, on the company units in charge of foresight. In fact, several strategies can be used. Here are some:

- Encouraging bottom-up initiatives
- Promoting interactions between employees from different departments
- Integrating foresight activities with other processes such as innovation, marketing and strategic management
- Leaving employees the freedom to share their opinions on future trends and drivers
- Giving employees some responsibility to identify trends and weak signals and to take action
- Promoting the creation of a wide network of partners and stakeholders inside and outside the company

In addition, some purely managerial levers can be used to give foresight a more operational role:

- Developing foresight indicators that highlight its added value
- Systematically interpreting the information derived from foresight activities through specific methods
- Matching specific methods of foresight with specific issues and contexts
- Integrating information and reporting foresight results to the whole company

Traditionally, strategic management experts have always emphasized the strategical need to focus on the future (Chandler, 1962; Ackoff, 1974; Hofer and Schendel, 1978; Hamel and Prahalad, 1994):

- In *Corporate Strategy* (1965) Ansoff describes the recommended decision procedure in a context of environmental turbulence and discontinuity (like the one faced by the US in the '50s).
- Andrews (1965) sees in the identification of trends the basis for economic strategy.

- Grant (1994), speaking of RBV (resource-based view), stresses the importance of understanding future potentialities.
- D'Aveni (1994), in his hyper-competition model, highlights the need to be ready for the future and to adapt quickly to change.
- For Stacey (1992) the future is an open system which must be pushed away from equilibrium, so that it can change and be truly innovative.
- Campbell and Goold (1991) propose the Ashridge model[3] to create a sense of mission.
- Hax and Wilde (1999) propose the Delta model[4] for "adaptive management" in a changing world.

The literature on strategic management emphasizes the need to take the environment's evolution into consideration during the process of strategic analysis.

The literature on foresight supports these views:

- Reger (2001) argues that the generation of technology foresight should essentially be based on the integration of concepts (such as vision) in the strategy of companies.
- Chermack (2004b) and Postma and Liebl (2005) emphasize the need to develop new ways to improve and use scenario techniques and tools for forecasting and anticipation, as part of a method for taking strategic decisions.
- Mendonça et al. (2004) propose to define reliable guidelines that can be used by organizations in turbulent environments, and to implement a procedure to manage wild cards.
- Van der Steen et al. (2010) emphasize the significant gap between futures studies and management. In practical terms, companies hardly make use of knowledge about the future: most futures studies are not used by managers and strategists, and do not affect the direction taken by companies.

All these approaches have one thing in common: they all try to shift the focus from abstract methodologies to real strategic management. The idea is to connect futures studies with managerial activities and with organizational development through a process of intelligence.

5.6 The two pillars of corporate foresight

Global trends know no borders and affect every aspect of society: they have the potential to profoundly change the way the world will function tomorrow, and may impact, as we have seen, faster than we might think. In order to innovate, we must learn to imagine scenarios that are completely different from current reality. But how do we imagine our technological, economic and social future? How do we actualize scenarios into new products or services?

There are specific organization models, processes and methodologies a company can use to stay focused on the future, and to monitor trends and weak signals on an ongoing basis. To maintain focus over time, it is necessary to implement new skills, to get creative, to listen and to observe, to eliminate background noise, and above all, to learn how to interpret signals and recombine them in a new light.

In the areas of innovation and business strategy, different trends are emerging with increasing force. In a complex environment, a company must be able to take into account a lot of different elements and to synchronize them with each other: attention to weak signals, creativity, collective intelligence, open-innovation business models, vision and strategic coherence. The skills required in a stable context may be completely different from the skills required when the wind of change is blowing, when the whole of society, together with politics, laws and technologies, is changing, so much so that the shape of whole sectors is altered, and companies are forced out of the market (just think of Polaroid and the advent of digital photography).

Being effective in a discontinuous context requires specific organizational and methodological skills. Bessant et al. (2005) identify twelve "strategies" that can be implemented in the first stage of innovation. Of these twelve, scouting, exploring multiple futures, using the power of the web (online communities, virtual worlds etc.), observing the new styles of consumption, brokering, fostering diversity and using idea generators (creativity techniques) are strongly associated with: detection of weak signals, networking and cognitive diversity to anticipate the future.[5]

In summary, the process of anticipation must be integrated into the management process and regarded as one of the most important assets for the formulation of corporate strategy. Specific tools and methodologies must be used. From the point of view of companies, the question of future anticipation can be analyzed in two perspectives: organization dynamics and management dynamics. Using the metaphor of an arch supported by two pillars (Figure 5.6), we could say that anticipation in the company is supported by organization and management, and actualized by tools and methodologies. To handle the issues described above, we propose the following:

1 At the organizational level:

   i   An internal solution based on the presence of a foresight unit, the separation of research from development, the commitment of the top management and a future-oriented culture
   ii an external solution based on networking and possibly acquisitions

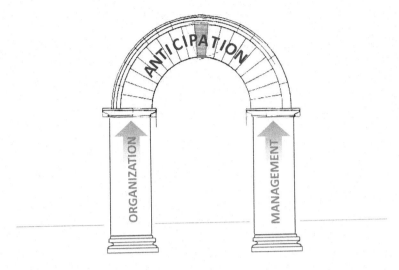

Figure 5.6 The two pillars of corporate foresight: organization and management.

2   At the management level: a methodology we have called "future cover-age approach", which can be used to analyze the consistency between vision, trends and future products.

Our discussion will focus on these two perspectives. From the point of view of organization, Chapter 6 will describe the ways in which a company can become proactive and be ready to seize the moment. From the point of view of management, Chapter 7 will describe how to verify consistency between trends (external perspective) and strategic orientation (internal perspective). In Chapter 8, we will propose our "future coverage approach" to measure how effectively a company's strategy for the future covers trends. In the third part, the concrete use of foresight and the application of our methodology will be illustrated in the Eurotech case study.

Notes

1   "Ignoranti quem portum petat nullus suus ventus est", from *Letters to Lucilius*, letter 71.
2   *Corporate foresight* can be found in the literature under different names and forms, depending on the type of activities performed. Some authors call it strategic foresight (Becker, 2002; Rohrbeck, 2008) highlighting its complementarity to the decision-making process; others prefer the term "corporate foresight" (Cuhls, 2003; Alsan, 2008) still others use the terms "organizational foresight" (Tsoukas and Shepherd, 2004) and Managerial Foresight (Ahuja, Coff and Lee, 2005). In this book we will use the most common and widely used "corporate foresight", in its broadest meaning.

3 The Ashridge model assists in thinking consistently about the mission. The mission has four defining elements: purpose, values, behavioral norms and strategies. These four elements are linked together and reinforce each other, giving the company a clear direction about decisions, strategies and policies.
4 According to the Delta model, the main company processes must be in line with the selected strategy. The model then provides guidance on how these processes should operate to give the right response in uncertain environments.
5 The other strategies are working with existing customers, probe and learn, mobilizing employees, corporate venturing, entrepreneurship and intrapreneurship.

6 The first pillar of corporate foresight
Organization

> "Take everything, but leave me my organization, and in two years I'll be at the top again".
> Henry Ford

6.1 The bygone era of research and development

Some studies have shown that half the current industrial problems could have been avoided through long-term research and a strong attention to changes in the environment, and that there is a strong relationship between these factors: sustainability and long-term profit on the one hand; investments in R&D (Fagerberg, 1987), competence and core capabilities of the company (Prahalad and Hamel, 1990) on the other. This is confirmed by the recent contributions of Philip Kotler and John Caslione (2009) in *Chaotics: The Business of Managing and Marketing in the Age of Turbulence*, and of Gary Hamel (2007) in *The Future of Management*. In other words, the current competitive environment, in which turbulence is becoming the norm and, consequently, uncertainty is the rule, increasingly emphasizes the need to be ready to seize the moment.

The future does not belong to companies which are too stable, which are not proactive: growing and sustaining a profitable survival in the long run is a big challenge, which requires a chameleonic ability to adapt, to anticipate the market and be always at the ready for the future. Due to the increasing complexity of competition dynamics and to the increasingly discontinuous conditions of the political, economic, social, cultural and technological environment, there is a stronger and stronger need to develop a wider peripheral vision, to "perceive" the future and to be quick to capture potential business opportunities. But how can management and organization set up the company for anticipation?

Recently, new approaches to innovation have surfaced, such as open innovation, technology brokering, collective innovation and so on. The business structure and dynamics are also evolving in relation to this new landscape. A large part of these new approaches deals with the structure and organization of research and development (R&D), which can certainly be considered the driver of innovation.

Nurturing R&D is vital to stimulate innovation. In fact, R&D is one of the means by which organizations increase their knowledge capital and use it to innovate (OECD Factbook, 2005). The nature of research activities is unique for several reasons, including a degree of uncertainty, non measurable results and a delayed effect on the market. Consequently, R&D has always been considered an expense, and R&D planning has always been constrained by negotiations on allocated resources.

According to Whatmore (2002), organizations can view R&D, despite its intrinsic level of uncertainty and complexity, either as a cost or as a driver of innovation, and manage it accordingly. The system can be organized according to the type of innovation it produces (e.g., Thamhain, 2003; Argyres and Silverman, 2004), and this is one of the dimensions that define the value of R&D (Chiesa and Masella, 1996). Furthermore, the organizational structure of R&D reflects the company's strategies (Eto, 1991).

In any case, the literature is in full agreement on the point that innovation requires a better organization of R&D (Zander, 1999; Volberda, 1998). But literature studies also agree that there is no single "best way", because the organization and management of R&D must be consistent with the objectives and importance of R&D (Von Zedwitz et al., 2004) and with the nature of the R&D process (Cavone et al., 2000). Moreover, Tidd et al. (1997) and Jacobs and Waalkens (2001) argue that the choice of the best form of R&D organization is based on four aspects: (1) technology-push versus market-pull, (2) centralization versus decentralization, (3) concentration in one country versus international distribution, and (4) creation of internal knowledge versus acquisition of external knowledge.

According to Nobelius (2004), R&D has been evolving towards more open and more future-oriented (Figure 6.1) forms: at first ('70–'80) it was an isolated ivory tower essentially focused on technology, which had very little interaction with the rest of the company, then it began to be more integrated with the other business functions and more attentive to the market, finally it became part of a partnership network with competitors, suppliers and customers. Today we are moving towards the separation of the two functions of research and development, which now operate in a real "arena" where the goal is to recognize future radical changes that will affect industry segments.

6.2 Research and development: A failed relationship

In most Italian companies, the two functions of research and development are performed within the same organizational unit. This solution seems to be the most natural, often justified by the small size of many companies. But this "natural" solution is conceptually wrong. We have realized it over

GENERATION	METAPHOR	CHARACTERISTICS	technology-push versus market-pull		centralization versus decentralization		national versus international		internal knowledge versus external knowledge	
			technology	market	centralized	decentralized	national	international	internal	external
1st	Ivory tower	Technology-push oriented, focused on scientific breakthroughs, little or no interaction with the rest of the company	x		x		x		x	
2nd	Business	Market-pull oriented, strategy-driven, relevant project management, internal customer concept		x	x		x		x	
3rd	Portfolio	Linked to both business and corporate strategies. Risk-reward methods to guide the overall investments	x		x		x		x	
4th	Integrative activity	Learning from and with customers, activities conducted in parallel by cross-functional teams	x	x	x		x	x		x
5th	Network	Focusing on collaboration with competitors, suppliers and distributors; ability to control product development speed, separation of R from D	x			x	x	x		x
6th	Arena	Research as distributed technology-sourcing: weak connections to research networks; ability to identify future discontinuities	x	x		x	x	x	x	x

Figure 6.1 Evolution of research and development.

Source: Nobelius, 2004.

time, like a married couple realizing as time goes by that husband and wife are not meant for each other. In other words, we might declare: "Research and development: the story of a failed relationship". But why is coexistence of R&D a structural error? Essentially for three reasons.

The first reason is the different temporal orientation: medium to long term (research), short to medium term (development). The consequence of this difference is simple: while research is oriented to the market of tomorrow, development is oriented to the market of today. As revenues are made in the market of today, this creates a bias within the organization towards the customers of today. What happens is that development tends to prevail over research. Tomorrow's customers can wait, nobody knows them, they do not make orders and they do not pay! The end result is that research is always in trouble, unable to define the offer of tomorrow, and when the future arrives, the company finds itself with obsolete technologies, an old product range and outdated designs.

The second reason why research and development cannot coexist is that research is technology push, whereas development is market pull. In order to develop new technologies and new designs, research must study technological evolutions of both the near and far future and imagine possible relationships between technologies, products and markets. On the contrary, development is essentially driven by current markets.

The third reason why research should be separated from development is that research is oriented to the exploration of new combinations of technologies, products and markets, whereas development is oriented to the exploitation of existing combinations. In other words, development is a stage in the virtuous cycle of marketing, design, production and sales aimed at maximum efficiency, in a framework of maximum continuity in terms of operational processes. Research on the other hand is a stage in the virtuous cycle of foresight, research, prototyping and test aimed at maximum innovation, in a framework of maximum discontinuity in terms of technological solutions, design and functionality of products and services. These two opposite cycles need to be balanced dynamically to ensure both maximum continuity (efficiency) and maximum discontinuity (innovation) as shown in Figure 6.2.

In line with the "edge of chaos" model (De Toni and Barbaro, 2010), organizations, dealing with a complexity which is always swaying between predictability and unpredictability, order and disorder, reversibility and irreversibility, determinism and chance, must necessarily position themselves at the edge of chaos. Stacey (1992) writes: "Successful organizations – that is, continually innovative organizations – cannot choose between tight, formal control systems and structures on the one hand and loose, informal processes

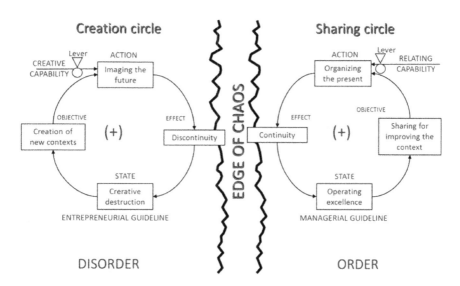

Figure 6.2 Balance between innovation and ongoing improvement.

Source: De Toni and Barbaro, 2010.

that provoke learning on the other. Whether they are large or small, successful organizations must have both at the same time. This is because they must all simultaneously handle both the knowable () and the unknowable (…).

The result is certainly organizational tension, paradox, and never-ending contradiction, but this provokes conflict and learning and thus is the source of creativity. Foster and Kaplan (2001) write: "Operational excellence will continue to be essential for the competitiveness. But it simply will not be enough. The assumption of continuity and its intimate link to operational excellence must give way to a more complex assumption of discontinuity and its intimate link with creative destruction. That is the challenge to management in the coming decades".

At the edge of chaos, the aim is to find a dynamic balance between continuity and discontinuity. Continuity is pursued by fueling the cycle of sharing, through the establishment of relations with all possible relevant actors in order to achieve operational excellence. This allows a constant pursuit of continuous improvement and a good *organization of the present*. In a complex market, however, organizations are also called upon to generate discontinuity, or ideas that are improbable for the competition, in the form of radical innovations. This can be achieved by boosting the creation cycle, that is, by investing in research and development or in connection and development (see Section 6.4), sometimes even tolerating inefficiencies that encourage creativity, thus fostering the *imagination of the future*.

It is therefore essential for organizations to activate both cycles: the cycle of creation or creative destruction, and the cycle of sharing or operational excellence. The cycle of sharing is aimed at efficiency (defined as static, i.e., here and now) obtained through continuous improvement, while the cycle of creativity is aimed at innovation. The joint effort towards efficiency (static) and innovation results in what is known as dynamic efficiency, that is, being efficient while evolving at the same time. The two key cycles for organizations are therefore efficiency and innovation, which, in a controlled imbalance at the edge of chaos, both concur to dynamic efficiency.

The separation of research from development[1] is implemented by a growing number of companies, especially in highly turbulent sectors like the chemical-pharmaceutical and the ICT. Research and development can coexist in the same unit only on the condition that change is not accelerated: only slow cycles allow to perceive changes, identify trends and develop products in a sufficiently stable period of time.

The separation of research from development makes it possible to focus at the same time on today's and on tomorrow's market by promoting anticipation activities (foresight). It also helps highlight the structural difference between the two markets.

We could view R&D as a spring system. If we do not split research and development (Figure 6.3b), the two entities will be polarized by the market of today and by the customers of today. Due to the different traction forces at play, the spring on the left will contract while the one on the right will

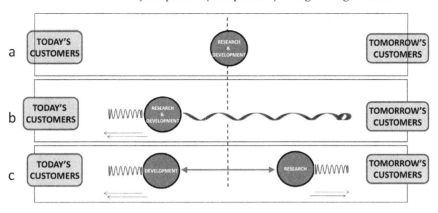

Figure 6.3 Separation of research from development.

stretch. If we separate research from development (Figure 6.3c), the two entities will be attracted respectively to the customers of tomorrow and of today in a more balanced fashion.

6.3 Foresight and research: A wedding announcement

In this era of acceleration and turbulence, companies require a new corporate function called Foresight or Anticipation, aimed at identifying new technology trends, new markets, new consumers, new regulations etc.

As already mentioned, corporate foresight (CF) is the study of weak signals (Ansoff, 1976 and 1987), of discontinuities in the environment and of emerging markets, for strategy and innovation policies (Becker, 2002; Rohrbeck and Gemünden, 2008). CF focuses on how companies can identify weak signals, collect information from the "periphery", anticipate emerging markets and trends and manage innovation, in order to prepare for an uncertain future. Foresight helps companies adopt a vision to interpret the complex forces driving change, to support the process of decision-making and to correctly handle R&D.

To ensure focus on innovation and on the markets of tomorrow, companies must adopt a peculiar R&D organization, and must absolutely support processes such as foresight. The matrix in Figure 6.4 gives a schematic view of the three different perspectives of foresight, research and development:

* Development has a short-term perspective: its goal is to design and develop new products;
* Research has a medium-term perspective and is aimed at (1) seeking new technological solutions for future product families; and (2) working on the business model (all things being equal, finding innovative ways to "stack" existing technology and to "sell" it to the market);

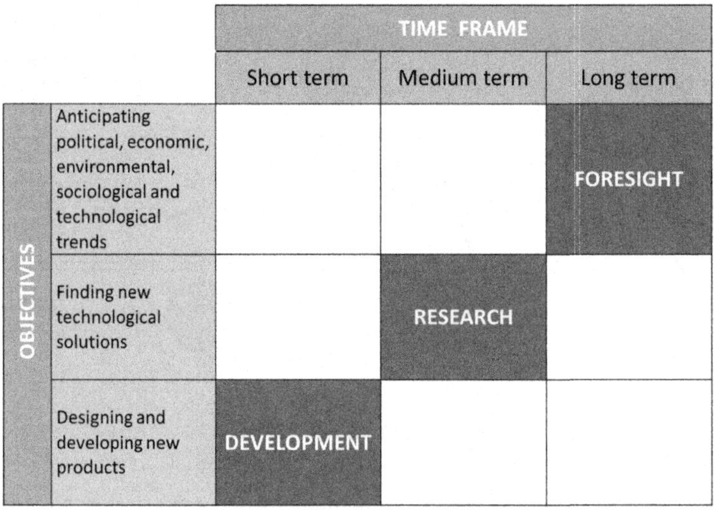

		TIME FRAME		
		Short term	Medium term	Long term
OBJECTIVES	Anticipating political, economic, environmental, sociological and technological trends			FORESIGHT
	Finding new technological solutions		RESEARCH	
	Designing and developing new products	DEVELOPMENT		

Figure 6.4 Differences between foresight, research and development.

- Foresight has the longest perspective of all, and aims at anticipating PEEST trends and orienting research towards products and businesses that are the most reasonable and aligned in terms of future market.

These different time perspectives imply a distinction between today's and tomorrow's market. In today's market customers are the drivers of innovation: innovation is pulled by the market (market pull) and the company is oriented towards *exploitation*. In tomorrow's market technological evolution is the driver of innovation: innovation is pushed by technology (technology push) and the company is oriented towards *exploration*.

Figure 6.5 graphically describes the separation of research and development and the connections between CF and the other functions, arranged according to today's and tomorrow's perspectives. Strategy is "in the middle" between today's and tomorrow's market: research is focused on tomorrow's market, while development is focused on today's market. Marketing is to development in today's market what foresight is to research in tomorrow's market. Marketing is on the left side of the diagram because it is more oriented towards the analysis of the current and future needs of today's customers. Finally, foresight is connected to research, in order to nurture it; to strategy, to decide which direction to take in accordance with the trends; to marketing, to investigate also the needs of tomorrow's customers.

CF can be seen as a function supporting research: foresight focuses on the long term, and can empower research by anticipating trends and generating new business ideas. In fact, CF can enable a "visionary" company to

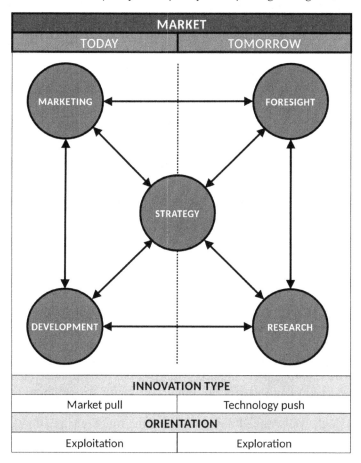

Figure 6.5 Connections between strategy, research, development, foresight and marketing.

activate systematic processes of exploration, creation and key trend monitoring that could have a potential impact on the business.

Using a metaphor, we could say that when couples split up, new love stories are born. From the separation of research from development, the first too concerned about the future and the second too concerned about the present, a new couple is born, research and foresight, which each share a great "interest" in the future. Research, after the end of her marriage to development, can find a new partner in foresight, more able to guide her in investigating and dealing with a complex and uncertain future. At the wedding of research and foresight, the best man is business strategy, which is also trying to draw marketing and product development together. These two may also get married sooner or later, to produce a finally happy community.

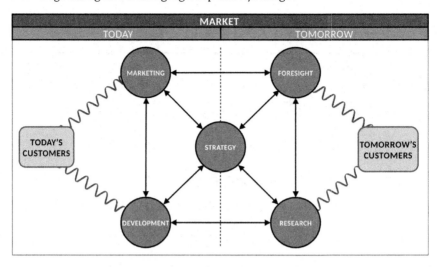

Figure 6.6 Balance between today's and tomorrow's customers.

Recalling the springs metaphor of Figure 6.3c, the separation of research from development allows to balance today's and tomorrow's customers. The introduction of a foresight function oriented to tomorrow's market – as opposed to marketing oriented to today's market – allows even more balance between the "pulling force" applied by the two sets of customers (Figure 6.6).

Finally, vision is an even more important factor for reaching the right balance between today's and tomorrow's perspective, because it can orient in a single well-defined direction all of the functions mentioned above (Figure 6.7).

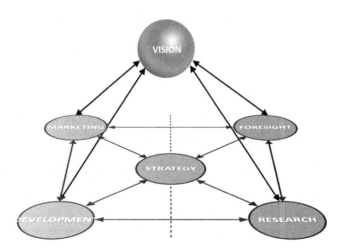

Figure 6.7 The importance of vision for research and foresight.

6.4 Connection and development: A new partnership

Products and services are becoming increasingly sophisticated. Companies (no matter how large) are no longer able to supervise all the technologies that become part of a product/service. For this reason, internal research is increasingly the result of brokerage, that is, the recombination of external knowledge with internal development activities. In other words, research and development is increasingly becoming connection – of internal and external knowledge – and development.

The open innovation approach assigns a different role to the R&D function. Generating new ideas, new knowledge and new technological solutions is no longer the fundamental task of R&D. In a landscape characterized by the presence and continuous growth of distributed knowledge, the new role of R&D is to connect and recombine all external and internal knowledge. In this sense, researchers are increasingly becoming "knowledge brokers", focused on enhancing distributed knowledge. This is why the internal research function is being replaced by connection, which fosters contacts and collaboration with external research units (indicated in Figure 6.8 as Research 1, Research 2 and Research 3).

Innovating mostly means borrowing significant contributions from a number of external actors and putting them together, in a word

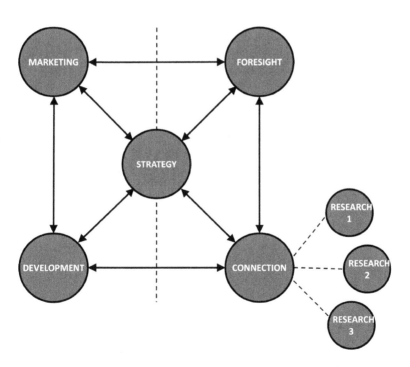

Figure 6.8 Research as connection between external and internal knowledge.

"connecting" external and internal knowledge. The obsolescence of the classical R&D model leads to a knowledge which is increasingly based on external sources; the key activity of knowledge connection is then performed internally. In other words, external knowledge is recognized, internalized and recombined.

As regards the connection function, a key role is played by the *technological gatekeeper*. Ashton et al. (1996) point out how often the success of an operation depends on a gatekeeper who collects information, performs a screening of the most relevant information and finally spreads it throughout the internal network. A gatekeeper is a professional who understands both the need for information of the internal units and the overall company objectives, who attends scientific conferences, has a good network of external contacts, possesses high communication skills and brings external information inside the company (Rothwell, 1992).

Research & development is the foundation of the classical "closed innovation" model, while connection & development is the foundation of the "open innovation" model (Chesbrough, 2003). Open innovation is based on the idea that, in a world like ours, where knowledge is widely distributed, companies cannot think of relying solely on their own research centers, but should both promote the use of external knowledge for their innovations (*inbound open innovation*) and consider trade agreements to share their internal knowledge with the outside (*outbound open innovation*).

Returning to our previous metaphor, research has just married foresight, but foresight is realizing that his partner is aging and hopes to find a younger one: connection precisely. Thus, the saying "love is the hardest thing" proves true indeed.

6.5 Acquisitions versus research

The alternatives to connection & development projects are mergers and acquisitions, performed with the aim of acquiring high-competence companies specialized in specific areas of know-how.

The classic path is internal, with connection and development (Figure 6.9), while the alternative route is external, with acquisitions and development (Figure 6.10).

Business acquisitions are extraordinary financial operations, typically for purposes of external growth. They can be vertical (the involved companies handle different stages of the production and distribution process of a product or service), horizontal (the involved companies operate in the same market or sector) and conglomerate (the involved companies operate in different and unrelated sectors or markets).

The typical reasons for acquisitions are: access to new customers or markets; acquisition of technological know-how (e.g., patents); faster growth; integration up and down the value chain.

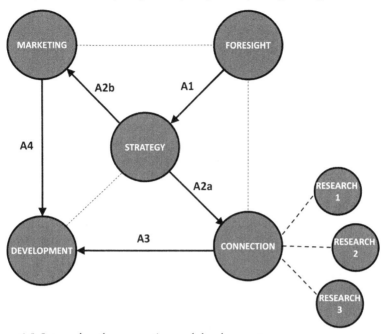

Figure 6.9 Internal path: connection and development.

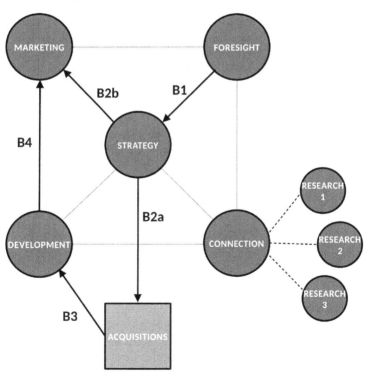

Figure 6.10 External route: acquisitions and development.

The external route ensures the acquisition of specific knowledge for development. In this sense, the company creates a leverage effect in order to speed up the availability of a strategical, innovative product and to capture a rising market trend.

6.6 Foresight as scouting

Highly innovative companies following an "open" approach focus on connecting with knowledge owners outside the boundaries of their organization. The more a company is able to create connections between external structures, the more it will be able to intercept different flows of knowledge and information and thus create new opportunities. This is why Connection is crucial for Foresight.

According to several authors, foresight functions and processes should be as integrated as possible with other business and intercompany processes (Cuhls and Johnston, 2006; Daheim, 2004, Fink et al., 2004). Rohrbeck (2008) adds that the foresight function within the company must also involve managers from other departments, who can act as "sensors" to collect as much useful information as possible for the anticipation of the future.

For the same purposes, Ashton et al. (1991) suggest to make use of external resources, in order to facilitate joint ventures and collaborations with other organizations. The authors classify these collaborations based on content, value and cost of accessing information. Wolff (1992) and Bürgel et al. (2005) suggest that, in order to promote technology scouting, full-time company managers should collaborate with consultants (scouts) who are technology or market experts. The internal positions are justified because foresight is considered a key activity that must not be outsourced.

Other authors (e.g., Hines, 2006) believe that the supporting role of consultants (scouts) is increasingly evolving towards functions of interconnection with other organizations or partners.

In this sense, foresight activities are related to scouting activities (Figure 6.11). Scouts can be external technology experts, managers of other companies, business consultants and researchers. They bring a different point of view into the company, and precious new information which substantially increases the resources available for analysis. Their presence is essential to enhance the company's peripheral vision, and thus improve foresight results (Becker, 2002; Daheim and Uerz, 2008). As always, people are the starting point for the discovery of trends and weak signals, and for scenario creation.

As far as technology is concerned, a technology scout is a specialist with a broad technical background, which identifies, evaluates and acquires new ideas to support the efforts of the company's R&D (Dougherty, 1989). The used devices are either actual acquisitions, licensing or co-development (Brenner, 1996; Wolff, 1992).

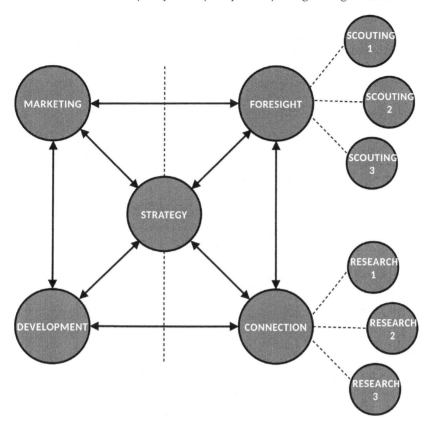

Figure 6.11 Foresight as scouting.

The goal of a technology scout is to identify new technological trends and developments and/or potential partners to jointly develop new opportunities. He focuses on generating opportunities rather than on problem solving (Brenner, 1996; Reger, 2001). Bodelle and Jablon (1993) identify three main scouting tasks: collecting information on R&D activities that are relevant in different geographic regions; initiating cooperations with R&D institutes; acquiring interesting technologies.

6.7 Ways of organizing foresight

In a survey of 54 multinational companies, Rohrbeck et al. (2009) highlighted the most common operators in charge of foresight: 79% specialized employees, 75% temporary project groups, 38% individual employees, 29% groups of employees (these forms were not mutually exclusive). The number of internal dedicated units appeared to be slowly on the rise.

Where does the need for foresight come from, and who are its promoters? From an organizational point of view, both top-down and bottom-up approaches can be found (Roveda and Vecchiato, 2006). A top-down approach is used primarily by companies which structure their foresight activities based on the scenario technique: they usually start by building global scenarios at the corporate level, then focus on business scenarios concerning the various divisions and eventually, at the lowest level, on scenarios about product design. The scenario hierarchy is reflected in a similar hierarchy of business units. This approach works well for homogeneous companies, which are very focused in terms of products and technologies, but influenced by geopolitical and sociocultural issues on a global scale (e.g., Shell).

In contrast, the bottom-up approach is used by companies which work on multiple business areas and are influenced by many different factors. In this case, the identification of all the factors is not possible at the corporate level and a combination of specialized expertise is needed at the lower levels of the organization (Roveda and Vecchiato, 2006).

Ashton and Stacey (1995) distinguish four different ways of organizing foresight:

1 A central unit responsible for all foresight activities;
2 Foresight objectives included into existing functional groups (business planning, marketing, R&D);
3 Decentralization of foresight activities in the various business units;
4 Dissemination of the responsibility for foresight throughout the company, without any formal structure.

Ashton and Stacey (1995) believe that one of the best ways to promote CF is to establish an ad hoc foresight unit. The authors argue that the best form of foresight depends on the company's product strategy and on its propensity to risk. While companies with a broad and diversified product mix and/or high-risk orientation seem to prefer decentralized or distributed structures, companies with a non-diversified product mix and/or low risk orientation seem to prefer centralized structures. Brockhoff (1991) also distinguishes between centralized and decentralized foresight activities. He suggests to adopt a decentralized approach for the collection and dissemination of information, but a centralized one for the organization, evaluation and processing of information. While data need to be collected everywhere, only a centralized unit can evaluate them in their entirety. More generally, a study of 60 companies availing themselves of foresight techniques reveals that only one third has a dedicated unit dealing with foresight on a stable basis; most companies prefer more temporary solutions, such as specific projects.

		CHARACTERISTICS							
		Structure	Type of Activity	Task	Allocated time	Analysis context	Internal staff	External links	Internal visibility
ORGANIZATIONAL FORMS	COLLECTING POST	Project	Activities inserted in other R&D activities. Many activities are outsourced	Researching and supplying pre-existent information on specific foresight areas	Not much	Micro-environment	Teams of experts and selected observators (selected based on task)	Consultants and specialised agencies	Limited
	OBSERVATORY	Autonomous unit	Autonomous activities	Researching pre-existent information and supplying new data on specific foresight areas	A lot	Micro-environment	Teams of experts and observators (specialised and fixed)	Experts	Good
	THINKTANK	Autonomous unit	Autonomous activities	Researching specific information areas. Creation of scenarios	A lot	Macro-environment	Teams of experts, futurists and researchers full-time	Experts, research centres and institutes	Very good
	OUTSOURCER	Project	Activities of selection of investigation areas. Research activities are outsourced Goals are decided internally	Researching specific information areas. Creation of scenarios	A lot	Macro-environment	Teams of experts (selected based on task)	Experts, research centres and institutes	Good

Figure 6.12 Organizational forms of foresight.

Source: Our elaboration from Daheim and Uerz, 2008.

Becker (2002) identifies three organizational forms for foresight: the *collecting post*, the *observatory* and the *think tank*. According to the author, these three forms differ by nature, intensity and variability of activities. They have been adopted by Daheim and Uerz (2008) who added a fourth one, the *outsourcer*. Each form has its own characteristics, described in Figure 6.12. According to Daheim and Uerz (2008), the application contexts of these four organizational forms are determined by two variables: the uncertainty of the external environment and the internal need for information.

For Gassmann and Gaso (2005), the collecting post is the best solution when the observation range is limited and there is little uncertainty about the future. The outsourcer solution works best with medium level uncertainty: it consists in selecting a team of internal and external experts, and in outsourcing research activities while setting all the goals internally. Reger (2004) considers external networks as a fourth level, where foresight takes place outside the company. These networks include, for example, university–industry partnerships, co-development with customers, joint ventures. The importance of external networks is also emphasized by Ashton et al. (1991) and Bürgel et al. (2005).

Both the observatory and the think tank are autonomous and well-established foresight units. These two forms are the most appropriate for highly uncertain environments. They can be implemented either at the corporate or business level, but at the corporate level their strategic impact is stronger. These stable networks have fast access to information and are especially suited for the identification of radical innovations (Ashton et al., 1991).

The think tank is the most advanced form of organization, consisting of an independent unit with a full-time dedicated staff and a wide network of external relations. Its activities include scenario development. This structure is generally highly respected, with an optimal degree of internal visibility. The generated results and outputs are not only disseminated throughout the company, but also considered very relevant to all the other functions.

In the practice, there are often hybrid forms, such as monitoring units at the corporate level combined with informal networks and ad hoc constellations or temporary projects at the business level (Gassmann and Gaso, 2005).

In many companies, foresight activities are not independent, but integrated into other functions, such as strategic planning, research or marketing. It depends on the configuration of foresight activities (more strategic, with a technological perspective or with a sociological market perspective). Lackman et al. (2000), for example, argue that foresight activities are often found in the marketing and planning departments. The authors point out that foresight location may have an influence on reporting, on resource allocation and on which kinds of projects are tendentially implemented. This is important, because insufficient resources and low priority assigned by the management are among the most common barriers against the establishment of effective foresight activities (Ashton et al., 1996; Bürgel et al., 2005). Bernhardt (1994) recommends a central foresight unit in the planning department, but not connected to marketing, as the author argues that too much focus on the market may lead to consider only incremental options and innovations, diverting attention from potential future disruptions.

In case foresight activities are not performed by a separate unit, strong connections are needed between foresight and strategy, marketing and research activities. These strong links increase the aptitude to perception.

In conclusion, there is no single organizational structure that fits all: foresight can be centralized or decentralized, internal or external, handled by full-time or part-time positions, or by a mix of all of the above.

The fact is that many companies consider foresight a core competence, to such an extent that they have created a dedicated CF function to study the future, which uses advanced models, projections, anticipation logic, weak signal detection from external sources, and identification of emerging trends across the PEEST environment. In large companies this function is called *Foresight Unit, Future Centre, Future Lab* (e.g., Nokia, Siemens, Deutsche Telekom, Shell, Telecom Italia). For some companies, even in the Italian industry sector, foresight is second nature: they have a real unit always on the lookout for future trends. Telecom Italia, for example, has created a unit that studies economic and technological developments and their influence on the market, the *Telecom Italia Future Centre*, where experts try to imagine how telecommunications could lead to a change in social ecosystems – from health care to entertainment and education – and which new business models could emerge in these ecosystems, in order to understand how to leverage specific assets to generate indirect revenues. Another example is Eurotech, which will be analyzed in a case study in Chapters 9, 10 and 11.

6.8 The promoters of foresight

Since the CF process is strongly related to imagination, creativity and openness to diversity, the question of foresight promoters is undoubtedly crucial for the success of foresight in a company.

A good "foresighter" must have a good peripheral vision, be imaginative and open-minded, with a strong multidisciplinary orientation (Rohrbeck, 2008). A thorough knowledge of one or more domains is necessary to fully understand the issues addressed; a broad general knowledge is also required, to gain access to new fields of information and connect them to one another. An open mind is ultimately necessary to ensure that beyond the dominant world view, original perspectives are also taken into consideration, and that external information is quickly identified and exploited.

Foresight is promoted by the top management, which often regularly participates in the process (Daheim and Uerz, 2008). In many cases, integrating the foresight process with decision-making and strategy translates into the fact that the head of foresight is also responsible for the strategic process (Becker, 2002; Rohrbeck, 2008). The role of the top management is crucial: often foresight is the CEO's responsibility, in accordance with the company's vision.

The impact of CF can be increased by the top management through a number of initiatives, both at the organizational and managerial levels, such as:

- Involving people who believe in the possibility of anticipation;
- Ensuring a high level of communication and participation;
- Separating research from development and creating both an internal network (through the scientific committee) and an external network (with universities, research centers, other companies);

- Promoting the transfer of knowledge between units and between research and development (e.g., by moving employees from R to D and vice versa); and
- Involving in the foresight process all the company functions and departments.

Note

1 See Leifer and Triscari (1987) and Chiesa (1996) for more details.

7 The second pillar of corporate foresight

Management

"The difficulty lies not so much in developing new ideas as in escaping from old ones".
John Maynard Keynes

7.1 The four branches of corporate foresight

The process of corporate foresight is not limited to technological investigation. Besides analyzing future technologies, companies also look to the future in terms of economic policy, legislation, behavior of consumers and competitors, and so on. As proposed by Rohrbeck and Gemünden (2008), the foresight process expands in four different directions (see Figure 7.1):

- *Political environment foresight*: identification, assessment and use of information concerning legislation, political environment and shifts in the political landscape;
- *Consumer foresight*: assessment and anticipation of consumers' needs and lifestyle, as well as of sociocultural trends;
- *Technology foresight*: identification and use of information about emerging technologies and technological discontinuities;
- *Competitor foresight*: assessment of competitors and identification of products and services, either in development or already available in lead markets.

Technology foresight is a systematic process which supports decision-making by identifying future technological and scientific developments (Martin, 1995; Porter, 2004). The basic steps of this process are: technology scanning, monitoring both of emerging technologies (weak signals) and existent technologies (discontinuities), assessment of opportunities and potential, information storage and dissemination (Reger, 2001).

Political environment foresight observes the trends and changes occurring in politics, laws and regulations (Roll, 2004; Day and Schoemaker, 2005). Especially for multinational companies in highly regulated sectors, such as transportation, the influence of laws and politics is sometimes more

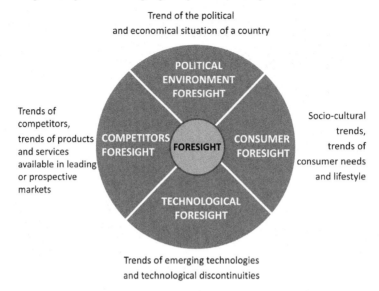

Figure 7.1 Corporate foresight orientations.

relevant than technological developments (Preble, 1988). The anticipation of changes in politics and legislation supports the development of proactive strategies. (Roll, 2004).

Consumer foresight gathers information on actual and potential customers and tries to identify their emerging needs (Brenner, 1996). The attempt to meet the future needs of consumers often leads to disruptive rather than incremental innovations, because the latter are based solely on customer feedback. Since the consumers' behavior essentially depends on changes in lifestyle and values, the aim of consumer foresight is precisely to assess these changes (Ruff, 2006; Trommsdorff and Steinhoff, 2007). Consumer foresight investigates the future from a sociological point of view.

Competitors foresight collects information about both known and potential competitors in terms of products and strategies. It could be defined as future-oriented marketing.

7.2 The corporate foresight process

The foresight process is critical for the quality of results. One of the fundamental tasks of a foresighter is to develop and structure this process, in addition to focusing on content (Hines, 2006). In 2006, the American futurist Andy Hines solicited the opinion of several experts and on this basis he structured a model in six stages, which represent the typical development of a CF process. Hines's stages are as follows:

- Framing (attitude, audience, work environment, rationale and purpose, objectives and teams)

- Scanning (the system, history and context of the issue and how to scan for information regarding the future of the issue)
- Forecasting (drivers and uncertainties, tools, diverging and converging approaches, and alternatives)
- Visioning (implications of the forecast, and envisioning designed outcomes), planning (strategy and options for carrying out the vision)
- Acting (communicating the results, developing action agendas and institutionalizing strategic thinking and intelligence systems)

Other authors (Becker, 2002; Bate and Johnston, 2005; Fink et al., 2004; Ratcliffe, 2006, from the viewpoint of scenario planning) have also formulated CF models based on specific stages, all very similar to Hines's model. Many companies use foresight techniques but do not apply a structured and ongoing process. A research commissioned by the EU (Becker, 2002), for example, showed that half of the 18 surveyed companies did not have a formal CF process. One of the reasons is the intrinsic nonlinearity of foresight activities, whereby sometimes too much formalism becomes counterproductive. Another reason is the top management's poor consideration for the foresight process, due to its long-term impact and its distance from daily business objectives. This may mean that foresighting activities are performed anyway, but without a reliable formal and methodological support.

An interesting view on foresight has been provided by Godet (1985), according to whom foresight essentially consists of three stages:

1   Collective thought
2   Preparing for a decision
3   Action

The collective thought stage includes six steps. The most important of these steps allow participants to identify key variables (steps 1 through 3), analyze stakes and stakeholders in order to ask better questions about the future (step 4) and reduce the uncertainty in these questions in order to create the most probable scenarios based on experts' opinions (step 5). The sixth step elaborates the most coherent strategic projects – those which are compatible with the identity of an enterprise/organization and at the same time represent the most probable scenarios in its given environment.

Preparing for a decision refers to the evaluation of strategic options (step 7) and of concrete strategic choices.

Finally, the action stage (step 9) is devoted entirely to the practical application of the strategic plan, which incorporates the use of "contracts" to meet strategic objectives, the development of a coordination and follow-up system, and horizon scanning (i.e., scanning for trends and changes in the business environment). Figure 7.2 compares the stages of the foresight process for Godet and Hines.

		STEPS	ACTIVITIES	OUTPUT
		Godet, 1985	Hines, 2006	
COLLECTIVE THOUGHT	1	• Problem formulated, system examined	SCOPING THE PROJECT • Setting objectives, selecting resources	• Teams • type and focus of foresight • Temporal frame of the analysis • Objectives
	2	• Diagnosis of firm, competence tree, strategic analysis	INTERNAL EVALUATION • Diagnosis of firm	• As-is situation
	3	• Key variables internal-external, structural analysis		
	4	• Dinamics of firm in relation to its environment, actors' games, strategic stakes		
	5	• Environment scenarios • Megatrends, wild cards, threats, opportunities, evaluation of risks	SCANNING • Collecting and analysing information • Creative imagery • Detecting disruptive events • Detecting key factors	• Trends and macro-trends • Factors of potential change • Possible disruptive events • Threats and opportunities
	6	• From identity to projects • Strategic options, possible actions (valorisation, innovation)	FORMULATING SCENARIOS • Creating a range of possible alternative futures • Creating scenarios • Creating connections	• Strategic options
DECISION	7	• Evaluation of strategic options • Multicriteria analysis	VISIONING • Evaluating organizational options and possible developments • Elaborating a preferred future scenario • Gap analysis between scenarios and vision	• Organizational implications • Vision
	8	• From project to strategic choices by the top management • Organization of objectives in a hierarchy	PLANNING • Moving from vision, scenarios and organizational implications to strategic planning	• Strategic plan
ACTION	9	• Plan of action and implementation • Contracts of objectives, coordination and follow-up, strategic watch	ACTING • Acting as decided and communicating the results • Creating a feedback to implement a process cycle and a learning cycle	• Decisions • Dissemination of results • Feedback

Figure 7.2 The foresight process.

7.3 Foresight methodologies

The purpose of CF is to assist decision-making through methods that allow to anticipate risks and opportunities (Glenn and Gordon, 2003). Available data that can be used in the foresight process belong to three categories (Castellucci, 1999), or a recombination of them:

- Information from the past (e.g., statistical methods)
- Knowledge of the present (e.g., monitoring)
- Abilities of the human intellect, i.e., logic, intuition, judgment and modeling (e.g., Delphi analysis)

More appropriately, the terms of hindsight, insight and foresight should be used with regard to the kind of data being analyzed and to the time span we are interested in:

- Hindsight: the ability to reflect and learn from the past
- Insight: the ability to interpret the present and respond to it
- Foresight: the ability to prepare for the future

Figure 7.3 shows the differences between hindsight, insight and foresight in relation to the questions we wish to answer and to the added value of these processes.

Kind of vision	HINDSIGHT	INSIGHT	FORESIGHT
Answer the question	What happened?	What causal relationship is there between x and y?	What happens if A occurs instead of B?
Value	Past experience and situations provide a good starting point to begin understanding the present	Understanding different relations helps up interpret our current and future situation within a changing environment	Modeling different scenarios allows us to prepare better and more rapidly to respond to unpredictable events
Analogy with a car	Rearview mirror	Windshield	GPS with traffic paths

Figure 7.3 Differences between hindsight, insight and foresight.

In the literature we can find several reviews of the methodologies that have been developed over the last 50–60 years in the field of futures studies, foresight, forecasting, strategic planning etc. Technological foresight techniques can be grouped into four categories (Castellucci, 1999):

1 Trend analysis
2 Expert judgment
3 Monitoring
4 Modeling

Trend analysis is based on the assumption that yesterday's trends and conditions might also apply tomorrow, and therefore it uses mathematical and statistical techniques to extend time series into the future. The advantage of this category is that it provides accurate and measurable predictions in the short term. The biggest disadvantages are the need for a large amount of reliable data, the inability to take into account causal mechanisms and the unreliability of long-term forecasts.

Expert judgment is related to the fact that there are people with higher knowledge. The advantage of these techniques is that they can provide good predictions even when data from the past are unavailable or difficult to obtain. The downside is that it can be difficult to identify and involve experts, and to ask them the right questions.

Technological monitoring is used to observe a specific technology or an area of interest on an ongoing basis, trying to identify developments that may affect the future. The downside of this technique is that to be effective it requires an enormous amount of filtered and selected data.

The last category is modeling. Modeling techniques are used to build models that represent in a simple way the structure and organization of a part of the real world. Unfortunately, models can never account for the complexity of true reality.

Other classifications are exploratory/regulatory and quantitative/qualitative (Lempert et al., 2003). While the former start from the present and move towards the future, extrapolating past trends and *what-if* causal

	EXPLORATORY / REGULATORY APPROACH		QUANTITATIVE / QUALITATITVE APPROACH		CATEGORY			
	Exploratory	Regulatory	Quantitative	Qualitative	Trend analysis	Expert judgment	Monitoring	Modeling
Action analysis	x	x		x	x			
Agent modeling	x		x					x
Framework analysis	x			x	x			
Analogies	x		x	x	x			
Analytical hierarchy process		x	x		x			
Backcasting		x		x				x
Bibliometrics	x		x		x			
Benchmarking			x		x			
Brainstorming	x	x		x		x		
Causal models	x		x					x
Checklists for impact identification	x			x				
Complex adaptive system modeling	x		x					x
Correlation analysis	x		x		x			
Cost–benefit analysis	x		x	x				
Creativity workshops	x	x		x		x		
Cross-impact analysis	x		x	x	x	x		
Decision analysis	x	x		x	x			
Delphi analysis	x	x		x		x		
Demographics	x		x					
Diffusion modeling	x		x					x
Econometrics and statistical method	x		x		x			
Economic base modeling	x		x					x
Environmental scanning	x			x			x	
Expert discussion	x	x		x		x		
Field anomaly relaxation method	x	x		x	x			
Focus group	x	x		x		x		
Future wheels	x	x		x	x			
Fuzzy logic	x			x		x		
Genius forecasting, vision and intuition	x	x		x		x		
Information visualization approaches	x			x				
Innovation system modeling	x			x				x
Interactive scenarios	x	x		x				x
Interviews	x	x		x		x		
Institutional analysis	x			x				
Long wave analysis	x		x					
Mitigation analysis		x		x	x			
Monitoring	x			x			x	
Morphological analysis	x	x		x	x	x		
Multicriteria decision analysis		x	x		x			
Multiple perspectives assessment	x	x		x	x	x		
Organizational analysis	x			x	x			
Participatory techniques		x		x		x		
Precursor analysis	x		x		x			
Relevance trees	x	x		x	x	x		
Requirement analysis		x	x	x	x			
Risk analysis	x	x	x	x	x			
Roadmapping	x	x	x	x				x
Scenarios	x	x	x	x		x		x
Science fiction analysis		x		x	x			
Simulation-gaming	x	x		x				x
Social impact assessment	x	x		x	x			
Stakeholder analysis		x		x	x			
State of future index	x	x	x	x				x
Strategic technology scanning	x			x			x	
Structural analysis	x	x	x	x	x			
Sustainability analysis	x		x		x			
System modeling	x		x					x
System simulation	x		x					x
Technological sequence analysis	x			x	x			
Technological substitution	x		x		x			
Technology assessment	x		x	x	x			
Text mining	x	x	x	x	x			x
Trend extrapolation	x		x		x			
Trend impact analysis	x	x	x		x			
TRIZ	x	x		x				x
Vision generation	x	x		x				x

Figure 7.4 Classification of corporate foresight techniques.

dynamics (Delphi, critical technologies, simulation modeling etc.), the latter provide a preliminary overview of a possible future and proceed backwards to determine whether it is feasible (scenario discovery). Exploratory methods are also called extrapolations, while regulatory methods are sometimes indicated as retrospections. A number of foresight techniques are classified in Figure 7.4 according to these categories.

Companies use a wide range of foresight methodologies. One study (Daheim and Uerz, 2008) lists the most widely used techniques, based on a survey of 40 companies. The preferred method seems to be trend analysis through publications and the media, followed by scenario analysis, road-mapping, other creative and participative methods, Delphi analysis and cross-impact analysis.

Finally, a key element of foresight is the width and depth of the analysis. Given the fact that none of these methods can be comprehensive, a compromise must be found between the width (the number of tackled issues) and the depth of the investigation (in terms of accuracy and precision). In order to obtain meaningful results, it is also necessary to find a middle ground between analytical rigor and imagination (Godet et al., 2009).

8 The "future coverage" approach

"In men, there is only one coherence: the coherence of their contradictions".
Guido Morselli

8.1 The problem of strategic coherence

In the literature, futures studies are widely recognized as a fundamental element of every strategy (Hamel and Prahalad, 1994). Since the '80s, the literature has highlighted the relevance of forecasting for economic trends, but this is equally true for technological trends (innovation, technology transfer, new products and applications etc.), for cultural and sociological trends (demographic changes, evolution of consumers' preferences etc.) and for political trends (new laws, norms and regulations). This aspect has been underlined by many scholars, among them Porter (1985).

According to Porter, the aim of corporate strategy is the acquisition and maintenance of competitive advantage in the company's sector, defined as "extended competition". Therefore, it is a problem of understanding and developing scenarios for handling industry competition. Moreover, the detection of trends and weak signals becomes even more essential in a turbulent context (Ansoff, 1987). While searching for new opportunities, innovation-oriented companies need not only analyze past mistakes and understand today's market; they also have to identify the possible scenarios involved in tomorrow's potential markets. This implies scanning the periphery of one's business (Day and Schoemaker, 2005), catching weak signals, monitoring trends, having a clear view of the company's present situation and subsequently analyzing its potential future paths.

Every company faces the challenge of adapting to its environment, thereby either surviving or failing (Aldrich, 1979). A company's objectives keep changing, both in response to external environmental factors and to internal development factors. Basically, an organization is a complex adaptive system which operates based on expectations and which modifies its behavior by learning, either from its environment, from its competitors' behavior, or from the evolution of the industry sector.

Given the importance of foresight and forecasting, the main problem we are facing today is how to integrate this process into the choices and decisions of the company (Schwarz, 2005) – more specifically, how to start implementing it and how to monitor its development, step by step, until completion.

Strategic fit (also called alignment, coherence, harmony) is crucial to a firm's ability to change and adapt to the context. Organizations are constantly looking for ways to develop both internal strategic fit (Miller, 1992; Porter, 1996) and external strategic fit (Venkatraman, 1989; Miles and Snow, 1994). Many scholars underline that when companies are obsessed with short-term profits, they tend to devote too much attention to the internal context and to ignore the evolution of the external environment, thereby failing to incorporate this precious information into their strategy (Coda, 1998). The literature on strategic management has always emphasized that in defining the company's strategy, it is of the utmost importance to consider the future evolution of the external context. Therefore, it is essential to resort to environmental scanning (Daft and Weick, 1984; May et al., 2000) to understand how to develop likely scenarios (Ansoff, 1965; Grant, 1994) and to incorporate the results into the decision making process (Nutt, 2007).

Nevertheless, it is still difficult for companies to integrate the foresight process into their particular strategy, and there is still a gap between collecting information and taking effective action (Reger, 2001; Van der Steen et al., 2010). This is why our main challenge is to help companies understand how trends concretely influence their business, how to update and revise their strategy in the middle of uncertainty, how to find effective methods to face change and to catch future opportunities.

The development of forecasts, the analysis of trends and scenarios and other foresight techniques are based on a complex interplay of different factors. A variety of tools and methodologies have been developed, with wide applications both in governmental policy-making and in corporate strategy. Preliminary conclusions suggest that foresight methods are indeed relevant to corporate strategy, but that they need to be made available and implemented in a more systematic way; besides, they have to be adapted to the needs and abilities of each specific company (Schwarz, 2008).

Companies need to develop methods for assessing their "strategic fit with the future"; in other words, they need processes to check the alignment between their strategic orientation (the internal perspective) and weak signals and trends (the external perspective). As of today, the literature does not provide us with precise and complete methodologies to assess the effective coherence between the company's vision, the company's products and the external trends.

We therefore propose a *"methodology of future coverage"*, the aim of which is to measure to what degree strategy is effectively aligned with trends and products. The methodology will then be tested in the Eurotech case study via a longitudinal analysis. In our view, our method gives a useful contribution to understanding how the company's vision and products match trends, and possibly provides supplementary information for improvement or reorientation.

8.2 The framework of our approach

The proposed methodology is based on foresight techniques and draws on the above discussion. It attempts to evaluate coherence between the external environment (trends) and the internal environment (vision and products). Corporate foresight supports this analysis by identifying external trends. Subsequently, trends are compared with vision and products, which make up the company's strategy. The comparison allows the company to understand if what is happening on a macro level (PEEST) and with its competitors and customers is aligned with its internal orientation. Figure 8.1 outlines the framework of the proposed methodology.

Once the scenarios and trends have been identified with foresight techniques, the methodology performs a preliminary analysis of the external and internal company dynamics: the external trends are compared with the company's vision to check that both are moving in the same direction – in other words, to ensure that the company's future orientation is coherent with the trends.

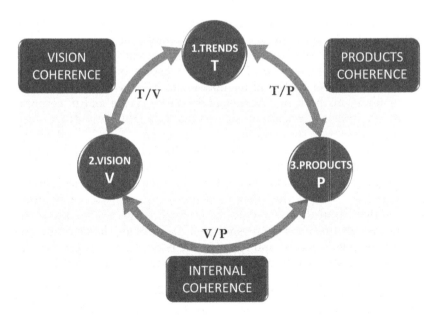

Figure 8.1 Framework of the "future coverage" methodology.

The second step is a completely internal one, aimed at verifying how effectively the products match the company's vision. This analysis determines whether the products are consistent with the intended trajectory, or in other words, whether the products manufactured today and the products being designed for the future match the company's plans and orientation, as expressed in the vision.

Finally, the last step evaluates the degree of coherence between the company's products and external trends, in other words, it verifies to what degree the products are effectively aligned with the prospective future of the industry sector.

The output consists of three values: alignment between vision and current trends, internal alignment between vision and products, alignment between products and external trends.

The methodology is made up of two macro-phases:

1 Study of the characteristics
2 Coherence analysis

The study of the characteristics investigates the three variables – trends/megatrends, vision and products (T, V and P, respectively) – and identifies their main characteristics. The coherence analysis compares the three variables T, V and P by pairs, thus conducting a trends–vision (T/V), vision–products (V/P) and trends–products (T/P) analysis.

Figure 8.2 highlights the two macro-phases and the six phases of the trends/vision/products coverage analysis, while Figure 8.3 shows the three variables (T, V, P) in the general company context.

The proposed methodology uses CF to analyze the company's strategy in terms of the company's vision and products, and to determine its level of coherence with industry trends. Finally, the method is consistent with the discussion presented in Chapter 5: the coherence analysis between trends, vision and products is in fact a coherence analysis between the future external environment and the company's internal context.

	MACROPHASES			PHASES		OUTPUT
METHODOLOGY OF FUTURE COVERAGE	a. EXPLICATION OF THE CHARACTERISTICS OF THE VARIABLES T, V, P		1	Explication of trend characteristics	T	Figure 11.1
			2	Explication of vision characteristics	V	Table 11.1
			3	Explication of product characteristics	P	Figure 11.2
	b. COHERENCE ANALYSIS OF THE VARIABLES T, V, P		A	Analysis of trends/vision coherence	T/V	Matrix 11.1
			B	Analysis of vision/products coherence	V/P	Matrix 11.2
			C	Analysis of trends/products coherence	T/P	Matrix 11.3

Figure 8.2 Macro-phases and phases of the "future coverage" methodology.

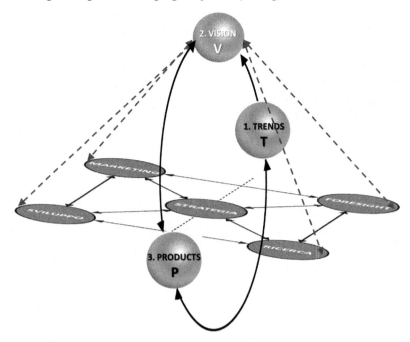

Figure 8.3 The three variables (trends, vision and products) in the company's general context.

8.3 The study of trends, vision and products

The study of the characteristics considers both the external and the internal environment: industry trends and scenarios (external context) are studied with foresight techniques; vision and strategy (internal context) are studied in terms of past, present and future products. Schematically, this macro-phase consists of three steps:

1 Study of trends' characteristics (T)
2 Study of vision's characteristics (V)
3 Study of products' characteristics (P)

The study of megatrends deals with the company's external environment: it takes into account possible scenarios and developments both in the industry of reference and in contiguous or complementary sectors (Gill, 1986). The study of trends depends on the main reference industry; it investigates the state of the art of technology (new technologies, research centers, connections to other sectors and different technologies etc.) as well as the overall PEEST environment in which the company operates.

Basically, we follows Porter's (1985) suggestion: when studying a specific sector, the focus should be on the competition and uncertainties typical of that sector. The focus is then widened to include the study of weak signals and trends from other sectors: a number of experts are contacted (not all of them coming from the company's specific sector) for a more profitable exchange of ideas and a better identification of the most probable scenarios, based on the availability of different sources and techniques.[1]

Trends' characteristics are identified in the following ways:

1 Researching the literature on industry trends
2 Using CF tools (Delphi analysis, technology roadmapping, brainstorming etc.)
3 Involving experts from different sectors

In strategic analysis, the term "vision" is used to indicate the projection of a future scenario which reflects the ideals, values and aspirations of the goal-setter. Vision could be defined as the desired future state of a company in business and in society. Scholars (e.g., Larwood et al., 1995; Kantabutra and Avery, 2010) see vision as a long-term, future-oriented endeavor. Vision, together with mission and values, is fundamental for any organization. It is essential to create a well-coordinated system and to make a desired scenario come true; it helps establish an identity, it gives a route to follow, it points to a horizon, it lights up a pathway from the actual situation to a possible future. An effective vision defines what an organization wants to be and gives it a clear direction, based on a series of indications connected to the idea of a possible future.

In our methodology, a study of the vision's characteristics is necessary to understand in what direction a company is moving or would like to move, and to assess its ideas about the future. This analysis can be conducted in many ways, but the assistance of the top management (CEO, CTO, CFO) is always required.

Products are the practical and operative manifestation of a company's strategy. They represent the actual state of company operations. However, future products must also be taken into consideration: products that are being studied in research labs, concept products still at the design or ideation stage – in other words, products upon which future operations will be based.

For a company to have internal coherence, its vision and products must be aligned. There has to be coherence between future objectives and what the company is actually accomplishing at the moment. Products must also be coherent with trends, to ensure that the company's everyday operations are consistent with the direction taken by the market. Moreover, the analysis can be conducted from a historical perspective, to highlight and understand the company's growth trajectory over time.

8.4 Coherence analysis between trends, vision and products

The coherence analysis is a triple comparison of the three variables previously studied: trends and vision, vision and products, trends and products. Both internal and external coherence is required. External coherence is

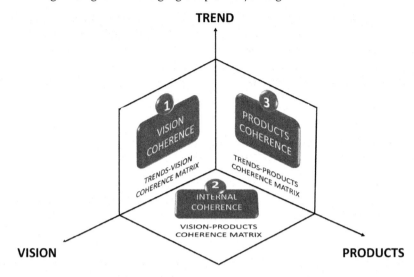

Figure 8.4 The Cartesian planes of the coherence matrixes.

necessary to ensure that both the company's vision and products are oriented in the same direction of industry trends. Internal coherence is also needed, to ensure that vision and products are aligned. In other words, there should be coherence between the company's vision of the future and the reality of what is actually occurring in the field.

The results of this analysis are a set of specific values: just as the inventory/sales index measures to what degree the inventory matches market demand, our "future coverage" index measures to what degree the vision corresponds to ongoing trends, to what degree the products reflect the vision and to what degree the products match trends.

Our coherence analysis is based on expert judgment according to the Delphi panel method. Experts give their subjective opinion on the variable pairs both verbally and numerically, giving marks according to a predetermined scale. The output of the coherence analysis consists of three matrixes (Figure 8.4).

Three comparisons are made:

1 Trends/vision (T/V) coherence analysis (vision coherence): this is an external–internal coherence analysis. The characteristics of trends and megatrends are compared with the vision's characteristics, to evaluate the coherence or lack of alignment between the vision and the trends and megatrends.
2 Vision/products (V/P) coherence analysis (internal coherence): this is an internal coherence analysis. Given the company's vision, the question is to determine whether the company's products are coherent with what the vision declares. This analysis is developed from a historical

point of view: the main products are analyzed, both the actual products and the past and future ones (e.g., products still in the design stage, which have not been developed or commercialised yct, or have been developed in the form of prototypes).

3 Trends/products (T/P) coherence analysis (products coherence): this is an external–internal coherence analysis. The characteristics of every product are compared with the characteristics of trends and megatrends, in order to identify similarities and discordances. Usually, the analysis takes into account both past and present products, including the most innovative ones, which are still prototypes or in the research stage. This allows to understand whether the company is growing in the direction indicated by the trends.

In Chapter 11, the methodology of future coverage will be applied to the Eurotech case.

Note

1 For example, the case study presented in Part 3 involved not only experts from informatics and electronics (i.e., the company's sector), but also from economics, sociology and biology.

Part III

Foresight in Eurotech SpA

9 Trends in the ICT sector

"Don't be a spider, be a honey bee".
Haruo Tsuji

9.1 Trends and megatrends

This chapter is an introduction to our case study. It presents an overview of the most important trends and megatrends in the ICT sector in order to identify and detail the issues and challenges that Eurotech is facing and will face in the future.

The ICT sector is definitely a context where acceleration, interconnection and discontinuity are ever-present conditions that have to be dealt with on an ongoing basis. In such a changing and uncertain situation, the resource of information has been taking on a more and more essential role both in the lives of men and in the strategies of organizations. The spread of personal computers, the development of broadband networks, the acquired habit of dealing with increasingly advanced technologies have all given momentum to the rise of new technologies and new service categories. Besides, ICT is a recent, constantly changing sector. Echoing Tsuji's statement, we can say that the ICT sector is like a very fast car: to be able to drive it, you have to look ahead. Finally, the ICT sector assimilates many ideas from different disciplines: not just computer science and electronics, but also biology, genetics etc., and this is why we talk about GRIN convergence (genetics, robotics, informatics and nanotechnology). Sometimes, this convergence generates strange and unexpected effects and is therefore highly eligible for foresight studies.

As regards industrial development, the three most interesting global megatrends for the next 5–10 years are the following:

1　West to East: the shift of economic power from the West to the East
2　Ageing: the demographic trend of progressively ageing global population
3　Resource availability: the reduced availability of strategic resources
4　Internet of Things: more and more information interconnecting people, objects and services, bonding together the real and the digital (machine-to-machine)

Obviously, these four megatrends do not include wild cards.

West to East. In the next 15 years, the current international system will undergo profound changes as regards the structure of international institutions, governance models and methods of production, exchange and consumption.

A new global, multipolar and highly interconnected system will be established. The difference in economic and political power between developed nations and emerging countries will shrink and new financial and social players, including non-institutional ones, will assume greater importance. The current configuration of global markets, including the recent past of general "Westernization", will give way to a new and more dynamic configuration. In politics and in the economy new management models will appear, more oriented towards locality (e.g., city states). Thanks to technology, learning will become much faster and gaps will close much faster, following a general trend towards unification.

More specifically, there will be a shift in socioeconomic and financial power from Western countries to emerging countries, particularly, but not exclusively, Asian ones. The countries that will benefit the most from this shift in the world's equilibrium are indicated as MINTS (Mexico, Indonesia, Nigeria, Turkey and South Africa). Up to the present day, the most favored emerging countries were indicated as BRIC (Brazil, Russia, India and China). In the short term, multinational corporations based in emerging countries will become increasingly powerful, while at present, and despite their often considerable size, they are still little known outside of their countries of origin. In the long term, network models and ecosystem models, in which the role of multinational companies is not yet clear, will spread all over the world. Already, three large global aggregations are emerging, centered respectively in the EU and the US for the West, in Russia and the Gulf states for central Asia, in China and India for the far East. The United States will maintain in the short term their political and military leadership and their leading role in the definition of global governance, but their margin of superiority will shrink over time, namely, in favor of China in the short term and of Africa in the long term.

Ageing. According to available data, the next 15 years will see an average global ageing of the world population. In the coming decades, demographic trends will alter the absolute values and relative ratios between the young and the elderly within nations, and the relative ratios between different nations and areas of the world. These demographic trends will follow divergent and sometimes conflicting paths in the various regions of the world, but globally the increase in the average age of the population will emerge as a common trend (from 26.6 years in 2000 to 37.7 years in 2050).

Ageing will have a particular impact on Europe, where between 2008 and 2060 the average age is expected to grow by eight years, from about 40 to about 48. This trend is influenced by two factors: the decline in fertility rates and the increase in life expectancy (in developed countries, plus

30 years in the last century). If a longer life is everyone's wish on the individual level, the global trend of ageing will put into question the economic and social sustainability (pension system, health care system, need to balance the needs of the elderly with those of younger generations etc.) of the models and infrastructures of present societies.

A key issue related to ageing will be the postponement of the limitations and diseases/disabilities traditionally linked to old age. As stated by the United Nations, in the future people everywhere shall be granted the possibility to age in security and dignity, continuing to participate as full right citizens in society. In other words, a longer life will also be a healthier one, which in turn will lower health care costs and promote better living conditions for the elderly population.

It will therefore be vital, for society as a whole, to integrate the elderly with disabilities, and more generally all people with disabilities, and to grant them equal opportunities and full access to physical, social, political, economic and cultural structures, to health care, education, information and communication. Future societies will thus enable people with disabilities to fully enjoy human rights and fundamental freedoms, promoting their participation at all levels.

Resource availability. In the coming decades, the problems related to resource availability will be more and more important in the international agenda. Global economic growth and population growth, together with richer (on average) consumers, especially in the OECD countries and in the new strong economies such as China, Brazil and India, will boost the demand for highly strategic resources (food, water, fossil fuels and minerals) which are already gradually decreasing, both in availability and accessibility. In the coming years, the fact that the growing demand for natural resources could vastly exceed the available offer will be a major global concern.

In particular, the debate is open on the problem of energy supply and of resource distribution: for water, extraction rates are already unsustainable in many parts of the world, and the increase in food production has seen diminishing returns in recent years. Obviously, the introduction of innovative technologies could change everything. For example, the debate on the oil supply crisis has come to an end thanks to the new "shale gas" technology, which allows to extract oil from marine gas deposits. Similarly, water supply would no longer be a problem if really efficient desalination technologies were developed, and the same goes for food production, food storage and preservation etc.

Humanity is responding to the increasing demand for resources by finding new ways to extract more value out of fewer available resources. In the near future, technologies and laws will change, and new markets will open up. Some analysts believe that there will be a big and purposeful global effort to attain greater overall efficiency, but the scarcity of natural resources may also result in an intensification of competition or an increase in conflicts – especially, but not exclusively, due to the effects of climate change. Either way, the coming decades will still be dominated by the double imperative of innovation and of environmental, social and economic sustainability.

Internet of Things. One very evident megatrend is the unstoppable spread of connectivity at all levels, and the pervasiveness of information systems. The Internet, already currently the most important global IT infrastructure, is expected to evolve towards an ever greater integration of networks and services, and the number of smart objects (either fixed or mobile) connected to the network is expected to grow exponentially. This interconnectivity no longer merely concerns people, services and information, but is rapidly extending to physical objects and will finally result in an integrated and seamless universal network, in which all elements will play an active role in the exchange of information about themselves and their environment.

The increase in connectivity will result in a greater and greater number of social and productive factors being technologically mediated; this technological mediation will extend the forms of interaction (e.g., speech, Google glasses) and at the same time open up opportunities for positive contamination. Creativity and innovation in technology and in the economy will become more closely connected to the areas of artistic and cultural creativity. In this context, the innovative forms of knowledge sharing, real-time interaction and co-creation will take on a particular significance, as will the emerging phenomenon of crowdsourcing. Predictably, this trend will lead to the enhancement of users' creativity, who in turn will take part in the design and co-creation of increasingly complex digital content.

The term *Internet of Things* refers to a scenario where the Internet connection is extended to most of the physical objects of everyday life, making it possible to control them remotely and to turn them into active elements able to autonomously exchange data and gain access to a diversified set of services and features. According to this vision, the physical and the digital world will become integrated: tiny computers embedded in common objects will make the information about these objects and their environment accessible and manageable in the digital world. These "smart" objects will also react autonomously to events taking place in their reference context, thereby realizing forms of ubiquitous computing (ambient intelligence).

The current business models, based on a static information architecture, will be challenged because the amount of potentially available information will require the development of new management models, such as intelligent data-retrieval systems, semantic search technologies, or smart technologies for real-time data processing. The ability to react to events in the physical world in an automatic, rapid and knowledgeable way will open up new opportunities for the management of complex and critical situations, but will also allow to optimize a variety of existing business processes. It will therefore provide an answer to the eternal dichotomy between optimization of the existing business model and creation of a new one. The real-time interpretation of data (big data and data analytics) from the physical world will lead to new services and generate economic and social benefits.

Both for society and for individuals, the Internet of Things will result in an improved quality of life. People will easily find any kind of information and will have their needs answered with greater attention, thanks to smart assistance systems that will make life more pleasant, fun, independent and safe. In the future, all the activities of daily life will be supported by the use of the Internet and by smart environments which will make human intervention less and less decisive. The development of the Internet of Things will lead to the creation of a network of people, objects and services steadily interacting between each other and with their environment.

9.2 ICT trends and megatrends

Humanity has travelled a long road from the first stone artifacts (the Levallois points) to complex microcircuits able to transfer information. Thanks to compression, the digital economy represents a paradigm shift. According to Negroponte (1996), value is no longer in matter (understood as an aggregate of atoms) but in bits. From a technological point of view, the 21st century can be seen as the century of the advent and spread of electronics, information and communication.

The current trend of "less is more" is based on devices that deal with information: we have gone from a lot of matter with little information to a little matter with a lot of information, because when information is added, much less matter is needed to do the same things. Just think of "drive by wire" processes and 3D printing, which produce no waste at all, thanks to computers.

In the field of information and communication technology, trends are dictated by four laws:

1 Negroponte's law (*digitalization*): Matter is changing from atoms to bits.
2 Moore's law (*miniaturization*): The price/performance ratio for memorization and computing power doubles every 18 months.
3 Metcalfe's law (*interconnection*): The value of a telecommunications network is proportional to the square of the number of connected users.
4 Gilder's law (*quantization*): The total bandwidth of communication systems triples every 12 months (at least three times faster than computing power in Moore's law).

Negroponte's law is the starting point of the other three laws: it is because matter is now made of bits that miniaturization, interconnection and quantization are possible. By definition, miniaturization uses less matter and allows it to be more easily distributed. At the same time, computing power is no longer concentrated in one place, but becomes available at any time and place by accessing the Cloud, which grants more rationality and efficiency both in terms of time and performance. This also means that major expensive infrastructures are no longer necessary, as virtual computers are unaffected by the limitations of the physical world.

A major trend is the increasing convergence of all sectors, which implies both a digital convergence and a process convergence. Digital convergence refers to the gradual integration of bits and atoms, while process convergence regards the progressive integration of different disciplines. In this sense, Marc Andreessen of Netscape says that "software is eating the world": in whatever business we are, we are always in the software business.

According to a McKinsey report, at least 80% of sectors will be impacted by the Internet of Things, in particular: medicine and life sciences will be impacted by bioengineering, manufacturing processes by nanotechnology, 3D printers and many others by the ubiquitous computer network.

As specifically regards the ICT sector, we have conducted a focus group.[1] The discussion has identified the following trends and megatrends:

1 *Acceleration of change*: The speed of technological evolution (the pace of change in the ICT sector) is continuously increasing.
2 *Technology essentiality*: Technology – understood as the set of tools with which man interacts with the environment to know it and transform it – has always been important to man, and with the advent of digital technologies, it is becoming even more important.
3 *Human–technology interaction*: Technology has changed many things for humans, both on the anthropological and on the sociological level, and in turn man selectively accelerates and catalyzes technological developments. In particular, the experts have underlined the following aspects:

   a   Irreversibility: After a disruptive technology is introduced, especially a technology so disruptive that it changes the surrounding environment, the process is irreversible.
   b   Conditioning: Technology opens up new possibilities for man, but at the beginning its full potentialities do not appear clearly.
   c   Human–technology transformation: Man and technology act in a double cycle of transformation. Man transforms technology, which in turn transforms man's life. This has always happened, but with the progressive acceleration of technological development, this transformation has even greater effects.

4 *Augmented reality*: For man, technology represents an extension of his capacities. For the environment, technology also represents an expansion of "intelligence", promoted by the diffusion of computers (pervasive computers create an "intelligent" environment, the network promotes the spread of information and the software provides data

logistics). All this contributes to the creation of an augmented reality, which according to the experts includes the following aspects:

a   Expansion and contraction: Technology works in two directions:

  i   From contraction to expansion: devices are becoming smaller and smaller but they allow expansion – for example, in computing, we find the chains "mainframe–PC–notebook–tablet" and "cellphone–smartphone–wearable smart things" where miniaturization allows expansion because of the diffusion and connection in a network.

  ii   From expansion to contraction: supercomputers provide the opportunity for high computing power, which in turn enables the study of scientific problems connected with micro- and nanotechnology. Currently we talk about Cloud computing, an IT infrastructure that provides computing power and data storage either in modality as-a-service or pay-per-use.

b   Invisibility: ICT technologies are becoming invisible to man; in other words, they have become part of our background: we are less and less aware of their presence and their use is more and more natural, almost like breathing.

c   Pervasiveness: Thanks to miniaturization, digital technologies for computation and communication have wider and wider effects. Objects are increasingly becoming "smart" and interconnected, thanks to pervasive computing.

d   Augmented reality: For man, technology represents an extension and a boost of his abilities. For example, a hammer extends the capacity of the human hand in terms of power, a car extends the capacity of the human foot in terms of speed, and a mobile phone today extends our ability to communicate. Such extensions also exist in the environment: miniaturized computers will be embedded in everyday objects, giving intelligence to inanimate things, and the environment will be full of information. Both humans and machines will be able to better perceive their reality – an augmented reality. In this sense, Intel defines technology as man's "sixth sense".

e   Connectivity: Digital technology allows the creation of a smart device network thanks to which humans will be able to overcome the limitations of physical space, becoming, in a sense, ubiquitous. The essence of technology is the creation of a wider and wider network of connections between things and people.

f   Informationalism: The development of digital technology implies that, more than ever, everything is based on information. Basically, the essence of all things is their information content, and in that sense Negroponte (1996) talks about the change from atoms to bits in his digitalization law.

g   Hypertextuality: Technology is becoming more nonlinear, dynamic and flexible because it increasingly follows the "logic of networks".

5 *Symbiosis*: The evolution of man is not only biological but also cultural and technological. Therefore, biotechnological evolution must also be taken into consideration, namely:

a   Technology–human transformation: Man and technology act in a double cycle of transformation. Technology acts on the environment and on man, changing him both on the anthropological and on the sociological level.

b   Organic–inorganic integration: The path of man now takes him towards biotechnological evolution and the possibility of symbiosis (think of the "digital native" generation).

c   Convergence: The evolution of digital technologies goes hand in hand with the simultaneous evolution of NBIC (nano-bio-info-cognitive) and all trends are converging in the same direction (more and more products employ a mix of technologies from different sectors).

9.3 The trend of man–machine symbiosis according to Eurotech

Eurotech is particularly focused on the trend of symbiosis, which will be discussed in this section.

Technology is the set of "capacities and means whereby man puts nature to his own service, by identifying nature's properties and laws in order to exploit them and control their interaction" (Gehlen, 1957).

The man–machine relationship is a complex interaction with strong mutual influences. Some of the most powerful technologies developed by man are related to communication (think about language, or writing). As men are inherently social beings, one of the major challenges of humanity has been the management of communication. The first technologies were strictly necessary for survival and based on the individual, but once the problem of finding food was solved, technology became social. Networks were created in order to leverage knowledge without having to rediscover (i.e., learn) things all the time, and tools were developed for information processing. The hominid species which developed itself the most was precisely the one most adept at learning, processing information and communicating.

At the present time in history, we possess powerful technologies for information processing. Still, language and writing have limited potentialities due to biological saturation. Computers overcome these limits and amplify human abilities, but above all, they increase our connection capacity. Thanks to an increasingly large bandwidth, it is now possible to store data at the nonlocal level and to use memory and computing power on-demand: the usability of communication tools has become extremely widespread.

Technology cannot be considered simply as a product of man, in a traditional cause–effect logic: rather, it retroacts on man in an advanced logic of circular causality. In this perspective of circular interaction between man and technology, the evolution of man is to be found in the complex interactions between biological evolution (Darwin), sociocultural evolution (Lamarck) and technological evolution (Dawkins, 1976). We can therefore speak of man–machine co-evolution, identifying biological, sociocultural and technological evolution as interacting elements.

In the words of Giuseppe Longo (2001):

> Technology is so important that it contributes to create man's cognitive (and active) categories, thus conditioning his development. The distinction between man and technology is not as clear as sometimes claimed, because technology concurs to form the essence of man: the evolution of technology has become the evolution of man. If today biological evolution is [appears] stationary, cultural evolution is faster than ever: but the separation between the two is artificial, since the two processes are now intertwined into one and the same biocultural, or biotechnological, evolution (*our translation, N.d.T.*).

In the mainframe era, there was one computer for many people. With the advent of personal computers, the ratio became one computer for one person. Today, in the era of the Internet and of distributed computing, a single person uses multiple devices. In the coming era of pervasive computing, a person will interact with a lot of interconnected computers. Finally, we will get to the biotechnology stage, the integration between biology and technology which is the paradigm of the future, when computers will be so widespread and integrated into the environment that they will weave an extremely dense fabric, the so-called computational exoskeleton. In the course of this evolution, what has been changing drastically is the ratio between the number of users and the number of computers, as shown in Table 9.1.

Table 9.1 Evolution of computing devices.

YEARS	DEVICES	USERS / COMPUTERS RATIO	PROCESSING POWER
1950–1980	Mainframe	$n : 1$	low
1980–2000	Personal computer	$1 : 1$	medium
2000–2010	Personal Digital Assistant (PDA), portable phones etc.	$1 : n$	medium
2010–2015	Smart devices (smartphone, smart appliances)	$1 : n^2$	high
2015 onwards	Internet of Things (pervasive computers, computational exoskeleton, smart dust)	$1 : n^n$	extremely high

Digital technology is heading towards the paradigm of pervasive computing and of the Internet of Things, as a result of the combination between miniaturization, integration, dissemination throughout the environment (embeddedness), network connection and invisibility of computing devices. In Mark Weiser's words, in the "pervasivity" scenario, computers exit man's conscious awareness (Weiser, 1991).

Pervasive computing is based on computers so small that they can be disseminated into the environment as smart dust, woven into fabrics or painted on walls to provide connection and computation to all the objects of everyday life.

Recently, the "smart" concept has become fashionable, and is increasingly used to indicate the enhanced intelligence which comes from the easier access to information provided by the widespread presence of ICT technologies. The "smart" concept is being increasingly applied to a variety of contexts: smart cities, smart environment, smart mobility etc.

In cities, for example, urban development does not only depend on the physical infrastructure (buildings, roads etc.), but also on the availability and quality of the computing and communication infrastructure. Also important is that all the miniature computers embedded into objects will communicate and interact with each other by transmitting data and information through networks of networks (in the logic of Grid computing or Cloud computing), which form the global structure of the computational exoskeleton.

More specifically, Cloud computing is a set of technologies that allow to store, archive and/or process data by using hardware/software resources distributed and virtualized on the Internet.

According to many authors, including anthropologist Arnold Gehlen (1957), technology has always been used by man to make up for his physical and mental weaknesses. In other words, technology represents an extension of man's body and senses, of his physical and psychological capabilities, and it also allows the creation of an augmented reality.

Throughout history, man has tried to enhance his abilities with artificial and technological tools; currently, the advent of digital technologies and the acceleration of technological development and of pervasive computing is prefiguring a new evolution scenario: the so-called Homo technologicus, perfectly adapted to the new technological and cultural setting.

The generation born in the '80s is considered the first example of humans "hybridized" with digital technologies. Several neologisms have been invented to describe them:

- "Homo zappiens"[2] (Veen, 2002): a mix between Homo sapiens and the skill of zapping, this expression is used to indicate those who naturally use a multitasking, discontinuous and nonlinear approach.
- "Digital Natives" (Prensky, 2001): those who were born and grew up with digital technology, as opposed to "digital immigrants", who were

born before its advent. As Alan Kay affirmed in 1982 at a meeting at PARC, the Palo Alto Research Center of Xerox, "technology is anything that wasn't around when you were born".

- "Symbionts" (Longo, 2001 and 2003): humans living in symbiosis with machines.
- "Net-Gens" (Tapscott, 2008): the generation of the Internet and of all communication networks.
- "Cyborgs without surgery" (Clark, 2003): cyborgs not surgically but culturally modified.

"Homo technologicus" is therefore a man who has been interacting with digital technologies since birth. These technologies include the remote, the mouse and the cell phone, which have been studied by many authors because they allow a completely new management of information: the children of today are skilled in controlling the information flow, in dealing with its over-availability, in selecting it appropriately and according to their needs. Their nonlinear behavior, their instinctive control of information, their knowledge of how to efficiently and effectively navigate through it, of how to communicate and to build a network of peers, will naturally bring about the development of critical skills for an interconnected and hyper-creative society. According to many authors (including Kurzweil, 2006), the next step in technological evolution is biorganic computing: technologies will interact more and more closely with humans who, in addition to living in an environment with widespread computing and smart objects, will wear an increasing number of computational tools (computer-shaped bracelets or earrings, nanocomputers woven into clothes' fabrics), and even have them implanted into their bodies (RFID tags, medication dispensers etc.).

According to John Smart's (2005) classification of the eras of human history in relation to biological, cultural and technological evolution (Table 9.2),

Table 9.2 The ages of human history.

AGES	LENGTH
Homo abilis age	1.000.000 years
Homo sapiens age	100.000 years
Tribal age/Cro-magnon	40.000 years
Agriculture age	7.000 years
Empires age	2.500 years
Scientific age	380 years (1500–1770)
Industrial age	180 years (1770–1950)
Information age	70 years (1950–2020)
Symbiotic age	30 years (2020–2050)
Singular age	(2050 onwards)

Source: Adapted from John Smart, 2005.

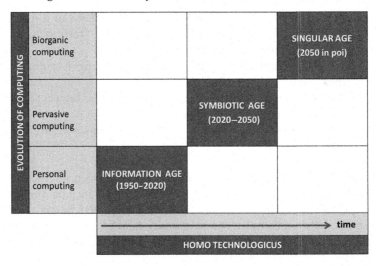

Figure 9.1 Man–machine evolution matrix (De Toni and Battistella, 2007)

man–machine coevolution will spread through three specific ages: the Information Age (currently under way), the Symbiotic Age (2020–2050) and the Singular Age (2050 onwards). In the course of these three eras, ICT technology will become more and more integrated with man, according to the coevolution matrix presented in Figure 9.1.

Notes

1 A focus group is a qualitative technique where a group of people are invited to speak, discuss and debate their personal views about a specific topic. The questions are asked interactively, and participants are free to communicate with each other under the supervision of a moderator.

2 "Homo zappiens" is a neologism describing young people born from the '80s onwards, who grew up with computers and therefore have much more familiarity with digital technologies than former generations (Veen, 2006).

10 Foresight in Eurotech
Organizational aspects

> "The most dangerous sentence in the world: that's how we've always done it!"
>
> Anonymous

10.1 Eurotech as a factory of ideas

Eurotech is an international company: its headquarters are located in Amaro (Udine, Italy), and it has eight controlled companies worldwide (Italy, France, UK, USA, China and Japan). It was founded in 1992 and went public in 2005. Its 2013 revenue was 66 million euro. It has 359 employees and two strategic business units operating respectively in the markets of nano-PCs (embedded computers, pervasive computers and Internet of Things platforms) and HPCs (high performance computers).

Eurotech is a medium-size company in the ICT sector. It was founded by six engineers with a starting capital of about 25,000 euro in 1992, and has been steadily growing until 2008 (around +50% yearly). Eurotech has a story of acceleration, which includes the stages of incubation (1992–2000), private equity and acquisitions (2000–2005), listing and acquisitions (2005–present day). Its revenues have been, in million euros: 3.9 (2000), 6.4 (2001), 8.3 (2002), 11.7 (2003), 18.8 (2004), 29.8 (2005), 50.7 (2006), 75 (2007), 91.7 (2008), 88.5 (2009), 99.3 (2010), 92.8 (2011), 78 (2012), 66 (2013).[1] Today Eurotech is an international group focused on innovation, applied both to products and to the business model. The company's strategy is focused on growth, and is sustained by two main drivers:

- A corporate culture based on innovation
- Openness to internationalization

Eurotech was born as a "factory of ideas", with the intent of miniaturizing computers for applications in still unexplored domains. This focus on innovation is evident in the words of its CEO, Roberto Siagri[2]:

> In the first stage, the short-term and the long-term vision coexisted, but over time the two visions have gradually become more and more

synergic. We have chosen to be a fabless company, a company of ideas betting heavily on innovation. (Siagri, pers. interview)

The company has built its first competitive advantage in a stable technology niche, and is now a leader in the consolidated field of Embedded Computer Technology (ECT). According to Eurotech, innovation in the ECT sector can only be incremental, and this is why the best choice is to innovate within the industry standard. After the first year (from 1996 onwards) and since 2000, between 5% and 10% of revenues[3] have been invested not solely in pursuing the process of incremental innovation, but also in looking for new possible disruptive innovations, considered the core of the system:

> The company's focus is on innovation. Disruptive innovation can be made using intuition, foresight and research. This is why our first revenues were immediately invested in research; other companies would have chosen to direct their capital elsewhere, but we felt we needed solid foundations for our growth. (Siagri, pers. interview)

Since 2000, Eurotech's vision has attached itself to the new scenario of pervasive computing and of the Internet of Things. Consequently, the company has decided to concentrate its foresight and research activities in this area, to identify, imagine, design and manufacture new products and new applications.

> Eurotech's strategy is now to explore new ways to use computers. For us, the emerging scenario of pervasive computing has always been an exciting challenge. But in order to take this new path, we had to adopt a new business model, and this required additional investments. In line with this, we decided to go public, in other words, to let go of control in order to preside. For the new business model, the main strategic line at the time was to put a lot of emphasis on research (12% of sales and 40% of employees) and to organize the company accordingly. We tried to combine innovation with both our external and internal processes, in order to grow more rapidly (Siagri, pers. interview).

The history of Eurotech is marked by ongoing success, as testified by the many product launches, innovation awards, strategic partnerships and the presence of *Fortune 500* companies among its customers. Table 10.1 presents a summary of Eurotech's main product innovations, while Tables 10.2 and 10.3 set out the company's milestones for networking and internationalization respectively.

The history of Eurotech has always been marked by a quest for technological leadership and by a strategy strongly based on research and foresight, focused on identifying future possibilities and then implementing possible scenarios in innovative products. As its CEO says: "Eurotech has always had a vision of the future, but this vision has changed over time, according to the growth stage of the company" (Siagri, pers. interview).

Table 10.1 Main product innovations in Eurotech's history.

YEAR	INNOVATION	TYPE
1995	First company to market a PC/104 module based on an Intel 32-bit 486DX processor.	Incremental innovation
1999	In collaboration with INFN, the company produces the innovative APEmille computer, with 1 TeraFlops of processing power.	Disruptive innovation
2000–2005	Improvements of existing technologies.	Incremental innovation
2006	First model of the Zypad wearable wrist computer.	Disruptive innovation
2006	Zypad wins the award for most innovative product at the Soldier Technologies conference in London.	Award
2006	Zypad wins the Frost & Sullivan award for most innovative product in the Ambient Intelligence category.	Award
2007	Eurotech invests in the UGV (Unmanned Ground Vehicles) sector by acquiring 20% of the US company Kairos Autonomi.	Disruptive innovation
2007	Production of Janus, a new HPC platform which can reach 8 PetaOps of processing power in two cubic meters and with only 10kWh of power consumption, the most powerful computer in its category.	Disruptive innovation
2008	At the "Well Net Tech Award" in Milan, Zypad is listed among the 60 products which really changed everyday life.	Award
2009	VDC gives Eurotech the Platinum 2008 award for embedded computing.	Award
2010	Production of ITH Security, for the development of intelligent viewing and surveillance system.	Disruptive innovation
2012	Production of PTC-PTL, a tracking and security system for the US railway network.	Disruptive innovation

Table 10.2 Networking and partnerships.

YEAR	EXTERNAL LINK	RESULT
1998	Partnership with the IRST Institute	Neuricam Spa spin-off. Creation of a new generation of tools integrating videocams with processors for visual recognition (smart digital eye).
1998	Ascensit spin-off	Development of a business model based on an open source software.
1999	Project with INFN (Italian Institute for Nuclear Physics)	Opening of the still unexplored HPC product line. Production of the innovative APEmille computer, with 1 TeraFlops of processing power.
2001	Collaboration with the NJUT (Nanjing University of Technology) research center	ICT research. Sponsor of a degree course in embedded system design.
2001	Partnership with the LITBIO consortium	Technological partner for supercomputer architectures and systems.
2003	Collaboration with the University of Trento and with ITC-IRST	Research activities in the field of pervasive (ubiquitous) computing.
2006	Partnership with Finmeccanica Spa	Exploring technological frontiers in the sectors of aerospace, defense, transportation and energy.
2008	Agreement on the development of HPC technologies	Eurotech and Intel receive an award for co-excellence.
2009	Member of the PROSPECT consortium	Connections with the largest HPC users (Julich Supercomputing Centre, Barcelona Supercomputing Centre, Leibniz-Rechenzentrum Garching) and with component suppliers.
2010	University of Bologna	Collaboration with the University of Bologna in the field of electronic engineering.
2011	Collaboration with the CNR	ITP4 HPC European technology.

Table 10.3 Internationalization and acquisitions.

YEAR	ACQUISITIONS	SECTOR	OBJECTIVES
1997	First collaborations with European distributors and marketing in the US, Asia and Australia	Industry	Developing international distribution
2001	IPS (Italy)	Industry	Completing product lines
2003	Parvus (Salt Lake City, UTAH, USA)	Defense, aerospace	Consolidating and increasing the company's presence in the US and acquiring know-how on subsystems
2004	Erim (Lyon, France – renamed Eurotech France)	Defense, industry, transportation	Entering a strategic market
2005	Arcom Control Systems Ltd. (Cambridge, England – renamed Eurotech England)	Industry, networking, transportation	Expanding/ strengthening international presence in strategic markets such as the US and Japan Completing the product range with complementary products Acquiring or increasing know-how
	Arcom Control Systems Inc. (Kansas City, USA – renamed Eurotech USA)	Industry, oil and gas	
2006	Applied Data Systems Inc. (Maryland, USA – 65% the property of Chengdu Vantron Technology Ltd, China)	Industry, commerce, medical	
2007	65% of Advanet Group (Okayama, Japan)	Industry, medical, transportation	
2011	The remaining 35% of Advanet Group	Industry, medical, transportation	
2012	Dinatec	Industry, medical, transportation	
2013	Parvus is sold (networking sector)	Networking	Refocusing on M2M and IoT technologies

Eurotech is very attentive to the present, to incremental innovation and to maintaining excellence standards, all the while also trying to introduce disruptive innovations. This is in turn reflected in the real separation between incremental and disruptive innovation which can be found at all company levels, from single operations to the organization's structure.

> Eurotech approaches the development of innovation using the Pareto rule: 80% incremental, 20% disruptive. Therefore, Eurotech's strategic line is both to innovate within standards and to identify and penetrate new and emerging markets, breaking traditional barriers through innovation. (Siagri, pers. interview)

Eurotech has always focused its research on key fast-growing areas and is now implementing cutting-edge technologies in the field which was once called Pervasive Computer Technology (PCT), and is now referred to as the Internet of Things. Eurotech's current vision is that pervasiveness will be the next paradigm of computing after mainframes, personal computers and PDAs (Personal Digital Assistant). The Internet era has huge potential for the ubiquity of telecommunications and the widespread dissemination of information. In line with this vision, the CTO (Chief Technology Officer) Giampietro Tecchiolli explains Eurotech's approach to augmented reality and invisible technology:

> The GRID of pervasive computing is called "computational exoskeleton" because, thanks to the dissemination and interconnection of computers at all macro and micro levels, reality will not only be made virtual, it will also be augmented. When we turn on the light, the mechanism of generation and transmission of electricity remains invisible to us. In the same way, in a not too distant future computation and processing capabilities will be so pervasive that we will no longer care who does it and how it gets to us. (Tecchiolli, pers. interview)

Figure 10.1 shows Eurotech's vision of product evolution, which is based on Christensen's model (1997). The market is split between nano-PCs and HPCs, according to two parallel paths:

- Path 1: From 1990 to 2010, office technology has been brought into the industrial sector by producing increasingly small and powerful PCs, and by using them both in embedded technologies and in HPCs.
- Path 2: Since 2000, the smartphone technology has been brought into the industrial sector, and its performances have been increased up to the level required by wearable and wrist computers.

Historically, one of the reasons why Eurotech decided to enter the HPC market was to reuse some of the technologies coming from the PC market

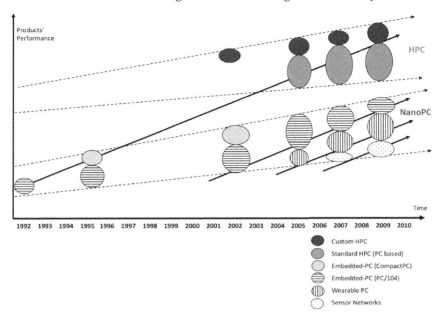

Figure 10.1 Evolution of Eurotech's products. (Adapted from Eurotech's internal documents.)

segment: this is an important strategy in an industry where the obsolescence of technology and of knowledge is very fast.

The idea is that by looking at markets that are not your own (for instance, in Eurotech's case, the consumer market) you can often see your future, it is already there. Therefore, a company must identify a valuable technology at a very early stage, when it is not yet ready for its market, and find the technological means to make it suitable for a more advanced market, where the company wants to position itself in the near future. But this can be very tricky, because if you wait for the technology to become widespread (choice B of Figure 10.2) there will already be too many competitors. You need to start out when the expectation is correct, in order to benefit fully from the upward trend (choice A of Figure 10.2).

Here are some examples of disruptive innovations in Eurotech's history:

- Embedded PCs: state-of-the-art PC technology is transferred to the PC/104 standard. Example: the PC/104 module based on the Intel 32-bit 486DX processor.
- Supercomputers: convergence is achieved between the nano-PC and HPC areas with a supercomputer design based on standard instead of custom processors, and on liquid cooling instead of air cooling. Example: The Aurora supercomputer.

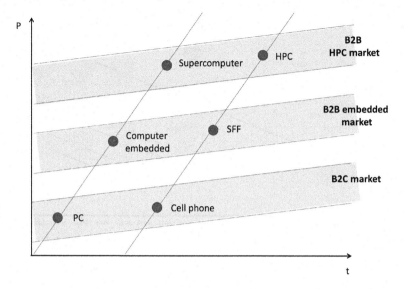

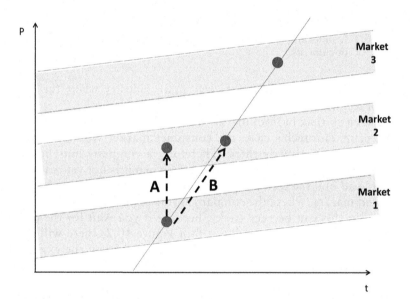

Figure 10.2 Possible choices.

- Wearable PCs: personal computers are miniaturized to such an extent that they can be worn like a watch or a piece of jewelry. Example: the Zypad wrist computer or the pendant which monitors physiological parameters.
- Internet of Things: implementation of a Machine to Machine (M2M) platform for data logistics.

10.2 Foresight, research and development in Eurotech

For Eurotech, R&D is undoubtedly a fundamental building block: the company defines itself as a "factory of ideas": production is outsourced, 30% of revenues are invested in R&D, and 32% of employees (359 total) are focused on the "innovation driver".

As for the structure of the Eurotech group, the function of research and foresight is located at the corporate level, while each company has its own development function. Therefore, development is separated from research and foresight. The organizational structure of Eurotech involves the separation of functions according to their relevance for present and future customers. In particular, development is related to the area of today's customers, while research and foresight are related to the area of tomorrow's customers. Research is separated from development, while foresight serves as nourishment both for research and for marketing activities.

It can be said that foresight, research and development represent the core system of innovation in Eurotech, the so-called innovation driver. In Eurotech, foresight activities are carried out by a real management unit and by a scientific committee.

The foresight management unit is made up of four Eurotech managers (two from strategy, one from research and one from marketing). Foresight deals with trend, market and technology analysis, as well as with surveying competitors and nearby markets. This is the real vanguard group in the company. The scientific committee is made up of external experts in different areas, who meet two/three times a year to identify opportunities and future scenarios. Some experts are from Eurotech's sector, that is ICT, electronics and information technology, while others come from complementary sectors like biology or sociology, in order to foster cognitive diversity and "cross-fertilization".

In general, *the internal organization must be designed in such a way as to favor internally generated innovation.* This is because the key inputs for innovation depend on formal and informal organizational structures, on human resources management tools, on control and communication procedures, and on motivational tools. But not only is it important to structure the organization so that it can support internal innovation; in a context of openness to possible futures, it is even more important *to structure the organization in such a way that it is willing and able to look outside its own boundaries and find external knowledge.*

Eurotech's future-oriented innovation strategy is strongly connected both to the internal organization (for internally generated scenarios), and to the external organization (based on partnerships and networking). This system is supported by a strategy of internationalization, acquisitions and minor interests, and by specific choices made by the top management concerning the soft factors that drive the spread of a corporate foresight culture.

Table 10.4 Employee breakdown in Eurotech.

FUNCTION	NUMBER	%
Foresight*	4	1%
Research	11	3%
Development	99	28%
Strategy	9	3%
Marketing	11	3%
Other (operations, sales, administration)	225	63%
TOTAL	359	100%

*Employees coming from research (1), strategy (2) and marketing (1) who perform two activities (foresight and research, foresight and strategy, foresight and marketing).

In Eurotech, research is a basic element of innovation. As already mentioned, Eurotech has adopted the "fabless company" model, and defines itself as a factory of ideas. This means that production is outsourced, and that the company can focus its efforts on research and development on the one hand, and on market supervision on the other. This is true both from the point of view of investments and from the point of view of human resources. In fact, R&D accounts for 30% of total investments and about 32% of the 359 employees work in the "innovation driver" (28% in development, 3% in research and 1% in foresight – as of 2014). There are five departments involved in innovation, foresight and strategic activities: research, development, strategy, marketing and foresight. Table 10.4 shows the breakdown of employees according to their functions in the organization.

10.3 The separation of research from development

As a rule, very innovative activities should not be too closely linked to day-to-day development activities. In Eurotech, research is not only conceptually and operationally, but also physically separated from development; this choice is seen as a best practice, a foundation of the company's organizational model. From a conceptual point of view, development addresses today's customers, while research addresses tomorrow's customers. According to the CEO:

> Development is tactics while research is strategy. Currently, development works on existing products with a very short-term focus, connected with what today's customers want. But as Morita, the co-founder of Sony, once said, if you ask customers you will always lag behind! This is why research should have a medium to long-term focus. What will be the future competitive scenario? Will technology

be different? And what about human–technology interaction? What will tomorrow's customers look for? (Siagri, pers. interview)

Eurotech refers to Christensen's innovation model (1997), which considers development as more pertaining to incremental/sustaining innovation, and research as more pertaining to radical/disruptive innovation. Therefore, Eurotech separates the two functions, so that while the former is more connected to current market needs (market-pull) and focuses on an "area of customer acceptance", the latter works outside this area, and is guided by PEEST (political, economic, environmental, sociological and technological) trends. As shown in Figure 10.3, Eurotech's organization is divided according to the required approach, either technology-push or market-pull.

In the CEO's words:

> The first approach [technology-push] starts from what technology can provide, while the second [market-pull] starts from what the market demands or is able to absorb. These are opposite approaches, but they can be combined effectively. For a company like ours, which bases its success on technological innovation and on market anticipation, it is essential that research be conducted with a technology-push approach, because this is the only way to maintain technological leadership while continuing to develop innovative solutions. The development part is a different matter. In order to effectively bring research results to the market, it is important to focus on an approach which starts from what

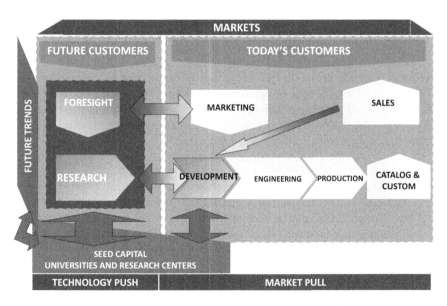

Figure 10.3 A representation of Eurotech's organizational model. (From Eurotech's internal documents.)

the market wants or might appreciate. In a word, the right approach for development is market-pull. (Siagri, pers. interview)

This means that research and development follow the technological curve in completely different ways. They need different organizational structures, and also different people with different ways of thinking. Research creates knowledge by completing ideas that come from external sources, or by turning foresight scenarios into product concepts. Development reengineers the concepts that come from research or tries to meet market needs, as identified by the marketing or by other development units at the corporate level.

Similarly, the results of the foresight activity are treated in two different ways: research interprets them favoring the "what", that is, scenarios and product concepts, while development interprets them favoring the "how", that is, the product design and the production process. End users provide feedback to development, while research receives inputs from foresight and from its knowledge network. So, from a structural point of view, if we consider links and knowledge exchange, development is more connected to marketing and to the other development units, while foresight is more connected to the research and strategy units.

> Research has to think 5–10 years ahead, imagining products for future customers. This is why it needs input from foresight. We are always looking for weak signals, networking, exploring weak connections, contacting experts from different fields and so on, in order to understand trends and imagine scenarios ... all these are good starting points, they create a context where researchers can conceptualize new ideas and innovate. Innovations are often disruptive, because researchers imagine potential products for a future which does not yet exist. (Siagri, pers. interview)

From a physical point of view, research is performed by a separate unit called ETH-Lab, located in Amaro (Udine) and Trento and headed by the CTO, while development units are present in every subsidiary in Europe, Asia and the USA. In addition, hierarchical control is centralized for research but decentralized for development.

> In order to maintain effective supervision over research, it is important that it is controlled at the corporate level. On the contrary, development is decentralized and distributed in the various subsidiaries of the group, so that each company can specialize according to its own strengths, understand local specificities and convert research results into commercial success. (Siagri, pers. interview)

Eurotech's innovation system can therefore be found both at the corporate and at the company level. The research center and the foresight unit are located at the corporate level, while development is decentralized at the company level (see Figure 10.4).

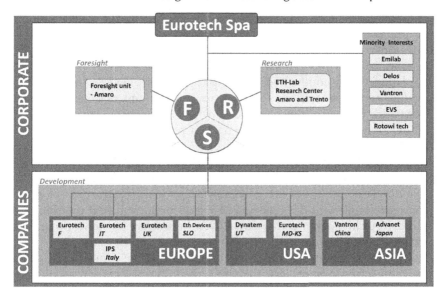

Figure 10.4 Structure of the Eurotech group.

10.4 The foresight unit

Foresight activities in Eurotech are aimed at anticipating change and imagining possible scenarios. The company seeks to obtain information by analyzing weak signals, by detecting the first signs of change, by intercepting and understanding trends, and by collecting and recombining the opinions and experience of experts. The foresight process takes place both inside and outside the company.

The tools are many and diverse: web search, database analysis, "visionary" books, Delphi panels, roadmaps, scenarios, wild card detection, creative techniques (Six Thinking Hats, brainstorming etc.) and trade shows on innovation. Nevertheless, the foresight process is based on informal methods without any explicit path or defined rule: the management believes that these activities should be conducted freely, without the constraints of a structured methodology.

> Foresight is not simply a matter of methodology, it requires putting together a previously separate and distinct knowledge, it requires intuition and imagination. (Siagri, pers. interview)

The organization is structured based on the Pareto 80/20 rule, applied both to internal and external sources. At the organizational level, foresight activities are supported by three groups: an internal foresight unit and two *ad hoc* teams, the scientific committee and the technology brokering unit. The foresight unit is made up of employees and carries out day-to-day monitoring and control, while the committee is made up of experts who meet two/three times a year. Technology brokering is an internal unit which handles networking activities and stays in contact with the outside. The process is not hampered by codified norms, so that it remains flexible and can adapt readily, modeling itself on the company's issues and objectives. Besides, a network of connections is critical to foresight, which strongly depends on exploration of new knowledge and on recombination of different and dispersed signals.

The 80/20 rule also applies to research and development. Research consists in 80% of technology brokering and networking and 20% of sedimentation and exploitation of external knowledge. On the contrary, development concentrates 80% of the time and resources on incremental innovation of standard technologies, saving only 20% of resources for networking, with the aim of tapping into non-core skills not present in the company.

The foresight unit is the real vanguard group in the company; it is composed of four top managers: the CEO, the CTO, the marketing manager and the strategy manager. This unit focuses the near totality of its resources and efforts on the detection of weak signals, striving to find, understand, connect and give meaning to new industry trends and possible directions of technological development.

> In order to successfully innovate, it is essential to have a person or a small team who thinks forward; a small portion of the organization has to be constantly projected into the future. (Siagri, pers. interview)

The foresight analysis must focus not only on the core business, but also on the neighboring areas, in order to gain insights from different sectors and to perceive the weak signals coming from the so-called white spaces[4] (Reger, 2004).

The activities of the foresight unit are strongly interrelated with the other functions. Foresight is not a mere "exercise on the future" without any practical application. On the contrary, it is strongly integrated within the company both in terms of innovation and strategy. Futures studies are closely interrelated with: the direction taken by research, the decisions concerning research investments, the identification of customers' future needs by the marketing department, the decision-making process, the definition of the company's vision and of future strategies.

Foresight is linked to marketing in that it supports it by providing reports on the current or expected socioeconomic situation, or by investigating sociological changes, such as changes in customer behavior. Foresight is also linked to the overall business strategy, in that it must be consistent with it: besides innovation, one of the most important functions of foresight is to orient decision-making. Finally, foresight is linked to research in that it orients innovation: it is a preliminary stage which provides inputs and insights for the research activity, it draws possible future scenarios from which new possibilities can emerge for technology and innovation. Research then generates new ideas suited to that particular scenario.

10.5 The scientific committee and the research network

Companies use both internal and external ideas as input for the innovation process, and use both internal and external market routes for the development of innovative products and services. Knowledge is widespread, innovation is the result of an iterative and distributed process, and companies seeking innovation can open up to external players and even lean on them.

A typical problem related to this issue is the large investment initially required for a still unknown commercial success rate. Unfortunately, investing in research involves no certainty that the products will be successful on the market.

Eurotech's solution to this problem has been the creation and development of collaborations and networks with universities and research centers, and of key partnerships with leading organizations in the ICT sector (IBM, Intel etc.). In Eurotech's organizational model, these networks of external knowledge have great strategic value.

Partnerships are selected not only on a technological, but also on a sociological basis. They cover a wide range of perspectives and orientations, sometimes with the aim of verifying the impact of innovation on specific customer groups. This networking perspective is strategically linked to innovation and to future-oriented strategy. Since 1998, the company has invested in scouting activities and in collaborations with leading research centers and universities: "We have asked universities not to solve our problems, but to help us see the future" (Siagri, pers. interview).

Starting in 2001, the company has strategically reorganized itself to foster innovation. It has promoted external collaborations and built a unique internal structure to support them. Research and foresight have also been developed with the help of external connections. All these have contributed to create what Eurotech calls "the knowledge network".

> For a technology-push approach to be effective, it is vital to have both a network of external relations and a knowledge network. This allows the parallel exploration, at limited cost, of several alternative routes. The center of gravity of technology-push research gets shifted asymmetrically towards the outside world, with a 80/20 ratio between external and internal. We employ 80% of external collaborations to explore alternative routes and to put together a lot of different factors. The roots of the tree of knowledge are research and foresight. The scientific committee is the first branch of our tree: it provides ideas directly and it connects with other branches and leaves. The remaining 20% is internal and uses internal resources: it is the Foresight unit. (Siagri, pers. interview)

Development is dealt with from a different point of view:

> Development has to do with what the market wants or is able to absorb. While research benefits from the simultaneous existence of several open fronts, development has to converge towards a product/service or a family of products/services. It is therefore preferable to limit the energy loss and interference from outside. Another peculiarity of development is that it necessarily relates to specific sectors and geographic areas: centralized control would not permit adequate understanding and exploitation of these specificities. (Siagri, pers. interview)

Eurotech maintains its peculiar attitude by supporting peripheral vision and by showing alertness in detecting new trends, mainly from the perspective of technological foresight. However, it also takes into great consideration the trends identified by sociological foresight, concerning the behavior of customers and competitors. To encourage exploration and surveys from various sources, Eurotech has set up a scientific committee, a team of experts who examine and discuss the various ideas in a multidisciplinary perspective. The committee provides support to the research and foresight units by focusing on the future evolution of technological scenarios and by nurturing Eurotech's knowledge network.

The scientific committee is designed as an open space where experts from different fields come together and try to imagine and shape the future, by interconnecting ideas from different scientific domains. The committee is composed with the precise aim of covering diverse and very specific areas: some are closely related to the ICT sector, such as computer science and electronics, while others are more loosely related to it, such as physics, biomedicine, economics and sociology.

The initiator of the committee's activities is primarily Eurotech's CTO, given that the strategic perspective of Eurotech sees research as the most important output of foresight. The committee's work allows crossfertilization[5] and access to cognitive diversity, which are essential to expand and enrich knowledge perspectives. Other important tasks of the committee are to determine the state of the art of technologies and new markets, to identify new trends and opportunities in various sectors, to consolidate partnerships with research institutions and to provide assistance to the research and foresight units.

10.6 The strategy of partnerships and acquisitions

As previously mentioned, business acquisitions are extraordinary financial operations, typically made for purposes of external growth. Acquisitions can be vertical (the companies involved deal with different stages of the production and distribution of a product or service), horizontal (the companies involved operate in the same market or sector of reference) or conglomerate (the companies involved work in different and unrelated sectors or markets).

Eurotech's acquisition strategy has the dual purpose of acquiring companies specialized in complementary products and/or expanding to new countries (e.g., the US and Japan) and new markets (e.g., defense).

As noted by the CEO, Eurotech has adopted a strategy of acquisitions in order to secure complementary skills and gain access to cognitive diversity and external knowledge. Eurotech has a strategy of Acquisitions & Development, that is, it invests in very young companies to stay in contact with the most recent technologies. This strategy can be seen as a means to support the internal organization of foresight, research and development: it helps build the external network and boosts the chances of finding new opportunities. Eurotech objectives in terms of internationalization and knowledge expansion are opening up to new markets and covering knowledge areas where the company's expertise level is low. Since 2005, the international expansion has been more oriented towards strategic innovation. For example, through the latest acquisition (Advanet) Eurotech has strengthened its skills and know-how in automation (Nikon and Canon), in process control (Mitsubishi Heavy Industries), in transportation infrastructure (Mitsubishi Heavy Industries and Matsushita Electric Industrial), in medical applications (Hitachi Medical Corporation and Toshiba Medical Systems Corporation) and has also acquired a complementary customer base. This in turn has allowed the company to consolidate its traditional business and to secure a reliable cash flow to fund innovation in an indirect way.

10.7 Minority interests as real options for innovation

New opportunities for growth may also come from expansion into new businesses. A tool commonly used by multinational companies is corporate venturing,[6] and Eurotech applies it to foresight by entering with minority interests (investments or participations) into smaller companies. If analyzed in a foresight perspective, these companies have great potential and are in line with the scenarios Eurotech envisions for the future. Minority interests are considered "innovation seeds" on which Eurotech bets for the future. "They are real options for innovation and for future markets" (Siagri, pers. interview).

For example, in the symbiosis scenario imagined by Eurotech, which implies a closer man–machine interaction, it is important to invest in technologies that support automation and miniaturization. Along these lines, the investment in Kairos Autonomi (25%) has been strategically important for the automatic steering system, and the investment in UTRI[7] (21%) has been important for miniaturized robot aircraft (UAV technology for anti-fire surveillance in military and civil contexts). For these unmanned planes, Eurotech won in 2006 the "Euroleader Award – Space & Satcom Navigation Sector".

10.8 Soft factors

Soft factors are also very important: they support Eurotech's innovation strategy in many ways:

- *Corporate culture and attitude:* the organization is open to external knowledge sources and external players. This makes it alert in sense-making (perception of the environment and attribution of meaning) and in understanding changes in speed and direction in terms of technologies, customers and competitors. Eurotech has a particular predisposition for peripheral vision and for exploring and investigating external sources. It is strongly oriented towards foresight activities, and is quick in perceiving new technology trends.
- *Top management commitment (and CEO leadership):* the CEO and other managers devote part of their time to monitoring and investigating new emerging and potentially disruptive trends, both internally, through president meetings and technical boards (internal committees which discuss the traditional business and the vision) and externally, by participating in conferences and forums on the future. This heavy commitment aims on the one hand to increase the amount of knowledge and to widen external networks, and on the other hand to spread the idea, both among employees and among external stakeholders, that Eurotech is a company focused on innovation and foresight. Given the strong belief in foresight's potential for innovation, the senior management's commitment is very high. This is in line with CF theory, according to which a strong commitment on the part of the management is essential to promote the use of foresight within the organization.
- *Communication:* CF results are disseminated within the company on an ongoing basis, both through formal and informal channels. Formal communication takes place in committees, working groups and conferences; informal communication occurs in personal interactions and social events, as well as through social networks.

10.9 Lesson learned for the organization

Eurotech's case study shows how foresight can be applied and how it can help identify the best strategies in advance and keep on innovating and developing new products. This ability to be or to become sensitive to trends and weak signals leads to greater attention, availability, willingness and readiness to listen and respond strategically and innovatively to internal and external changes in the PEEST environment.

Figure 10.5 sums up organizational variables and management best practices. Figures 10.6 and 10.7 show the driver of strategy and innovation oriented to the future. The driver is based on a core where foresight and research are closely connected with each other and with an external

VARIABLE	FEATURES	EUROTECH
STRUCTURE	Definition of the organizational unit/function	Definition of the foresight unit aimed at innovation and long-term strategy.
	Dimension of the organizational unit/function	Small CF unit.
COORDINATION	Specialization	The CF unit and of its relations to the other company functions are permanent and institutionalized.
	Training	Employees are trained in foresight activities: they learn from specific methodologies and from past projects.
DECISION-MAKING PROCESSES	Vertical centralization	Foresight activities refer directly to the CEO.
	Horizontal decentralization	Strong commitment of the other functions.
NETWORKS	External relations	Importance of external relations for foresight and for research.
CONTROL SYSTEM	Formalization of procedures	Procedures are not strictly formalized.
	Internal and external cohesion mechanisms	Importance of the scientific committee.
TECHNIQUES	Formalization of foresight techniques	The "future coverage" methodology is applied every two years.

Figure 10.5 Organizational variables in the Eurotech case study.

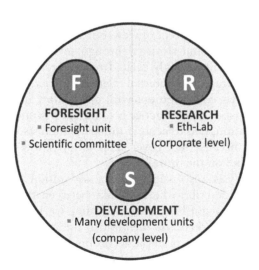

Figure 10.6 Eurotech's core system for innovation.

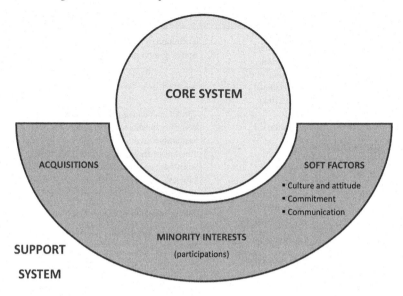

Figure 10.7 Eurotech's system for innovation.

network. This makes it possible to imagine scenarios and future products, and to give Development ideas and concepts to prototype and produce. The support system consists of acquisitions that fund innovation, of minority interests and of soft factors. These strong links increase the "sensemaking attitude" (Weick, 1979): a network model is adopted, made of large hubs where information flows, along with trends, are proposed to peripheral units.

From an organizational point of view, our case study suggests the steady support of innovation and strategy through several practices. One is to build a dedicated unit strongly related to research (the Foresight unit). Another is to encourage both internal relations and external networks (e.g., scientific committee, collaborations with universities and research centers, R&D partnerships). A third practice is to pursue a strategy of acquisitions to finance innovation, and to acquire minority interests in small but smart companies, both because they cover areas of low know-how, and because they represent a bet on the future.

The case analysis also suggests the separation of research from Development and describes the key links between the CF unit and the other functions, distinguishing them according to the two perspectives of current and future markets. As mentioned, the main role of Foresight is to nurture research and to orient it according to trends. Research in turn provides feedback to foresight, assessing the opportunities for investigation and evaluating the practical applicability of ideas.

As discussed in Chapter 5, the separation of research from development is a much debated topic among academics. The literature has recognized the different managerial approaches required to deal with R&D, highlighting the "creativity versus efficiency" contrast and distinguishing basic and applied research from the development of new products. As Eurotech's case study shows, the separation of R&D can be recommended in contexts of rapid knowledge obsolescence, due to accelerated changes in the PEEST environment and in the specific sector, and should be coupled with an internal strategy of strong attention to future possibilities and with an ongoing search for balance between sustaining/incremental innovation, and radical/disruptive innovation. Along these lines, foresight can be tied to the concept of ambidextrous organization.

The study shows that the effort required to focus on innovation and on tomorrow's markets can be supported by a specific organizational and strategic structure, and explores the ways in which Eurotech organizes its R&D activities in order to look more closely at the future. It also shows how the separation of research from development can be practically implemented, it underlines the importance of a dedicated foresight unit (with the main purpose of directing vision, orienting decision-making and nurturing research), and it discusses how processes and tools can be applied to support a future-oriented strategy.

The present chapter highlights the potentialities of an approach which anticipates weak signals and trends based on the analysis of internal and external sources. The separation of research from development, the use of foresight methodologies and the creation of a supportive structure for strategic decisions could be of extremely high value in driving the innovations of tomorrow.

Notes

1 One subsidiary was sold in 2013.
2 The statements quoted in this chapter refer to the years 2008–2010.
3 Thirty percent of revenues is invested in R&D, including a percentage devoted to radical innovation.
4 The term comes from graphics, where a "white space" is a blank on the page, a space left without signs: the space between letters, between columns, between lines, between drawings. In futures studies, a white space is an area not yet investigated.
5 The term comes from biology and botany, and indicates fertilization obtained by the fusion of gametes from individuals belonging to different species. Transposed to innovation, the term indicates the interaction and exchange, between two or more cultures, of knowledge which becomes mutually beneficial and productive (Lapierre and Giroux, 2003).
6 Corporate venturing is a direct and formalized bond, usually between a large company and a small independent business. Both companies contribute financially and in terms of management and technology, sharing risks and benefits for mutual growth. It is a partnership in which each company invests in the other in exchange for dividends on future earnings.
7 Today Rotowi Technologies.

11 Foresight in Eurotech
Managerial aspects

> "In formal logic, a contradiction is the signal of defeat, but in the evolution of real knowledge it marks the first step in progress toward a victory".
> Alfred North Whitehead

Our discussion will now focus on the application of the proposed methodology of future coverage to the Eurotech case study. Coherence has been assessed between trends and vision, between vision and products, and between trends and products, according to the framework of Figure 8.1.

11.1 Trend analysis (T)

As we have seen in previous chapters, the ICT sector is a particularly dynamic and complex environment in continuous transformation, due to the strong acceleration of technological change (Kurzweil, 2006). The exponential progress of digital technologies in terms of speed, miniaturization and interconnection creates an ever-changing environment characterized by strong acceleration.

The analysis of trends and megatrends highlights that since the last years of the 20th century we have been experiencing a true revolution, based on the new digital information and communication technologies. In this sense, the evolution of man and the evolution of computers are converging towards what is called "biotechnological evolution". The main trends in computer evolution point to increased miniaturization, dissemination, integration into the environment (embeddedness) and invisibility (ubiquitous or pervasive computing).

From an anthropological point of view, this trend indicates the advent of the so-called *Homo technologicus* or *Homo zappiens*, born of the symbiosis of man and technology. It is evident that humans and computers are integrating more and more: from personal computers to handheld computers (cell phones, PDAs), to the more recent wearable computers (embedded in clothes and jewellery), to future microcomputers that will be directly

MEGATREND		TREND	
M1	ACCELERATION OF CHANGE	T1	Acceleration
M2	TECHNOLOGY ESSENTIALITY	T2	Essentiality
M3	HUMAN-TECHNOLOGY INTERACTION	T3	Irreversibility
		T4	Conditioning
		T5	Human-technology transformation
M4	AUGMENTED REALITY	T6	Expansion and contraction
		T7	Invisibility
		T8	Pervasiveness
		T9	Augmented reality
		T10	Connectivity
		T11	Informationalism
		T12	Hypertextuality
M5	SYMBIOSIS	T13	Technology-human transformation
		T14	Organic-inorganic integration
		T15	Convergence

Figure 11.1 Trends (T) in Eurotech's industrial sector.

implanted under our skin and into our bodies (see the latest research on medical applications), the future is already traced.

Figure 11.1 lists the trends and megatrends identified in our coherence analysis. The fifteen trends have been clustered into groups to determine the five megatrends of biotechnological coevolution.

The identification of trends and their combination into megatrends are both key phases, essential to get both an analytical and a synthetic perspective.

11.2 Vision analysis (V)

Eurotech's philosophy has been inspired by the vision and ideas of Mark Weiser (1991), the father of ubiquitous computing: "The most important technologies are the ones that disappear, they wave themselves in the fabric of everyday life until they are undistinguishable from it".

This is also the company's vision: "The pervasive presence of digital technologies will free our minds from trivial and repetitive tasks, giving us the time to address the essential challenges of humankind: to improve our knowledge of man and of the universe". Eurotech's CEO notes: "As we enter the new millennium, the pervasiveness of digital technologies is defining a new scenario: distributed information, widespread knowledge, and digital economy. In the words of John Smart, human–machine interaction will become constant and more natural, even second nature".

In Eurotech's vision, invisibility will be achieved through the progressive diffusion of technologies and their integration with everyday life and everyday objects. From a technical point of view, the notion of invisibility will lead to a revolution in ubiquitous computing: extremely miniaturized embedded computers will become "smart dust".[1] More broadly, this notion also suggests that we are now entering the symbiotic era of human– machine interaction, and that biology and technology are progressively converging. Computers will disappear, in the sense that they will no longer be seen or even perceived, they will no longer be noticed as objects in the external environment. People will simply use them all the time without even noting their presence. Essentially, computer pervasiveness consists of three aspects:

- Miniaturization
- Dissemination
- Connection

Eurotech's mission is summarized in the following words: "Digital technologies for a better world". In practical terms, this means integrating stateof-the-art computation and communication technologies into miniaturized and user-friendly solutions.

The company focuses on studying and developing cutting-edge technologies that can offer innovative solutions that anticipate market evolution and future scenarios. For example, Eurotech strives to position itself at the edge of innovation by entering niche markets with high growth potential. In the words of its CEO, "Eurotech's strategic direction is to define and penetrate new and emerging markets, breaking traditional barriers through innovation. With this vision in mind, Eurotech has focused its research and development on key high-growth sectors like pervasive computing, in order to create innovative, integrated solutions (which include software, hardware, middleware and support services) offering the flexibility and scalability needed to capture new market opportunities".

The many aspects of the company's vision, based on the considerations and beliefs of the top management and of the internal foresight team, are listed in Table 11.1.

Table 11.1 Eurotech's vision (V).

EUROTECH'S VISION	
V1	Computing evolution: supercomputers, pervasive computers
V2	Acceleration
V3	Network-humanizing technology
V4	Interconnection
V5	Informationalism
	Symbiotic era, Homo zappiens

11.3 Product analysis (P)

Eurotech's market is pervasive computation: nano-PCs, embedded computers, wearable computers, high-performance computers and M2M (machineto-machine) platforms. All these devices create an infrastructure of digital communication, originally named "computational GRID", which is now called the "Internet of Things".

Eurotech's research and development focuses on two main areas: (1) pervasive embedded computers for the Internet of Things, with special attention to wearable computers, and (2) green supercomputing, with the objective of creating large Cloud computing data centers collecting and processing data coming from all the computers connected on the Internet. For nano-PCs, the potential markets are mainly defence, transportation, the medical and industrial sectors; for supercomputers, the traditional customers are universities, research institutes and computer science centers, but increasingly also the private sector for industrial design, medical and cyber-security applications.

Three among the most relevant Eurotech products have been identified for our analysis. To represent the company's past we have selected embedded PCs, the products with which Eurotech started its business in 1992; to represent current products we have selected the Zypad wearable computer (for the pervasive computing area) and the Aurora supercomputer (for the HPC area); to represent future products we have selected the *Everyware Cloud* IoT integration platform.

Figure 11.2 briefly describes the features of the selected products. Figure 11.3 shows Eurotech's products and their applications.

PRODUCTS		CHARACTERISTICS
P1	EMBEDDED PCs (PC/104 modules)	• highly miniaturized • highly reliable for use in critical environments • integration of intelligence and connectivity
P2	SUPER COMPUTERS (Aurora)	• parallel machines providing a computation power ranging from tens of Teraflops to PetaFlops • low energy consumption per computation unit • reduced dimensions • reduced TCO (Total Cost of Ownership) • easily accessible technology thanks to standard components • G-station – personal supercomputer
P3	WEARABLE COMPUTERS (Zypad)	• small computers that can be worn on the wrist, belt etc. • "hands-free" operation • high computing power (smartness) • non-stop Internet connection
P4	INTERNET OF THINGS (Everyware Cloud)	• free connectivity • integrated hardware, software and support services • end-to-end and machine-to-machine applications

Figure 11.2 A brief description of Eurotech's products (P).

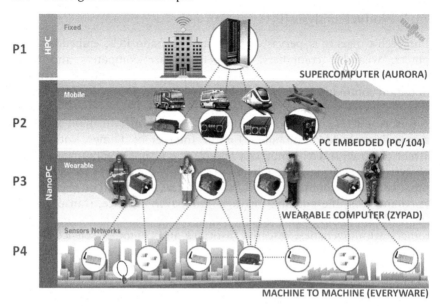

Figure 11.3 Eurotech's products (P).

11.4 Trends–vision coherence analysis (1)

Matrix 11.1 presents all the comparisons made between the trends and the vision in the case study, and shows how Eurotech's vision reflects all the technological trends and megatrends previously identified.

As regards the applied method, the evaluation is conducted by experts who jointly make a discrete evaluation (from 0 to 3) of the coherence and alignment of a single characteristic of the vision with a single trend: 0 means no alignment, 1 low alignment, 2 mid-level alignment and 3 high alignment. The methodology then proceeds algorithmically with the calculation of average values and percentages, and finally returns an "index of future coverage" indicating the coherence level between T and V (and between T and P or V and P in the other coherence matrixes): in other words, the methodology evaluates how much the company's strategy for the future effectively "covers" the possible future. The values referring to a single trend or megatrend, or to a single aspect of the vision, give the index of future coverage on the last horizontal line, while in the last column they return an index of presence which measures the influence of trends and megatrends on the vision (or of megatrends on products, of the vision on products etc.).

Coherence analysis can be a useful orientation tool in that it tells a company in which direction to move in order to stay innovative and in line with trends. It shows which characteristics of the vision are less comprehensively mirrored in trends: in the Eurotech case, interconnection (52%) and informationalism (60%). It also shows which trends and megatrends

MEGATREND	TREND	V1 Computing evolution: supercomputers, pervasive computers		V2 Acceleration		V3 Network–humanizing technology		V4 Interconnection		V5 Informationalism		V6 Symbiotic era, homo zappiens		INDEX
M1 Acceleration of change	Acceleration	3	100%	3	100%	2	67%	2	67%	2	67%	2	67%	78%
M2 Technology essentiality	Essentiality	3	100%	3	100%	3	100%	1	33%	1	33%	3	100%	78%
M3 Human–machine interaction	Irreversibility	1		2		0		0		1		2		
	Conditioning		33%	3	78%	2	56%	1	22%	1	44%	3	89%	54%
	Human–technology transformation	2		2		3		1		2		3		
M4 Augmented reality	Expansion and contraction	3		2		2		2		2		2		
	Invisibility	3		0		2		3		3		3		
	Pervasiveness	3		0		2		3		3		3		
	Augmented reality	3	100%	2	33%	3	86%	3	95%	2	90%	3	95%	83%
	Connectivity	3		1		3		3		3		3		
	Informationalism	3		1		3		3		3		3		
	Hypertextuality	3		1		3		3		3		3		
M5 Symbiosis	Technology–human transformation	2		2		3		1		2		3		
	Organic–inorganic integration	2	67%	1	56%	3	89%	1	44%	1	67%	3	100%	70%
	Convergence	2		2		2		2		3		3		
			80%		73%		79%		52%		60%		90%	73%

Matrix 11.1 Trends/vision (T/V) coherence analysis.

are less comprehensively reflected in the vision; in our case, the megatrend of human–technology interaction (54%).

In the Eurotech case study, the comparison between megatrends and vision has revealed a substantial consistency of the corporate vision with the industry megatrends. As indicated by a coverage index of 73%, Eurotech presents rather high levels of alignment between trends and vision and can therefore be considered a visionary and innovative company. Hypothetically, we could define a value higher than 66% as high coherence, typical of a future-oriented company with good propensity towards innovation, a value between 33% and 66% as medium coherence, and a value lower than 33% as low coherence.

11.5 Vision–products coherence analysis (2)

The internal alignment analysis considers the vision and the products (Matrix 11.2). For Eurotech, this analysis indicates substantial coherence.

EUROTECH'S VISION		EUROTECH'S PRODUCT LINES							
		PAST		PRESENT				FUTURE	
		P1		P2	P3			P4	
		EMBEDDED PCS	INDEX	SUPER COMPUTERS	WEARABLE COMPUTERS		INDEX	MACHINE TO MACHINE	INDEX
V1	Computing evolution: supercomputers, pervasive computers	0	0%	3	100%	3	100%	100%	3	100%
V2	Acceleration	0	0%	2	67%	3	100%	83%	3	100%
V3	Network-humanizing technology	0	0%	3	100%	3	100%	100%	3	100%
V4	Interconnection	2	67%	1	33%	3	100%	67%	3	100%
V5	Informationalism	1	33%	1	33%	2	67%	50%	2	67%
V6	Symbiotic era, homo zappiens	0	0%	1	33%	3	100%	67%	1	33%
			17%		61%		94%	78%		83%

Matrix 11.2 Vision/products (V/P) coherence analysis.

Three separate analyses have been conducted. The first one considered examples of past products (embedded computers) and returned a value of 17%, the second dealt with present products and returned a value of 78%; the third examined a future product and yielded the highest value (83%). We can note that the coherence values get higher as time goes by, proving that the vision is best mirrored by actual or future products than it was in past products.

This analysis can be used as a tool for diagnosis in two ways: to highlight which characteristics of the vision are not found in products, or to highlight which products are more aligned with the vision. From the analysis of Eurotech, we find that all the characteristics of the vision are found in the products and that the products are aligned with the vision, in medium– high degree for supercomputers (61%) and in very high degree for wearable computers (94%). Eurotech therefore can be said to have excellent internal coherence.

11.6 Trends–products coherence analysis (3)

The comparative analysis of trends and products was conducted by comparing every formerly analyzed product family with the identified scenarios.

Matrix 11.3 synthesizes the trend–product coherence analysis for past products (26%), present products (75%) and future products (76%). This analysis can be helpful in two ways: it helps identify the most innovative and future-oriented products (those most consistent with trends), and at the same time highlights the trends and megatrends which are not reflected in the products (namely, the trends with few coherent products are those on which the company could begin to invest).

		EUROTECH'S PRODUCT LINES								
		PAST		PRESENT					FUTURE	
		P1		P2		P3			P4	
MEGATREND	TREND	EMBEDDED PCS	INDEX	SUPER COMPUTERS	INDEX	WEARABLE COMPUTERS	INDEX	INDEX	MACHINE TO MACHINE	INDEX
M1 Acceleration of change	Acceleration	1	33%	3	100%	2	67%	83%	2	67%
M2 Technology essentiality	Essenziality	2	67%	3	100%	2	67%	83%	3	100%
M3 Human-technology interaction	Irreversibility	0	0%	1	22%	1	44%	33%	1	22%
	Conditioning	0		0		1			1	
	Human-technology transformation	0		1		2			0	
M4 Augmented reality	Expansion and contraction	2	19%	3	90%	3	81%	86%	3	100%
	Invisibility	0		2		2			3	
	Pervasiveness	1		2		3			3	
	Augmented reality	0		3		3			3	
	Connectivity	1		3		3			3	
	Informationalism	0		3		2			3	
	Hypertextuality	0		3		1			3	
M5 Symbiosis	Technology-human transformation	0	11%	3	78%	3	100%	89%	2	89%
	Organic-inorganic integration	0		1		3			3	
	Convergence	1		3		3			3	
			26%		78%		72%	75%		76%

Matrix 11.3 Trends/products (T/P) coherence analysis.

The most innovative products are indicated by the comparison of the three analyses. For instance, embedded PCs show low coherence with trends. This does not mean that the company must no longer rely on these products; it simply indicates that they are suitable for today's market but may not be sufficient to win the competitive challenge of tomorrow. Eurotech started its business in 1992 with embedded PCs, which have been greatly improved over time and which still represent the core of its market. As regards the other three products, the analysis highlights growing levels of "orientation to the future": wearable computers (72%), machine-to-machine (76%) and supercomputers (78%). These considerations provide useful indications as to where and how the company should invest in order to keep its products consistent with the trends' orientation.

As for trends and megatrends, we can observe that the megatrend of "human–technology interaction" is scarcely present in today's products, with a value of 33% (22% if we consider only future products). On this basis, it seems that Eurotech could invest in some research to improve the related products, possibly adding features addressing this megatrend.

Obviously, this methodology should be applied to all the company's future products. In our analysis, some returned values are low due to the fact that the methodology was applied to a limited set of products. Furthermore, the values should be interpreted and reviewed in relation to business strategy: for example, the company may decide not to diversify according to trends but to focus on one prominent trend instead.

11.7 Validity evaluation

The proposed methodology allows to verify whether the company's strategic direction is coherent with the trends, and can be applied quite easily because of its simplicity. The analysis confirms that Eurotech is a particularly innovative company; its vision and products are aligned and coherent with the direction of trends in the ICT industry. Moreover, the past–present–future comparison shows that the strategy is effectively following a coherent path: the vision has always been coherent with trends (73%), while products are getting more and more aligned both with the vision (internally) and with trends (externally), as demonstrated by the growing figures 17–78–83% for internal coherence and 26–75–76% for product coherence. In other words, while the vision was already aligned with trends, the products have been gradually improving in alignment. Figure 11.4 presents a synthesis of the case study in a dynamic perspective.

From a practical point of view, the methodology of future coverage can be used as a *diagnostic tool* for a rapid clinical outline of the coherence of industry megatrends with company strategy: in other words, it can tell us how well the strategy takes the future into account. The three

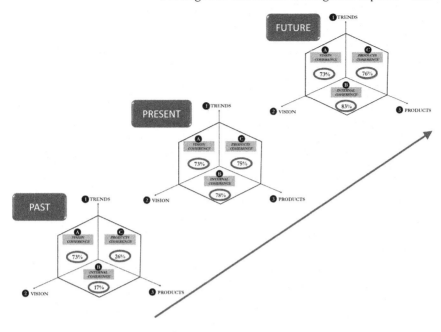

Figure 11.4 Application of the methodology in a dynamic perspective.

indexes of vision coherence, product coherence and internal coherence reach the highest values when the company has a real foresight capability. Moreover, the analysis of future coverage highlights the variables that influence the investigated industry at the level of trends and megatrends, and tells us which trends are (or are not) mirrored in the company's vision and products.

The matrixes provide a schematic representation of the company's strengths and weaknesses. Low values ring an alarm bell: they detect anomalies, indicating the points where the company's strategy deviates from the route traced by industry trends. In the case of the megatrends–products relationship, for example, a particular megatrend may be scarcely represented in products, or a particular product may not be aligned with megatrends. Based on this diagnosis, the management can resolve a new course of action in terms of both vision and products, in order to bring the company's strategy into alignment with trends.

From a dynamic perspective, the methodology of future coverage can be used as a tool to verify the correspondence between trends and company strategy over time. By repeating the analysis periodically, the company can understand its strategic path towards the future more clearly. Besides, the methodology can be used to compare the degree of "orientation to the future" of different companies in the same sector.

11.8 Lesson learned for the management

A successful company is always ready and proactive in front of the social, technological and political–economical complexity of a competitive environment. The challenge of facing this complexity becomes even greater in our accelerated and dynamic environment. If this turbulence is not managed, chaos will overcome the company. It is therefore necessary to develop a pre-alarm system to keep things under control. Therein lies the reason for the important and difficult, but also the fascinating, task of actively monitoring and exploring emerging trends and developing alternative scenarios. Companies can learn to formulate possible scenarios and use a *what-if* logic to imagine the actions that may result. They can rethink their management and organization from the perspective of the exploration, perception and monitoring of key trends, and align their strategy, in terms of vision and products, with industry trends.

We propose the methodology of future coverage to help companies understand, through the evaluation of coherence among trends, vision and products, whether the business strategy is oriented in the right direction.

This methodology can be a valuable tool in support of strategic management: in a context of turbulence, companies need to be aware of the most probable evolution of the market. But this kind of analysis must not remain a mere exercise; instead, it must be integrated into the company's strategy so that it can have concrete effects. In this sense, our methodology can help managers understand whether the vision and the products are aligned with the trends, it can highlight a company's weaknesses and can assist in the decision-making process, so that the company is always "ready in advance". Both futurists and managers need reliable tools to measure the degree of readiness for the future; we believe that our methodology fills a gap by helping companies to determine it.

The proposed methodology identifies possible problems, generates new insights and enhances decision-making. It is not about predicting the future or depicting scenarios, but about being able to understand both the evolution of the external PEEST environment and the internal coherence. It is about being ready to face uncertainty and complexity and to include them in the decision-making process. It is about developing the company's capacity to proactively navigate the external landscape.

The use of this methodology enhances the confidence both of the management and of employees in the decision-making process, and helps develop flexibility in dealing with future issues. Another advantage is that it clarifies the company's internal situation (vision and products) in reference to a changing external world, through simple schematic tables which visually highlight the company's strengths and weaknesses, providing readily available and easy-to-use information.

In our opinion, Corporate Foresight has a real strategic value in helping companies innovate and react to the latent vulnerabilities of an accelerated and turbulent environment. It must absolutely be supported both at the organizational and managerial level. In this context, our methodology of future coverage can really help companies investigate and prepare for a complex and uncertain future.

Note

1 The term "smart dust" describes the dissemination into our environment of a myriad tiny devices (as small as grains of sand) with computing and communication capability.

Part IV

Imagination reveals the future

12 Conclusion

"Art is a step toward what is arcane and concealed".
Khalil Gibran

The future always passes through imagination

As a conclusion, we would like to take our readers on a journey inside the complexity of the future, by looking at the future through imagination.

To understand where the world is going, it might be a good idea to pay a visit, from time to time, to a great modern art exhibition such as the Venice *Biennale*. It is in such places that the future is already present. Artists have enough inspiration and creativity to imagine and convey the future ahead of time. An artist interprets and gives a meaning to the present and expresses his imagination in relation to it; he is a visionary who recounts a possible future, engaging in a dialogue with his public through the symbolic nature of his work. No one could be more responsive to weak signals, and more able to see in the present an omen of the future. Back in 1912, the Austrian writer and satirist Karl Kraus argued that "Art is what the world becomes, not what the world is". For the German philosopher Martin Heidegger, art is the ever-changing place where truth is determined. He denies the role of technology as prevalent means of experiencing truth for the modern man and proposes art as a path to salvation. Art is essentially artwork, the act of opening and unveiling. Artistic nature is reflected in the ability to disclose a new "web of signification" (the World) and to keep it open, without contracting the meaning in a closed and definitive message. However, the artwork is also materiality (the Earth). Art is therefore a struggle between the World and Earth, and truth is a product of this struggle taking place within the artwork. Also, the movement of truth is constantly evolving: confronted with art, we have the opportunity to meditate and to ask questions, relentlessly seeking the future.

The ability to create new meanings is a feature of imagination and creativity. For the Italian philosopher Umberto Galimberti, creativity is divergent thinking, the transgression of rules and of shared rationality. Imagination is therefore at the border between reason and madness. Reason is a system of rules governed by the principle of noncontradiction, which makes behaviors predictable and languages univocal, which determines them by establishing boundaries. Madness is instead the confusion of all codes, what is known as chaos. Behind all creativity is the sacrifice of the creator, who descends into the prerational abyss and thence infers something profoundly new. And more often than not, artists are the ones who make this sacrifice: they go down into the dimension of the undifferentiated, draw from their own folly and then re-emerge, bringing back a small fragment of the future. Imagination is at home among artists.

Imagination has this extraordinary ability: it allows an individual to mentally anticipate a situation that has not yet entered the visual field. He allows him to "see", or rather "fore-see" the consequences of a gesture, an action and a behavior. It is a typically human talent, resulting from the activity of certain areas of the cerebral cortex probably located in the frontal lobes. In fact, the large number of processing nerve cells make it possible to implement an association activity based on simulated "montages" of fragments of experiences. To put it more simply, it is as if we had a mental kaleidoscope in our brain, in which certain memories of experiences were assembled into a single image, giving us a view of how the problem we are facing will present itself if linked to the various factors that are associated with him. This ability to imagine is typical of foresight when all the weak signals and trend are put together, assembled in different forms (scenarios) and interpreted in order to "put yourself in the shoes" of the future.

The difficulty is that our visibility is limited. We physically see only part of the road, the other we have to imagine it. We need to connect mentally (and in the most correct way possible) our experiences and knowledge to "simulate" situations that have not yet entered our field of vision. The arts are therefore exciting because they look at reality with new eyes and attempt to convey experiences in visual and symbolic forms which recount endless ways of viewing the world, not so much as it is, but as it might present itself to our eyes. It is not a simple exercise; yet we are condemned to learn how to do it because, in a world that moves at ever higher speed, visibility becomes shorter and shorter.

Throughout our lives, we accumulate experiences through our mistakes. Each of these experiences required a certain number of errors, or even traumas, but these errors taught us not to repeat the wrong choices. It is learning by experience. But, in some cases, learning by experience is catastrophic. If, for example, you climb Everest without knowing the dangers, there is no more time to learn from mistakes. You die first, due to cold, hunger, bad weather and lack of oxygen. This applies to many other things. In particular, it applies to the choices that concern our future. If you go to the future without knowing the problems, learning by errors is no longer necessary. It is too late.

But the man is able to use another type of learning: this allows him to imagine future situations and understand the consequences, thanks to mental associations. This ability is the result not only of a complex brain but also of a mental training that must begin early and then continue with a variety of creative stimuli. It is a typical human mechanism that has always been the basis of imagination and inventions, such as machines, ideas, strategies and projects, to solve problems that are not yet real but promptly imagined. Through imagination, man has managed to achieve great achievements. For Albert Einstein, the reason is clear: "Logic will get you from A to B. Imagination will take you everywhere". The conquest of the Moon, for example, took place, thanks to a series of mental simulations. To get the astronauts up and bring them home safe and sound, it was necessary to mentally simulate (and solve) the problems before they even occurred: problems related to gravity, temperatures, communications, fuels, tools navigation and vehicles. In other words, we have learned to do something completely new, that is, to go to the moon without ever having gone there. It was an imagined learning. In the same way, when we want to do a journey in the future, it would be catastrophic to learn by mistakes. We must be able to mentally simulate the problems (and solve them) before they even arise.

The future cannot be built solely by remaining into the sphere of the systematic and methodical – as we have tried to convey in this book by highlighting methods, processes and structures. In order to overcome existing paradigms, it is essential to "see" new possibilities and innovative solutions with the eyes of imagination. Imagination traces infinite, sometimes inaccessible pathways, and gives men and their organizations many prospective futures. It is the realm of alternatives, the place where visions multiply and intertwine, transforming the horizon of reality.

For Kant, "imagination is a necessary ingredient of perception itself": through imagination, it is possible to transform experience, the world of reality, doomed to mutability and change. Imagination is for those who want to evolve, and evolution is made of new projects, of future scenarios, of willingness to co-evolve with the environment. The future belongs to those who can imagine it.

Afterword
Foresight is possible

Ugo Morelli

In today's world, prediction of the future cannot be our purpose. Prediction has never been easy, and in this time of great changes such claim would not be credible. What is possible, however, it letting current events speak for themselves, learning to be attentive to their possible consequences, identifying the priorities that count and anticipating evolution with appropriate professional skills.

Just as we can learn to take risks, and learn to make better choices, we can likewise develop the managerial skills needed to anticipate relevant processes and to promptly grasp the opportunities they offer. The theme of anticipation is emerging at the different levels of research, in view of possible business applications both in government policies and in corporate organizations. It is a meaningful coincidence that nowadays the concern for anticipation appears to be shared between the interests of research, the needs of public governance and the transformations under way in company management and in the economy.

Among the different ways of gathering knowledge of the world, anticipation is one of the most ancient, and it is also one of the main indicators of the deep relationship existing between wisdom and knowledge. Faced with terrible and harrowing situations, and more generally confronted with the uncertainty of the future, in the course of our cultural evolution we have reacted, at least in part, by resorting to soothsayers and to multiple forms of *prediction*. We have created lots of deities, in which we have confided and to which we have entrusted our destiny, assigning to each of them a role in some specific field of our experience.

As the most relevant phenomena in the life of the human species have begun to show a certain empirical recurrence, we have started not only to identify a principle of *probability*, but also to give a voice to current events, recognizing their richness, understanding how they were already pregnant with the future. The recognition – the Aristotelian *anagnorisis* – of frequent signals; the assessment of probability of events either associated or associable with these signals (*association* is one of the most common modes of reading and analysing the world's signs); the verification of the probability of occurrence of those same events; the construction of time series for the most common occurrences: all these have composed a form of knowledge in which wisdom is a decisive factor, linked to the possibility of *anticipating* the occurrence of the events and phenomena of the world.

Together with association, which is an extremely important element of depth psychology constructs, we also use *projection* in our attempts at anticipation. According to the Kleinian psychoanalytic tradition, projective mechanisms are put in place as a defense against the invasiveness and uncertainty of the world, and can either lead us to model the world according to our own projects, or deceive us into believing we can control other people and external events, making them conform to our expectations. The danger involved is clear: going beyond what exists may expose us to disappointment and disenchantment, whose consequences are not only feared but also often avoided in advance.

In our inclination to project and look forward, trying to anticipate events and to change our minds according to emerging innovative possibilities, there is something dramatic which is deeply embedded into human experience: the fear of novelty, the fear of the future, which expresses itself, in the words of the psychiatrist E. Pichon-Rivière, in *epistemophilic anguish*. And fear, as we know, cannot be controlled. That anguish appears whenever we find ourselves following (*philia*) an unprecedented rationale or an unusual knowledge structure (*episteme*). The development of the *conflict* between our propensity to project ourselves into the new and the anguish caused by that same projection produces the level of *returning tension* that we, either individually or collectively, are able to sustain and to experience. The returning tension is a construct put in place during a process of research on the relationship between the body–brain–mind system and beauty, understood as a possibility of resonance with the world which has the capacity to generate a particularly meaningful extension of the neurophenomenological model of self, group and collectivity.

Apparently, it is that same extension which opens up to the sense of the possible and to the possibility of investing in the search for innovation. It is well known that the concept of beauty, and the approach to beauty, generates anxiety. If the word "awesome" is used to praise beauty, there must be a reason, as Luigi Pagliarani, who theorized the anguish of beauty, has said.

Foresight, or anticipation, is therefore a particularly demanding and complex process with uncertain outcome, but at the same time attractive and potentially generative.

Seeing the possible in the existing; acting as midwives to assist its birth; placing ourselves inside what might be possible and appropriating it, at least partially: perhaps these guidelines can help us capture the meaning of *foresight management*. Experimental trials are beginning to highlight the neurocognitive correlations of our ability to recognize the possible in the present.

The relationship between memory and imagination, for example, seems to be supported by neural substrates involved in the construction and elaboration of events (Addis D.R., Wong A.T., Schacter D.L., "Remembering the Past and Imagining the Future: Common and Distinct Neural Substrates During Event Construction and Elaboration", *Neuropsychologia* 2007; 45: 1363–1377). There are studies which confirm the absence of imagination in cases of cerebral limitations (Hassabis D., Kumaran D., Vann S.D., Maguire E.A., "Patients with Hippocampal Amnesia Cannot Imagine New Experiences", *Proceedings of the National Academy of Sciences of the United States of America* 2007; 104: 1726–1731).

The relationship between foresight management and the performance of businesses and institutions is becoming a well-defined field of study and research (Amstéus M., *Managerial Foresight and Firm Performance*, Linnaeus University Press, 2011). The fields of application expand and become diverse, increasingly encompassing the global and controversial issues of our time, and their complex management. In some areas, foresight studies take on the characteristics of participatory *backcasting analysis* (e.g., Robinson J., Burch S., Talwar S., O'Shea M., Walsh M., "Envisioning Sustainability: Recent Progress in the Use of Participatory Backcasting Approaches for Sustainability Research", *Technological Forecasting and Social Change*, 2011, vol. 78, no. 5, pp. 756–768).

One of the most frequently explored approaches concerns competency for the understanding of the future and for foresight practices compatible with an integral perspective. This area of study is based on an *enactive* approach to cognition and leads to a competency model described as *embodied foresight*. Action research is proposed as an important contribution to the development of embodied foresight (Floyd J., "Action Research and Integral Futures Studies: A Path to Embodied Foresight", *Futures*, 2012, vol. 44, no. 2, pp. 870–882). This particularly original perspective is also followed by other authors (Floyd J., Burns A., Ramos J., "A Challenging Conversation on Integral Futures: Foresight & Embodied Trialogues", *Journal of Futures Studies*, November 2008, 13(2): 69–86).

Anticipation of the future and foresight management are the focus of research of a well-known expert in innovation like Alberto Felice De Toni, currently Rector of the University of Udine. Together with Roberto Siagri, an entrepreneur and untiring explorer of the boundaries of innovation, and Cinzia Battistella, a researcher at the Free University of Bozen-Bolzano, he has written the present book, *Corporate Foresight, Anticipating the Future*, which has recently been published in Italy by EGEA, the Bocconi University publisher.

The book consists of four parts; each has its own completeness, and in the fourth, with some surprise, we can see three engineers attempting to explore the relationship between art, imagination and innovation.

The family of concepts and research constructs which make up this cutting-edge work, stimulating and fruitful, include creativity, understood as a distinctive trait of the human species; imagination, which makes it possible to conceive of what is not there yet; anticipation of existence, precisely as the search for the conditions in which to listen to the present in view of possible futures; innovation, either technological, of products, processes, organizational forms or knowledge.

The cognitive cues proposed in the authors' analysis of the prerequisites of anticipation are many and varied. If change is accelerated, interconnected and discontinuous, we soon realize, with some bewilderment, that we do not currently have the mental capacity required to confront it. The "exponential times" mentioned by the authors lead us away from every certainty. The probable and the plausible come forward as research fields and necessary practices when the existing and the present no longer suffice. On the other hand, going against the so-called dominant design is hard for us humans. We have to disobey in some way. Alberto De Toni has long maintained, as he does in this book, that "innovation is a successful disobedience". If the dominant design can be equated with reliance on tradition, it is difficult and at the same time necessary to recognize that, as we have argued over time, *tradition is nothing but successful innovation.*

Innovation can arise from a process of hybridization with unusual codes and languages, as it can also emerge from uncommon applications of existing solutions. The decisive step proposed by the authors is the transition from prediction to anticipation. Besides examining in depth the roots of anticipation, the study identifies organization and management as the two pillars of foresight. The detailed presentation of foresight methodologies provides especially useful information for the development of applications in various fields, from business to social processes. The thorough analysis of Eurotech, a company whose history is of particular relevance to anticipation, provides a meaningful example, very helpful to fully understand the requirements and developments of foresight management.

The whole text is infused with a strong tension towards change, and encourages us to observe the world from the point of view of the possible, by coming to terms with the ghosts of tradition that often threaten innovation.

Innovation is possible and requires investments to be realized. Of course it may be challenging, but it has never been as needed as today. Therefore, we must make the most of our imagination. The fact is that humans know very well how to hypothesize: *Homo hipoteticus* is one of the terms used by the biologist and epistemologist Giorgio Prodi to describe man. Then again, this hypothetical capacity is the condition that can allow us to go beyond the usual, beyond what is so obvious as to appear granted.

As Aristotle writes: "Just as it is with bats' eyes in respect of daylight, so it is with our mental intelligence in respect of those things which are by nature most obvious" (*Metaphysics*, Alpha Book, 993b 7–9). Still, there must be a reassuring convenience in not seeing what would otherwise be obvious but, precisely because it is obvious, does not emerge and is unable to assert itself.

Heinz von Foerster used to argue that we often place ourselves in the position of "not seeing that we do not see".

Why are we doing this? We are certainly able to see, at least in part. There are things that we do not see but, by contrast, we see other things. What happens, though, when not only do we not see, but we are also unable to see that we do not see? In this predicament, the conditions are unsuitable for exercising doubt on the things of the world, and existing states of equilibrium appear natural to us. This appearance of naturalness, which so reassures us, bestowing regularity upon what had once been discontinuous, is also a bearer of conformity and continuity. In such circumstances, what can be created – and apparently will, sooner or later – is a feeling of emptiness, of absence of something, perhaps the result of the incidence of the domain of normality and of the boredom that may ensue.

Terrence Deacon has theorized the generative value of *absentiality* in connection with the themes of uncertainty, chance, emergence, creativity, imagination. Absentiality is, for Deacon, a property of the living; not a property like any other, but a constitutive property. As such, living beings are incomplete, and this is why they tend to evolve; the specificity of living beings is to be found in the tension between what they are not yet and what they can become. The process of becoming is uncertain by its very nature, and what emerges from that space of uncertainty is a possible evolution, the chance to imagine and create the unusual, especially for the human species (Deacon T., *Incomplete Nature*, Norton & Co., New York, 2011).

The risk we run is often that of being so absorbed in the urges of *presence* that, while analyzing and trying to manage it, we lose sight of the *absence* from which presence originates and to which it refers.

Working in the present while searching for an *anticipatory* position means being aware of the weight of absence on presence (aware of "no longer" and "not yet"), aware of the fact that no presence is self-sufficient and that the quality of what is, or rather, of what becomes, depends on how the present and the absent (memory–imagination) are stretched. That stretch takes on the characteristics of the *returning tension* mentioned above, proposed as a distinctive feature of creativity and of aesthetic experience in the *Homo sapiens* species (Morelli U., *Mente e bellezza. Arte, creatività e innovazione*, Allemandi, Torino 2010).

For every generative process which presents itself as a forerunner, it is important to carefully examine the weight of presence (of *habit*, of reassurance, of continuity, of conformism, of the "formative context", as defined by R. Mangabeira Unger, of saturation) on absence. This is one of the fundamental aspects of the problem.

According to a metaphor suggested by Luca Mori, the present, full and saturated, is like a container in which the things that already exist pile up against the walls to the point of exerting pressure on them. Nonetheless, everything seems to work because the existing things are in balance while they saturate the whole. In this state of saturation, as soon as a space or a slot opens up, the most likely outcome is that what saturates the presence gets ejected into the void that has become available, making it look as if it were already inexorably and satisfactorily full of what is. It follows that the dynamics of emptying, receiving and processing the void are very difficult to implement, in an age committed to producing only fullness and even more fullness.

We tend not to be particularly familiar with utopias, intended as places that are not there yet, nor with *ucronias*, which project onto the future certain trends observed in the present, nor with *eutopias* or *dystopias*, or other forms of in-depth representation of the state of things to come.

It is difficult for us to examine and submit to criticism the modern paradigm of *necessity*, which is based on a Newtonian mechanism and has a mechanistic and deterministic character. It is equally difficult to shift towards a paradigm of observation, attention, understanding and analysis focused on *chance* – which combines both a principle of indeterminacy referred to the observer and a principle of probabilistic determinability oriented to the future and to the consequences of actions. These two difficulties definitely limit our ability to think of ourselves as truly capable of anticipation.

In-depth research is required on the aesthetics of change and on the constraints and possibilities of their emergence. The problem is particularly arduous and, despite the progress made by research on the brain–mind system, we have certainly not yet addressed the question raised many years ago by William James: "Something definite happens when to a certain brain-state a certain 'consciousness' corresponds. A genuine glimpse into what it is would be *the* scientific achievement, before which all past achievements would pale" (*Psychology, The Briefer Course*, Henry Holt & Co., New York, 1892).

In order to develop a reflection on the aesthetics of change, we must first ask ourselves the following questions. What do we know at present about the aesthetic experience and about the human mind in general? Besides, what do we know about the correlation between the dynamics of the aesthetic experience and the changes which modify meanings and tastes? Not only do we not know much, but also we tend to relegate the aesthetic experience to that particular kind of situation where someone is viewing a work of art. More rarely, we observe that experience extending into our lives. As a rule, we do not recognize the presence of the aesthetic experience when we are learning or when we change our mind, when we are presented with a transformation of symbols and tastes, or even when we have an intuition about a new scientific hypothesis. In all these situations, our relationship to the world is interrupted and reorganized. A psychology of the aesthetic experience is thus primarily a means to analyse our shifting viewpoints, our difficulty and our ability to change our mind, the emergence of innovative processes and results.

In the hypotheses today available on the origins and evolution of the aesthetic experience, notably derived from studies of paleoanthropology, cognitive neuroscience and psychology, we can identify two main guidelines:

- One supporting the "sudden" advent of the aesthetic experience, presumably caused by an evolutionary leap
- The other more inclined to endorse the viewpoint of a gradual and slow emergence of symbolic skills and aesthetic experience

Even while leaving open the question of the relationship between symbolic experience and aesthetic experience, there seems to be a challenging road ahead for those trying to understand something more about this distinctive character of human experience. However, the possibility is still remote of developing a model of change for

- ideas,
- symbols, and
- tastes and aesthetic preferences.

For a long time, the aesthetic experience has been considered exceptional compared to the so-called normal flow of experience, something supplementary and not linked to other processes of knowledge. Underlying this dominant orientation is, in all likelihood, an idealized vision of the mind as separate from the body. The beliefs related to the unnatural nature of the mind have a remote origin and have solidified over time. The Hellenistic propensity to see the "breath of life" (*psyche*), the spirit, as separate from the body, has certainly had a function in the process of semantic self-elevation of the *Homo sapiens* species but, up to the mentalistic aporias of cognitivism, this vision has continued to fuel the dualism with which the mind–body relationship, and aesthetic experiences in particular, are considered.

The combination or alliance between the natural sciences and the phenomenological approach can help us understand the natural conditions of the aesthetic sense and meaning. In particular, a neurophenomenological perspective could actually integrate different paths of explanation and comprehension that can help us recognize some of the distinctive features of the human aesthetic experience.

Some of the most challenging issues that have to be addressed concern the conditions for the establishment of "aesthetic conformism". It is crucial that we try to understand how habit is formed and how a symbolic order is created, expanded and intensified, together with the complex distinctions of a dominant aesthetic taste. At the same time, we need to ask ourselves how and for what reasons that order gets interrupted, explodes and gives life to an emerging state and then to a new order, which ends up creating another "aesthetic conformity".

Habituation and explosion, in the transformation of something into art and in the aesthetic experience in general, thus become two aspects of the same research topic, on which the available knowledge is particularly scarce.

Ideas, symbols and preferences seem to bear a close resemblance to the aesthetic experience, both in terms of emergence and in terms of conformism, both in terms of habituation and in terms of explosion. This is why scrutinizing the dynamics of aesthetic experience can help us understand the evolution of ideas, symbols and preferences. The aesthetic experience can therefore be configured as an ideal-typical situation, in the same manner as the tip of an iceberg, with its phenomenology and dynamics, may shed light on other phenomena and aspects otherwise unexplored or insufficiently traced back to verifiable explanations.

Some research carried out in recent years seems to prove that habituation overrides explosion over time. The dominant trend is in fact the preservation of the existing order, and conformism has a tendency to prevail over change, either of ideas, symbols or preferences. In the arts, the persistence of taste tends to be even more tenacious, and plays a critical selective function in respect to innovation and to experimentation with new trends and original emergences. Yet, despite this prevailing tendency, the explosion continues; it suddenly appears, unexpected but inevitable, breaking the force of habit, subverting the symbolic order and destroying consolidated ways.

Recent studies in the economy of art and of the immaterial have developed the construct of "activation costs" as a way of evaluating accessibility to artistic expressions and artistic events, such as performances, exhibitions and happenings. Activation costs mainly focus on the price people are willing to pay in terms of time, effort and resources to access an artistic event, an exhibition, a performance.

In order to complement and further specify this category, it may be interesting to see activation costs as the consequence of a psychodynamic relational process, both individual and collective, which goes way deeper than its concrete manifestation. Perhaps we might better understand the nature of this construct by exploring the psychological processes underlying its operation. When we attempt to analyze, as is both appropriate and necessary, mental processes and phenomena of experience in their instinctual and mechanical perspective, and especially in relation to the change of aesthetic taste, ideas and preferences, what emerges is the complexity and richness of these phenomena, but above all the need for further study and research.

Change, notably in the aesthetic experience but also in the evolution of taste and preferences, has to do with the fear and horror caused by the destabilization of the existing order. The story of contemporary art, starting from the linguistic shift and the resulting crisis at the beginning of the 20th century and onwards, is a clear example of this dynamic.

Is this the horror that art feels for itself, or is it the horror that art elicits in the audience? This is a dilemma (misplaced from a scientific point of view) contemporary art often deals with, and it is also the leitmotif of the dialogue between P. Virilio and E. Baj (*Discorso sull'orrore dell'arte*, Eleuthera, Milano 2002–2007), where the contemporary work of art is reduced to "an icon of itself, devoid of intrinsic meaning".

Let's start from here, but we might as well start from a number of other places.

First of all, *Homo sapiens* cannot perform any gesture or sign, nor produce any sound, without generating meaning. We are sense-makers by constitution, and giving meaning is not a choice. How meaning is generated, and why exactly *that* meaning; how meaning circulates and how and why it changes or remains unaltered, is an important research topic. But the fact that meaning is always generated is an undeniable reality, which relates to the natural–cultural comprehension of the mind (see the fundamental work of Giorgio Prodi, *Le basi materiali della significazione*, Bompiani, Milano 1977; but also the masterly report of Valentino Braitenberg, *Alla ricerca dell'intelligenza elementare. Come ancorare i pensieri alla mate-ria*, Mosaicoscienze review, Castiglione delle Stiviere (MN), September 23, 2007).

Contemporary art, like any human sign, like any gesture and any sound, and also like any element of the semiosis in which we are immersed, is symbolic and significant.

Another important question is how and why, at some point, one element separates from the semiotic pluriverse and takes on a peculiar and distinctive connotation, such as to be transformed into art. How *transformation into art* takes place is an interesting line of research, starting from the very creation of the "art" category and following its deepest evolutions over time. The hypotheses are many, and each deserves some thought and further exploration.

Secondly, we must consider not so much the horror that art may elicit in the public, much less the horror that art feels for itself, but art as a representation of the inner–outer world and of the horror inherent to that world; not only that, but also the subtle and profound tangency between art and horror, between art and terror, in the affective and cognitive dimension of creation and of aesthetic fruition. Apparently, the same psychodynamic processes, liminal, unheard, unpredictable and inexpressible, but above all irreducible, which are at the origin of the aesthetic experience, are also at the origin of terror and horror. The dimension of the shocking, the wonderful, the ineffable and the sublime, which emerges as distinctive, characterizes both emotional experiences. If contemporary art were able, even partially, to capture that dimension, it could be rightfully called "the first art": the art which would mark the symbolic childhood of humanity, a humanity able to look within itself, and not only see itself from outwards, for the first time. Perhaps we, symbolic infants, are now able to express ourselves through contemporary art as we never did before, and we are surprised to see ourselves; we are surprised to be able, at least for a while, "to see that we do not see".

And behind it all, there is probably only the intuition of the sociologist Gianni Pellicciari: "Exercise doubt and wait to see what chance may offer you".

Afterword

Perceiving the future or creating it?

Renato Quaglia

In an essay of many years ago on the political economy of music, Jacques Attali suggested that future changes in society are best revealed by its noises, arts and festivals, rather than by statistics: "If the political organization of the twentieth century is rooted in the political thought of the nineteenth, the latter is almost entirely present in embryonic form in the music of the eighteenth century".

Attali saw the transformations that have taken place throughout the history of music production and listening as anticipations of momentous social and political changes. "In the codes that structure noise and its mutations we glimpse a new theoretical practice and reading: establishing relations between the history of people and the dynamics of the economy on the one hand, and the history of the ordering of noise in codes on the other; predicting the evolution of one by the forms of the other; combining economics and aesthetics; demonstrating that music is prophetic and that social organization echoes it" (Attali, *Noise*). Music and its evolution can unravel the constitutive and compositional mechanisms of social dynamics. Music exists in order to interpret and give a sign to change: it becomes the announcement of a future society.

Does the artist anticipate (*fore*-see) the future, or does the observer of his work turn into concrete novelty the signs and forms unwittingly and abstractly drawn by the artist? Who is the real producer of future visions? Who creatively processes groundbreaking artistic signs? Who, as an observer, will associate these with other signs and, going beyond the artist's desire or thought, will see the work of art merely as a starting idea upon which to create (on his own, without the help of the artist) a true vision of innovation and future?

In some cases it is the artist who anticipates a trend, who reveals the imminence of its appearance, actualizing an intuition (the observer captures the wonder of that form, of that unexpected concept and, by echoing it, amplifies it). In other cases, the observer himself is the driver of change, the one who captures the spirit of the times and the possibility of transformation; the observer, who is already searching everywhere for inputs and innovative ideas, finds in the artist's work (whose vision is original, eccentric) the signs and concepts that give him a starting point and a set of instruments to fulfill his deep need for change.

Perhaps it is always an activity of coproduction between the observer (whose gaze is not neutral because he is looking for something) and the artist (who has created something that does not belong to the predictable), both incomplete and insufficient on their own: the artist who challenges the world in order to create, through his work, a different one, and the observer who sustains that vision (literally: lifting it upward) and uses it as an instrument of real action, of transformation of the world.

Returning to music and to its ability to anticipate the future, Attali leads us through a reinterpretation of some crucial moments. In the perspective he invites us to take, the 18th-century work of Mozart or Bach is not only sublime music, but also a harbinger of the bourgeoisie's dream of order and stability which will manifest itself only in the following century. Their music represents, well in advance and more explicitly than any 19th-century political theory, the bourgeoisie's desire to definitively discard the French Revolution and the Napoleonic period.

Again connecting musical phenomena to the historical, economic and social phenomenology, the sacred and counterpointed operas of Cherubini do not only represent wonderful examples of unparalleled complexity: they also announce the imminent revolutionary zeal with an intensity rarely attained in the political debate of the time. Similarly, Janis Joplin, Bob Dylan or Jimi Hendrix describe the contradictions, tensions and energies released by the societies of the '60s much better than any theory of development crisis and consumerism. "The standardized products of today's variety shows, hit parades, and show business are pathetic and prophetic caricatures of future forms of the repressive channeling of desire" (Attali, *idem*). In that essay on the economy of music, it is argued that primitive polyphony, classical counterpoint, tonal harmony, twelve-tone serial music and electronic music have appeared in succession because, amid the background noise that pervaded society and its discourse, music was detecting the changing of the times, the need for a new order … maybe what we now call "weak signals"?

When he is an outcast, the musician sees society in a political light. When he is accepted, funded, well adjusted to his role, "he is its historian, the reflection of its deepest values". If we observe symmetrically the history of music and the history of social organization, we can see that the most important social and economic changes are actually preceded by a decisive change in musical codes.

The so-called *modal* music, based on the eight modes of Benedictine origin, greatly develops its harmonic possibilities just prior to the beginning of a profound change in the social and economical structure of Western Europe, which will lead to the expansion of Renaissance trade.

In three centuries, from the 14th century to the 16th, during the transition from the feudal world to the more complex organization of Communes and

Seigniories, European courts replace jongleurs with minstrels. Jongleurs are halfway between high culture and popular culture, they improvise, they are anarchists, wandering clerics. Minstrels (from the Latin *ministerialis*, functionary) know how to read music, and music begins to be written down, so that digressions are no longer allowed, let alone improvisations. Minstrels are remunerated and only play what the lord commands them to play, that very lord a jongleur would never have submitted to. Jongleurs asked for hospitality, court musicians are manservants, "like the cook or huntsman of the prince, reserved for his pleasure". Even Bach's work contract, in the middle of the 18th century, is still that of a domestic.

Until the 17th century, music is governed by the ancient logic of ownership: one *owns* music, one does not listen to it. But again, music is the first to find the path of change from the ancient to the modern age, towards commoditization, towards the division of roles, responsibilities, hierarchies, towards a new social order. The first concert to draw a profit was given in 1672 by John Bannister, a violinist at the English court of Charles II, in his own home. Bannister charged a fee for admission, thus anticipating the valorization of desire, the commercialization of art, of every relationship and every performance. We are entering the modern age, the industrial revolution is yet to come, but music is already starting to quantify the cost of the different components of its value and production chain. It is no accident that one century later, the first concert hall was established, not by representatives of the aristocracy or the clergy, but by a group of Leipzig drapers who converted a private house into a paying concert hall. People start paying to hear music, churches and palaces are no longer the only places where one can hear (*have*) music, financed by nobles and princes. Music announces the division of labor, a concept that will only take root in the following century. The musician no longer sells himself to a lord: he sells his labor to a pool of customers, who are sufficiently rich to buy his performances, but not rich enough to claim his exclusive services. We are only at the beginning of yet another, profound change in music statutes, which announces the arrival of bourgeois individualism, of the organization and commoditization of desire and production. "The concept of representation logically implies that of exchange and harmony. The theory of political economy of the nineteenth century was present in its entirety in the concert hall of the eighteenth century, and foreshadowed the politics of the twentieth" (Attali, *idem*).

The constitution of great orchestras begins in the seventeenth and eighteenth centuries. In these orchestras, musicians are arranged in a semicircle, different instrument groups are represented, each performing its score and contributing, in contrast or affinity with the other groups, to the overall sound of the whole. Does not all this evoke the parliamentary democracy of the following century? In the 19th century, the unlimited use of symphony orchestras with mighty sound power also announces the industrial macrosomia of the United States, England, France and Germany in the twentieth, when the industry will impose the exaggeration of its power role above any other productive aggregation.

At the beginning of the 20th century (11 March 1913), Luigi Russolo wrote the Futurist manifesto *The Art of Noise*, theorizing the use of pure sounds to compose a music which denies harmonic sounds: it is the anticipation of the disorders and social disruptions that some years later will mark the second half of the century.

Music is not only a range of sounds ordered rationally: behind pure syntax there is a *sense* of music. Music is a "dialectical confrontation with the course of time", says the French philosopher Michel Serres. But in a lesson of the sixties, not about the future but about art, the Italian poet Attilio Bertolucci said to an audience of students: "We have given you clues to decode the painting that is in front of you, but maybe you will derive from it many other images and suggestions: do not be discouraged and, if possible, do not take offence: painting is akin to music, and you do not ask music to tell you something specific".

In Attali's interpretation of the relationship between music and political economy, the impending future (especially political and economic) finds in music the announcement of its own coming (music itself becomes a weak, or strong, signal).

Predicting the future, knowing beforehand, being ready, maybe turning this knowledge to one's advantage, is an ancestral desire, which implies that time flows and carries with it events that elude our present capacity of determination. Edward Lorenz, the pioneer of chaos theory, argued that satisfactory forecasting models are hard to obtain, and gave the example of "the flap of a butterfly's wings in Brazil". But the anxiety of prediction is such that mass culture has given to that theory the opposite meaning to that advocated by its author: that almost imperceptible facts can in fact determine consequences that alter the course of events, rather than subject it to many variables. But is the future knowable a priori, because already written? Does it arrive some day and ask to be announced, or is it produced day after day? Is it to be disclosed or, rather, determined?

In the first six months of 2013 in Italy, the alleged turnover of magicians, fortune tellers and the like has reached 8.3 billion. There are no precise economic analyses, but the turnover has increased by 18.5 percent, from 7.5 billion to 8.3 billion, and is clearly on the rise if compared to a few years ago. A considerable number of occultists – 160,000 – make 30,000 predictions every day for four out of ten Italians who apparently believe in the gift of clairvoyance, since they are willing to pay from 50 to 1,000 euros for a consultation. Women interrogate them about relationships, love and health. Men focus on work and money.

Work is a burning issue these days, on which people want to know if their hopes will be confirmed or denied; this trend is confirmed by another research on the topic, conducted by CICAP (the Italian committee for the investigation of claims on the paranormal). Primarily, people ask for predictions about their job, trying to exorcise the nightmare of losing it or not finding it, either for themselves or their children. They also seek reassurance on ongoing business, health, and love lost or found. Magicians and fortune tellers are increasingly contacted by finance professionals, executives and entrepreneurs, who wish to know how the crisis will develop and how long it will last.

A study by Codacons (the Italian association for the defense of consumer rights) has estimated that 13 million Italian citizens are turning to the world of occultism, 1 million more than in 2011 and over 3 million more than in 2001. It is impossible to guess how many people read daily, weekly or monthly horoscopes, looking for indications and warnings about their future. An interesting indicator could be the space reserved by all publications, including the most authoritative newspapers and television channels, to the astral themes of showmen and showgirls, however lightly touched by fame (Theodor Adorno wrote a sharp essay on this subject, "The Stars Down to Earth").

The future, as we know, will not fall upon us unexpectedly at some distant time, undefined and distinct from our present. It will not appear one day knocking at our door, like a salesman, displaying all the new things it carries along. The future is being determined today, it depends on our actions (or inaction) of today and will be a result of them. It has already begun and we know from the outset that nothing will be like before, that the rules of the game are already profoundly changing.

In the most difficult negotiations, in politics as in everyday life, we tend to defer to the future what we cannot solve today. The choices on which there is no agreement, the decisions that today would be unpopular, get postponed to a future time, to which we delegate the courage to do all the things that we should have decided today (or yesterday) and that we hope someone will do for us. But the future is not a time that is determined elsewhere, away from us. It is the outcome of our decisions and the expression of our potential. Sure, we do not know the exact moment when a sign of change will manifest itself as the future ("the future arrives like London buses – says Angela Wilkinson, OECD – not one at a time, but two or three at once, and never when expected").

If anything, the risk is to stand still and keep waiting for the future. The Italian journalist and artist Leo Longanesi once harangued an opponent with these words: "On the other side there was the future, and you loudly fled in the opposite direction!" and, worried about his contemporaries' view of the future, he left us this image for future reference: "He looked at the future as cows watch trains go by".

According to the analysts of major international institutions, the most advanced economies in the world are building a future made of competence and merit, tolerance and curiosity. Temporary employment, which is replacing permanent employment and is seen today as a symbol of uncertainty, insecurity and overexploitation, will settle into a new way of working, not definitive nor totalizing, in people's lives. In coming years, a different model of employment and professionalism will set in: each person will be part of a multiple, complex and plural working system. We will manage simultaneously several jobs and tasks, none of them sufficient, on its own, to fill the working day or to ensure the expected income. We will juggle two or three careers, work two or three jobs at the same time, be part of two or three working environments (with their corollary: colleagues, office managers, internal conflicts, friendships, suppliers, contributory roles etc.).

Customer pools, critical issues, goals to be achieved, complexity in relationships...all of these will increase and expand. We will definitively move beyond 20th-century Fordism, not by cancelling the division of tasks and responsibilities, but by multiplying their application to an indefinite number of contemporary settings. Companies will absolutely need to know how to combine traditional product expertise with new skills, other than those of their value chain and eccentric if compared to the more predictable ones, in order to overcome the limitations of specialized and unidirectional thinking, and to find unexpected and unsettling points of view. Correspondingly, a reshuffling of roles and positions will take place, together with a change in the concept of specialization.

We will have to blend skills together, adding identity to identity, becoming centaurs. But not in the mythological sense: in myths, centaurs were proud, overbearing, quarrelsome, rude. Among them, however, there was Chiron, the wounded centaur who healed the wounds of those he met. We must all become Chirons.

As St. Augustine wrote in *The Confessions*: "For these three do exist in some sort, in the soul, but otherwise do I not see them: present of things past, memory; present of things present, sight; present of things future, expectation".

As we juggle multiple professions (and therefore multiple contexts, multiple lives, multiple Pirandellian masks for our public persona), we will sometime rediscover the meaning of St. Augustine's words, warning us that whichever temporal projection we may turn to, the starting point (the one always conditioning our vision) remains the present, the here and now, the current moment.

Then perhaps the present is all the possible presents, defined in this book as weak signals, emerging trends and possible paths of evolution. And in the face of continuously changing conditions and settings, which at every step suggest different possible scenarios, it would be wise to imitate Beethoven who, in his deafness, read the music he could no longer hear, and saw it full of all the possible interpretations.

Changes are constantly taking place, and it is crucial to distinguish among them, to cultivate some and deflate others, to make a selection, like betting on one horse at the races or on many horses in different races (for this reason, research and development must be separated).

The Italian writer Giuseppe Tomasi di Lampedusa, in his novel *The Leopard*, puts these words in the mouth of the Prince of Salina: "Everything needs to change, so everything can stay the same". This dialogue between the Sicilian nobleman Don Fabrizio, Prince of Salina, and his nephew Tancredi, a supporter of Garibaldi, takes place in 1860, at the time of the unification of Italy. What the nobleman meant was that Sicilian nobility had to support the Savoy monarchy and expel the Bourbons, now defeated, to maintain its privileges. He was in fact inciting the Sicilian nobility to yet another about-face, so that things could remain unchanged.

Reversing the premises of this statement, we could say that an organization that remains anchored to the rules, the ways, the "system of dominating ideas" (Richard Normann) that have made it successful can lose, over time, its position, its achievements, its meaningful results (its distinctive competence, Selznick would say) if it is unable to redefine its views on management, organization, product and process. An organization that continually reshapes itself – even considerably – may on the other hand preserve and strengthen its identity and its position.

Remaining "within the scope of one's specific skills" equates to considering one's characteristics immutable, and is likely to expose a company to the danger of being unprepared, in a word, of surrendering to the future. On the contrary, a company that is willing and able to change its organization and its management mode will have the means to reaffirm its own ethics.

Hence a strategy must be adopted, a strategy that is the result of a development process in knowledge.

According to Normann, a new emerging strategy must not attempt to change the organizational and managerial structures all at once, but certainly it must commit to break the system of dominating ideas, because they are the cornerstones of strategic management.

Dominating ideas are the present of a company (or institution), they have been created by the currently ruling leadership; nonetheless, they have to give way to the new strategy, because they are a reflection of the past.

Dominating ideas almost always reflect a "reality of the past", instead of a reality of the present, let alone of the future; and sometimes they have been so successful that we cling to them, even when in fact we should abandon and replace them. In the present there are always good reasons to defend dominant ideas, but still greater risks: in front of a new context, new factors, a different set of problems, the solutions we adopted in the past, which in the past assured our success, are probably no longer adequate and need not be replicated (although it may be reassuring to think that they did work, and instinctively repeat the pattern of the once successful formulas). Those old ideas, those outdated recipes that once led us to victory, today could well become for us "the failure of success".

The responsibility and the ability to take the existing structure by surprise, to overcome its defense and resistance, should be entrusted to *prime movers* (those who defrost old structures and build new ones). They will be perceived as invaders and they will be fought, as the heralds of the future always are. But again Normann exhorts the natives: "Love your invaders, they are your salvation".

The future is not what we would like it to be, but what we might encounter walking in its direction. We must be able to change in order to build a future that will be a consequence of our current choices, in order to manage the complexity of the changes that will affect us. Similarly, we must be willing to weave our skills with those of the experts of change, to integrate experience and knowledge from different sources, refusing to repeat, in our solitude and inside our little closed world, the patterns of the past: although they once guaranteed our success, they are now proving inadequate and outdated, because the context is already profoundly different from the one that saw them victorious.

As Chéreau wrote about Siegfried, the hero of Wagner's *Ring of the Nibelung*: "The central part ... is precisely this: a hero has been created who would actually have had all the attributes of freedom, but nobody remembered to tell him ... so Siegfried remains unaware and incomplete".

References

"We don't read and write poetry because it's cute.
We read and write poetry because we are members of the human race.
And the human race is filled with passion".

Professor Keating, *Dead Poets Society*

Ackoff R.L. (1974) *Redesigning the Future: Systems Approach to Societal Problems*, John Wiley & Sons, New York.

Adorno, T. (1994) *The Stars Down to Earth*, Routledge Classics, London.

Ahuja G., Coff R.W. and Lee P.M. (2005) Managerial Foresight and Attempted Rent Appropriation: Insider Trading on Knowledge of Imminent Breakthroughs, *Strategic Management Journal*, 26(9):791–808.

Aldrich H. (1979) *Organizations and Environments*, Prentice-Hall, New York.

Allais M. (1992) An Outline of My Main Contributions to Economic Science, Nobel Prize in Economics Documents 1988-1, Nobel Prize Committee.

Alsan A. (2008) Corporate Foresight in Emerging Markets: Action Research at a Multinational Company in Turkey, *Futures*, 40:47–55.

Amara R. (1981) The Futures Field (Report), Menlo Park, California, Institute for the Future.

Andersen P.D. et al. (2005) Sensor Foresight – Technology and Market, *Technovation*, 24(4):311–320.

Anderson J. (1997) Technology Foresight for Competitive Advantage, *Long Range Planning*, 30(5):665–677.

Andrews K. (1965) *The Concept of Corporate Strategy*, Dow-Jones Irwin, Homewood.

Andriopoulos C. and Lewis M.W. (2009) Exploitation-Exploration Tensions and Organizational Ambidexterity: Managing Paradoxes of Innovation, *Organization Science*, 20:696–717.

Ansoff H.I. (1965) *Corporate Strategy: An Analytic Approach to Business Policy for Growth and Expansion*, McGrawHill, New York.

Ansoff H.I. (1976) Managing Strategic Surprise by Response to Weak Signals, *California Management Review*, 18(2):21–33.

Ansoff H.I. (1980) Strategic Issue Management, *Strategic Management Journal*, 1:131–148.

Ansoff H.I. (1987) The Emerging Paradigm of Strategic Behavior, *Strategic Management Journal*, 8(6):501–515.

Argyres N.S. and Silverman B.A. (2004) R&D, Organization Structure, and the Development of Corporate Technological Knowledge, *Strategic Management Journal*, 25:929–958.

Arnold H.M. (2003) *Technology Shocks: Origins, Management Responses and Firm Performance*, Physica-Verlag, Springer, Heidelberg.

Arrow K.J. (1962) The Economic Implications of Learning by Doing. *Review of Economic Studies*, 29:155–173.

Ashton W.B. and Stacey G.S. (1995) Technical Intelligence in Business: Understanding Technology Threats and Opportunities, *International Journal of Technology Management*, 10(1):79–104.

Ashton W.B., Johnson A.K. and Stacey G.S. (1996) Monitoring Science and Technology for Competitive Advantage, *Competitive Intelligence Review*, 7(1):115–126.

Ashton W.B., Kinzey B.R. and Gunn M.E. (1991) A Structured Approach for Monitoring Science and Technology Developments, *International Journal of Technology Management*, 6(1,2):91–111.

Attali, J. (1977) *Noise: The Political Economy of Music*, University of Minnesota Press, Minneapolis, MN.

Ayres R.U. (2000) On Forecasting Discontinuities, *Technological Forecasting and Social Change*, 65(1):81–97.

Baricco A. (2006) *The Barbarians: An Essay on the Mutation of Culture*, Rizzoli, New York.

Bate J. and Johnston R. (2005) Strategic Frontiers: The Starting Point for Innovative Growth, *Strategy & Leadership*, 33(1):12–18.

Battistella C. and De Toni A.F. (2011) A Methodology of Technological Foresight: A Proposal and Field Study, *Technological Forecasting and Social Change*, 78(6):1029–1048.

Becker P. (2002) Corporate Foresight in Europe: A First Overview. Report of the Institution for Science and Technology Studies, Bielefeld. Retrieved from https://cordis.europa.eu/pub/foresight/docs/st_corporate_foresight_040109.pdf.

Becker P. (2002) Corporate Foresight in Europe: A First Overview. Retrieved from https://cordis.europa.eu/pub/foresight/docs/st_corporate_foresight_040109.pdf.

Bellamy E. (1888) *Looking Backward: 2000–1887*, Ticknor & Co., Boston.

Berger G. (1957) L'accélération de l'histoire et ses conséquences, in Berger G., de Bourbon-Busset J. and Massé P. (Eds.) *De la prospective*. Textes fondamentaux de la prospective française, Paris: L'Harmattan, 2007. Textes réunis et présentés par Philippe Durance.

Bergman J. et al. (2006) Managing the Exploration of New Operational and Strategic Activities Using the Scenario Method – Assessing Future Capabilities in the Field of Electricity Distribution Industry, *International Journal of Production Economics*, 104(1):46–61.

Bernhardt, D.C. (1994). I Want it Fast, Factual, Actionable – Tailoring Competitive Intelligence to Executives' Needs. *Third International Symposium On National Secu-rity & National Competitiveness: Open Source Solutions Proceedings*, 2:12–24.

Bessant J. et al. (2005) Managing Innovation Beyond the Steady State, *Technovation*, 25(12):1366–1376.

Bishop P. (1980) How to Prepare Professional Futurists, in Bishop P. and Hines A. *Teaching about the Future*, Palgrave MacMillan, New York, 2012.

Blackman D.A. and Henderson S. (2004) How Foresight Creates Unforeseen Futures: The Role of Doubting, *Futures*, 36(2):253–266.

Blind K., Cuhls K. and Grupp H. (1999) Current Foresight Activities in Central Europe, *Technological Forecasting and Social Change*, 60(1):15–35

Bodelle J. and Jablon C. (1993) Science and Technology Scouting at Elf Aquitaine, *Research-Technology Management*, 36:5:24–48.

Borges J. L. (1941) An Examination of the Work of Herbert Quain, in *The Garden of Forking Paths*, English translation by Andrew Hurley, London, 1998.

Bradbury R. (1952) *A Sound of Thunder*, Doubleday, New York.

Breiner S., Cuhls K. and Grupp H. (1994) Technology Foresight Using a Delphi Approach – A Japanese-German Cooperation, *R&D Management*, 24(2):141–153.

Brenner M.S. (1996) Technology Intelligence and Technology Scouting, *Competitive Intelligence Review*, 7(3):20–27.

Brockhoff K. (1991) Competitor Technology Intelligence in German Companies, *Industrial Marketing Management*, 20(2):91–98.

Brown S.L. and Eisenhardt K.M. (1997) The Art of Continuous Change: Linking Complexity Theory and Time-Paced Evolution in Relentlessly Shifting Organizations, *Administrative Science Quarterly*, 42(1):1–34.

Bürgel H.D., Reger G. and Ackel-Zakour R. (2005) Technologie-Früherkennung in multinationalen Unternehmen: Ergebnisse einer empirischen Untersuchung, in Möhrle Möhrle M.G. and Isenmann R. (Eds.) *Technologie-Roadmapping – Zukunftsstrategien für Technologieunternehmen*, Springer-Verlag, Heidelberg – New York, 27–53.

Burmeister K., Neef A. and Beyers B. (2004) *Unternehmen gestalten Zukunft* (Corporate Foresight), Murmann, Hamburg.

Calvino I. (1969) *The Castle of Crossed Destinies*, English translation by William Weaver, London, 1976.

Campbell A. and Goold M. (1991) *Building Core Skills, Paper for the Ashridge Strategic Management Centre*, Ashridge Executive Education, Ashridge, Berkhamsted, Hertfordshire.

Castellucci F. (1999) Le tecniche di previsione tecnologica, in Sobrero M. (Ed.) *Gestione dell'innovazione: strategia, organizzazione e tecniche operative*, Carrocci Editore, Roma.

Cattell K. (2002) Foresight, Space and E-Commerce, *Facilities*, 20(3–4):145–162.

Cavone A., Chiesa V. and Manzini R. (2000) Management Styles in Industrial R&D Organisations, *European Journal of Innovation Management*, 3(2):59–71.

Chandler A. (1962) *Strategy and Structure: Chapters in the History of the Industrial Enterprise*. MIT Press, Cambridge, MA.

Chandy R. and Tellis G. (1998) Organizing for Radical Product Innovation: The Overlooked Role of Willingness to Cannibalize, *Journal of Marketing Research* 35(4):474–487.

Chéreau, P. and Boulez, P. *Wagner – Der Ring des Nibelungen*, Bayreuth Festival, Bayreuth, Germany.

Chesbrough H. (2003) *Open Innovation: The New Imperative for Creating and Profiting from Technology*, Harvard Business School Press, Boston.

Chiesa V. (1996) Separating Research from Development: Evidence from the Pharmaceutical Industry, *European Management Journal*, 14:638–647.

Chiesa V. and Masella C. (1996) Searching for an Effective Measure of R&D Performance, *Management Decision*, 34(7):49–57.

Christensen C. (1997) *The Innovator's Dilemma: When New Technologies Cause Great Firms to Fail*, Harvard Business School Press, Boston.

Clarke I.F. (1979) *The Pattern of Expectation 1644–2001*, Jonathan Cape, London.

Clark A. (2003) *Natural-Born Cyborgs*, Oxford University Press, Oxford.

Clark K.B. (1996) Competing through Manufacturing and the New Manufacturing Paradigm: Is Manufacturing Strategy Passé, *Production and Operations Management*, 5(1):42–58.

Coates J.F. (1985) *Issues Identification and Management: The State of the Art of Methods and Techniques*, Palo Alto, CA: Electric Power Research Institute.

Coda V. (1988) *L'orientamento strategico dell'impresa*, UTET, Torino.

Coda V. (1998) *Strategia Aziendale*, UTET Libreria, Torino.

Cohen W.M. and Levinthal D.A. (1990) Absorptive Capacity: A New Perspective on Learning and Innovation, *Administrative Science Quarterly*, 35:128–152.

Collins J. and Porras J. (1994) *Built to Last*, HarperCollins Publishers, New York.

Copernicus N. (1543) *De revolutionibus orbium coelestium*, in F. Barone *Niccolò Copernico, Opere*, Torino, UTET, Nuremberg, 1979.

Cornish E.S. (2004) *Futuring: The Exploration of the Future*, World Future Society, Bethesda.

Cuhls K. (2003) From Forecasting to Foresight Processes – New Participative Foresight Activities in Germany, *Journal of Forecasting*, 22(2–3):93–111.

Cuhls K. and Johnston R. (2006) Corporate Future-Oriented Technology Analysis. *Presented at the Second International Seville Seminar on Future-Oriented Technology Analysis: Impact of FTA Approaches on Policy and Decision-Making*, Seville, Spain, 28–29 September.

Daft R. and Weick K.E. (1984) Toward a Model of Organizations as Interpretations Systems, *Academy of Management Review*, 9(2):284–295.

Daheim C. (2004) Z-Punkt Report 2004.

Daheim C. and Uerz G. (2008) Corporate Foresight in Europe: From Trend Based Logics to Open Foresight. *Technology Analysis & Strategic Management*, 20(3):321–336.

D'Aveni R. (1994) *Hypercompetition: Managing the Dynamics of Strategic Maneuvering*, Free Press, New York.

D'Aveni R.A. (1995) Coping with Hypercompetition: Utilizing the New 7S's Framework, *Academy of Management Executive*, 9:45–57.

Dawkins R. (1976) *The Selfish Gene*, Oxford University Press, Oxford.

Day G.S. and Schoemaker P.J.H. (2004a) Driving through the Fog: Managing at the Edge, *Long Range Planning*, 37(2):127–142.

Day G.S. and Schoemaker P.J.H. (2004b) Peripheral Vision: Sensing and Acting on Weak Signals, *Long Range Planning*, 37(2):117–121.

Day G.S. and Schoemaker P.J.H. (2005) Scanning the Periphery, *Harvard Business Review*, 83(11):135–148.

De Geus A. (1997a) *The Living Company*, Harvard Business School Press, Boston.

De Toni A.F. and Tonchia S. (2005) Definitions and Linkages between Operational and Strategic Flexibilities, *Omega – The International Journal of Management Science*, 33(6):525–540.

De Toni A.F. and Battistella C. (2007) Dal 'sapiens sapiens' all''Homo technologicus': la co-evoluzione uomo-macchina, Multiverso, Retrieved from http://www.multiversoweb.it/rivista.

De Toni A.F. and Barbaro A. (2010). *Visione evolutiva. Un viaggio tra uomini e organizzazioni, management strategico e complessità*, Ed. Etas.

Dioguardi G. (1991) *Organizzazione e bricolage*, Donzelli, Roma.

Dougherty E. (1989) Tech Scouts: R&D's Globetrotters, *R&D Management*, 31(10):44–50.

Doz Y.L. and Kosonen M. (2008) The Dynamics of Strategic Agility: Nokia's Rollercoaster Experience, *California Management Review* 50(8):95–118.

Drucker P. (1992) *The Age of Discontinuity: Guidelines to Our Changing Society*, Transaction Publishing, New Jersey.AU:

Dushnitsky G. and Lenox M.J. (2005) When Do Incumbents Learn from Entrepreneurial Ventures? Corporate Venture Capital and Investing Firm Innovation Rates, *Research Policy*, 34(5):615–639.

Eto H. (1991) Classification of R&D Organizational Structures in Relation to Strategies, *IEEE Transactions on Engineering Management*, 38(2):146–156.

Fagerberg J. (1987) A Technology Gap Approach to Why Growth Rates Differ, *Research Policy*, 16:3–5.

Fink A. et al. (2005) The Future Scorecard: Combining External and Internal Scenarios to Create Strategic Foresight, *Management Decision*, 43(3):360–381.

Fontana, L. (1946) *Manifesto Blanco*, Galleria Apollinaire, Milano.

Foster R.N. and Kaplan S. (2001) *Creative Destruction: Why Companies That Are Built to Last Underperform the Market – And How to Successfully Transform Them*, Doubleday, New York.

Fuld-Gilad-Herring Academy of Competitive Intelligence (2002). Competitive intel-ligence report.

Galbraith C.S. (1952) *Designing Organizations: An Executive Guide to Strategy, Structure, and Process*, Jossey-Bass.

Galileo (1610) *Sidereus Nuncius (the Starry Messenger)*, Thomas Baglioni, Venice.

Gallivan B. (2002) How to Fold Paper in Half Twelve Times: An Impossible Challenge Solved and Explained, pamphlet for the Historical Society of Pomona.

Gassmann O. and Gaso B. (2005) Organisational Frameworks for Listening Post Activities. *International Journal of Technology Intelligence and Planning* 1(3):241–265.

Gehlen A. (1957) *Die Seele im technischen Zeitalter* (translated as *Man in the Age of Technology* (1980), Columbia University Press, New York.

Gemünden H.G., Salomo S. and Holzle K. (2007) Role Models for Radical Innovations in Times of Open Innovation, *Creativity Innovation Management* 16(4):408–421.

Georghiou L. (1996). The UK Technology Foresight Programme, *Futures*, 28(4): 359–377.

Gerybadze A. (1994) Technology Forecasting as a Process of Organisational Intelligence, *R&D Management*, 24(2):131–140.

Gill R. (1986) *Scenario Planning: Managing for the Future*, John Wiley & Sons, Chichester.

Glenn J.C. and Gordon T.J. (2003) *Futures Research Methodology* – V2.0. AC/UNU Millennium Project.

Godet M. (1987) Scenarios and Strategic Management, Butterworths, traduction de. Godet M. (1985), Prospective et planification stratégique, Economica.

Godet M., Durance P. and Gerber A. (2009) Strategic Foresight the Prospective Use and Misuse of Scenario Building, research working paper (#10), LIPSOR Working Paper.

Gould S.J. (1982) *The Panda's Thumb: More Reflections in Natural History*, Norton & Company, New York.

Grant R. (1994). *L'analisi strategica nella gestione aziendale*. Il Mulino.

Greenspan A. (2007) *The Age of Turbulence: Adventures in a New World*, Penguin Press, London.

Grove A. (1996) *Only the Paranoid Survive*, Doubleday, New York.

Grupp H. and Linstone H.A. (1999) National Technology Foresight Activities around the Globe – Resurrection and New Paradigms, *Technological Forecasting and Social Change*, 60:85–94.

Hamel G. (2007) *The Future of Management*, Harvard Business School Press, Boston.

Hamel G. and Prahalad C.K. (1994) *Competing for the Future*, Harvard Business Publishing, Brighton.

Handy C. (1996) *The Age of Paradox*, Harvard Business Review Press, Boston. *Harper's Magazine*, 1856. Retrieved from http://harpers.org/archive/1856/.

Harris S.D. and Zeisler S. (2002) Weak Signals: Detecting the Next Big Thing, *The Futurist*, 36(6).

Hax A. and Wilde D. (1999) The Delta Model: Adaptive Management for a Changing World, *MIT Sloan Management Review*, 36(6):21–28.

Hayes R.H. and Pisano G.P. (1994) Beyond World-Class: The New Manufacturing Strategy, *Harvard Business Review*, 72(1):77–84.

Heraud J.A. and Cuhls K. (1999) Current Foresight Activities in France, Spain, and Italy. *Technological Forecasting and Social Change*, 60(1):55–70.

Herodotus (2013) *The Histories, Herodotus*, translated by Tom Holland, with intro-duction and notes by Paul Cartledge, Penguin, New York.

Hines A. (2006) Strategic Foresight: The State of the Art, *The Futurist*, 40(5):18–21.

Hofer C.W. and Schendel D. (1978) *Strategy Formulation: Analytical Concepts*, West Pub. Co., St. Paul.

Horton A. (1999) A Simple Guide to Successful Foresight, *Foresight*, 1(1):5–9.

Ilmola L. and Kuusi O. (2006) Filters of Weak Signals Hinder Foresight: Monitoring Weak Signals Efficiently in Corporate Decision-Making, *Futures*, 38(8):908–924.

Irvine J. and Martin B.R. (1984) *Foresight in Science, Picking the Winners*, Pinter Publishers Ltd.

Jacobs D. and Waalkens J. (2001) Innovation. Modernisation in the Innovative Function of Companies, Background Study AWT, n. 23, Kluwer, Deventer.

Jain S.C. (1984) Environmental Scanning in U.S. *Corporations. Long Range Planning*, 17(2):117–128.

Jaques E. (1991) *Requisite Organization: The CEO's Guide to Creative Structure and Leadership*, Casar Hall & Co., Gloucester.

Jones-Smith K. and Mathur H. (2006) Fractal Analysis: Revisiting Pollock's Drip Paintings, *Nature*, 444:E9–E10.

Kahn H. (1967) *The Year 2000*, Calman-Levy.

Kaivo-oja J. and Marttinen J. (2006) Foresight Systems and Core Activities at National and Regional Levels in Finland 1990–2008. Finland Futures Research Centre, Turku School of Economics. Retrieved from https://www.utu.fi/fi/yksikot/ffrc/julkaisut/e-tutu/Documents/eTutu_2008-6.pdf.

Kameoka A., Yokoo Y. and Kuwahara T. (2004) A Challenge of Integrating Technology Foresight and Assessment in Industrial Strategy Development and Policymaking, *Technological Forecasting and Social Change*, 71(6):579–598.

Kandinsky, W. (1947) *Point and Line to Plane: Contribution to the Analysis of the Pictorial Elements*, Howard, Dearstyne.

Kantabutra S. and Avery G.C. (2010) The Power of Vision: Statements That Resonate, *Journal of Business Strategy*, 31(1):37–45.

Keenan M. (2005) *Technology Foresight Training Programme*, UNIDO.

Kijkuit B. and Van Den Ende J. (2007) The Organizational Life of an Idea: Integrating Social Network, Creativity and Decision Making Perspectives, *Journal of Management Studies*, 44(6):863–882.

Kim Chan W. and Mauborgne R. (2005) *Blue Ocean Strategy*, Harvard Business Review Press, Boston.

Klaus Weyrich of Siemens. Cited in Stadler C. (2011) *Enduring Success: What We Can Learn from the History of Outstanding Corporations*, Stanford University Press, Stanford, CA.

Kotler P. and Caslione J. (2009) *Chaotics: The Business of Managing and Marketing in the Age of Turbulence*, Sperling & Kupfer, New York.

Kuhn, T. (1962) *The Structure of Scientific Revolutions*, Chicago University Press, Chicago.

Kurzweil R. (2006) *The Singularity Is Near*, Viking Press, New York.

Lackman, C.L., Saban, K. and Lanasa, J.M. (2000) Organizing the Competitive Intelligence Function: A Benchmarking Study, *Competitive Intelligence Review*, 11(1):17–27.

Lambe C.J. and Spekman R.E. (1997) Alliances, External Technology Acquisition, and Discontinuous Technological Change, *Journal of Product Innovation Management*, 14(2):102–116.

Lane, D.A. and Maxfield, R. (1997) Foresight, Complexity and Strategy, in Arthur, Durlauf and Lane, eds., *The Economy as a Complex Evolving System 2*, Addison-Wesley, Redwood City, CA.

Larwood L., Falbe C.M., Kriger M.P. and Miesing P. (1995) Structure and Meaning of Organizational Vision, *Academy of Management Journal* 38(3):740–769.

Laszlo E. (1996) *Evolution: The General Theory*, Hampton Press, New York.

Leifer R. and Triscari T. (1987) Research versus Development: Differences and Similarities, *IEEE Transactions on Engineering Management*, 34:71–78.

Lempert R.J., Popper S.W. and Bankes S.C. (2003) *Shaping the Next One Hundred Years: New Methods for Quantitative Long-Term Policy Analysis*, The RAND Pardee Center, Santa Monica, CA.

Lichtenthaler U. (2008) Open Innovation in Practice: An Analysis of Strategic Approaches to Technology Transactions, *IEEE Transactions on Engineering Management*, 55:148–157.

Lichtenthaler U. (2009) Absorptive Capacity, Environmental Turbulence, and the Complementarity of Organizational Learning Processes, *Academy of Management Journal*, 52:822–846.

Lindberg C. and Herzog A. (1998) Life at the Edge of Chaos, *Physician Executive*, 24(1):526–544.

Linneman R.E. and Klein H.E. (1983) Using Scenarios in Strategic Decision Making, *Business Horizons*, 28(1):64–74.

Longanesi, L. (1947) *Parliamo dell'elefante*, Longanesi, Milano.

Longo G. (2001) *Homo technologicus*, Meltemi, Roma.

Longo G. (2003) *Il simbionte. Prove di umanità futura*, Meltemi, Roma.

Lorenz, E.N. (1963) Deterministic Nonperiodic Flow, *Journal of the Atmospheric Sciences*, 20(2):130–141.

Marion R. and Uhl-Bien M. (2001) Leadership in Complex Organizations, *The Leadership Quarterly* 12:389–418.

Martin B.R. (1995) Foresight in Science and Technology, *Technology Analysis & Strategic Management*, 7(2):139–168.

Masini E. (2006) Rethinking Futures Studies, *Futures*, 38(10):1158–1168.

May R.C., Stewart W.J. and Sweo R. (2000) Environmental Scanning Behavior in a Transitional Economy: Evidence from Russia, *Academy of Management Journal*, 43(3):403–427.

McHale J. (1978) The Emergence of Futures Research, in Fowles J. (Ed.) *Handbook of Futures Research*, Greenwood Press, Westport, 5–16.

McMaster M. (1999) Foresight: Exploring the Structure of the Future, *Long Range Planning*, 29(2):149–155.

Meadows D.H., Meadows D.L., Randers J. and Behrens W.W. (1972) *The Limits to Growth a Report for the Club of Rome's Project on the Predicament of Mankind*, Universe Books, New York.

Mendonça S., Pina e Cunha M., Kaivo-oja J. and Ruff F. (2004) Wild Cards, Weak Signals and Organisational Improvisation, *Futures*, 36:201–218.

Mercier L.S. (1771) *An 2440 in L'anno 2440 di Louis-Sébastien Mercier*, Laura Tundo, (ed.), 1993, Dedalo, Bari, Italy.

Mietzner D. and Reger G. (2005) Advantages and Disadvantages of Scenario Approaches for Strategic Foresight, *International Journal of Technology Intelligence Planning*, 1(2):220–230.

Miles I. (1999) Foresight and Services: Closing the Gap? *Service Industry Journal*, 19(2):1–27.

Miles R.E. and Snow C.C. (1994) *Fit, Failure and the Hall of Fame: How Companies Succeed Or Fail*, The Free Press, New York.

Miller D. (1992) Environmental Fit versus Internal Fit, *Organisation Science*, 3(2):59–78.

Mintzberg H. (1979) *The Structuring of Organizations*, Prentice-Hall, Englewood Cliffs NJ.

Mitchell W. and Singh K. (1993). Death of the Lethargic: Effects of Expansion into New Technical Subfields of an Industry on Performance in a Firm's Base Business, *Organization Science*, 4(2):152–180.

Morel B. and Ramanujam R. (1999) Through the Looking Glass of Complexity: The Dynamics of Organizations as Adaptive and Evolving Systems. *Organization Science*, 10(3):278–293.

Morrison E.W. and Milliken F.J. (2000) Organizational Silence: A Barrier to Change and Development in a Pluralistic Worl, *The Academy of Management Review*, 25(4): 706–725.

Müller A. (2006) Strategic Foresight in Companies, PhD Thesis, University of St. Gallen, St. Gallen, Switzerland.

Mureika J.R., Dyer C.C. and Cupchik G.C. (2005) On Multifractal Structure in Non-Representational Art, *Physics Review*, arXiv:physics/0506063, E72.

Negroponte N. (1996) *Being Digital*, Alfred A. Knopf, Inc., New York.

Nobelius D. (2004) Towards the Sixth Generation of R&D Management, *International Journal of Project Management*, 22:369–375.

Nutt P.C. (2007) Intelligence Gathering For Decision Making, *Omega – The International Journal of Management Science*, 35(5):604–622.

O'Connor G.C. and DeMartino R. (2007) Organizing For Radical Innovation: An Exploratory Study of the Structural Aspects of RI Management Systems in Large Established Firms, *Journal of Product Innovation Management*, 23(6):475–497.

OECD Factbook 2005 (2005), OECD, Paris.

Olson E.E. and Eoyang G.H. (2001) *Facilitating Organization Change. Lessons from Complexity Science*, Jossey-Bass/Pfeiffer, San Francisco.

O'Reilly C.A. and Tuschman M.L. (2004) The Ambidextrous Organization, *Harvard Business Review*, 82:74–83.

Patton K.M. (2005) The Role of Scanning in Open Intelligence Systems, *Technological Forecasting and Social Change*, 72(9):1082–1093.

Pascale R.T. (1999) Surfing the Edge of Chaos, *MIT Sloan Management Review*, 40(3):83–94.

Peters T. (1992) *Liberation Management: Necessary Disorganization for the Nanosecond Nineties*, Macmillan, London.

Peters T. (2006) *Re-imagine! Business Excellence in a Disruptive Age*, Penguin, London.

Phillips W., Noke H., Bessant J. and Lamming R. (2006) Beyond the Steady State: Managing Discontinuous Product and Process Innovation, *International Journal of Innovation Management*, 10(2):175–196.

Pittaway L. et al. (2004) Networking and Innovation: A Systematic Review of the Evidence, *International Journal of Management Reviews*, 5–6(4–5):137–168.

Popper K. (1934) *Logik der Forschung, first published in English as The Logic of Scientific Discovery*, Hutchinson & Co., 1959.

Porritt J. (2005) *Making the Net Work: Sustainable Development in a Digital Society*, Stylus Publishing, Sterling VA.

Porter A.L., Ashton B., Clar G., Coates J.F., Cuhls K., Cunningham S.W., Ducatel K., Van der Duin P., Georghiou L., Gordon T., Linstone H., Marchau V., Massari G., Miles I., Mogee M., Salo A., Scapolo F., Smits R., Thissen W. (2004) Technology Futures Analysis: Toward Integration of the Field and New Methods, *Technological Forecasting and Social Change*, 71(3):287–303.

Porter M. (1985) Technology and Competitive Advantage. *Journal of Business Strategy*, 5(3):60–78.

Porter M. (1996) What Is Strategy? *Harvard Business Review*, 74:61–78.

Porter M. (2004) *Techniques for Analyzing Industries and Competitors*, Simon & Schuster, New York.

Postma T. and Liebl F. (2005) How to Improve Scenario Analysis as a Strategic Management Tool?, *Technological Forecasting and Social Change*, 72:161–173.

Prahalad K. and Hamel G. (1990) The Core Competencies of the Corporation, *Harvard Business Review*, 68(3):79–91.

Preble J. (1988) The Selection of Delphi Panels for Strategic Planning Purposes, *Strategic Management Journal*, 5(2):157–170

Prensky, M. (2001) *Digital Natives, Digital Immigrants, On the Horizon*, 9(5):1–6.

Prigogine I. and Stengers I. (1990) *La querelle du déterminisme, six ans après*, La querelle du déterminisme, Gallimard, coll.

Raisch S. et al. (2009) Organizational Ambidexterity: Balancing Exploitation and Exploration for Sustained Performance, *Organisation Science*, 20(4):685–695.

Rasetti M. (2007) Complessità: sfide e confini della nuova scienza, Convegno Conoscere la complessità, CSI Piemonte, Torino 22–23 November 2007.

Ratcliffe J. (2006) Challenges for Corporate Foresight: Strategic Prospective through Scenario Thinking. Foresight Management in Corporations and Public Organizations New Visions for Sustainability Conference, Helsinki, Finland, 10 June, 2005.

Reger G. (2001) Technology Foresight in Companies: From an Indicator to a Network and Process Perspective, *Technology Analysis & Strategic Management*, 13(4):533–553.

Reger G. (2004) Coordinating Globally Dispersed Research Centres of Excellence – The Case of Philips Electronics, *Journal of International Management*, 10: 51–76.

Rochlin, G.I. (1993) Defining High-Reliability Organizations in Practice: A Taxonomic Prolegomenon, in K. H. Roberts (ed.), *New Challenges to Understanding Organizations*, Macmillan, New York.

Rohrbeck R. (2008) Harnessing a Network of Experts for Competitive Advantage – Technology Scouting in the ICT Industry, *R&D Management*, 40(20):169–180.

Rohrbeck R. (2010) *Corporate Foresight: Towards a Maturity Model for the Future Orientation of a Firm*, Physica-Verlag, Springer, Heidelberg and New York.

Rohrbeck R. (2011) Best-Practices in Corporate Foresight. In: *Corporate Foresight. Contributions to Management Science*, Physica, Heidelberg. pp. 123–175.

Rohrbeck R. and Gemünden H.G. (2008) Strategic Foresight in Multinational Enterprises: Building a Best-Practice Framework from Case Studies, R&D Management Conference 2008: Emerging Methods in R&D Management, Ottawa, Canada.

Rohrbeck R. et al. (2009) Benchmarking Report: Strategic Foresight in Multinational Companies, European Corporate Foresight Group.

Roll M. (2004) *Strategische Frühaufklärung: Vorbereitung auf eine ungewisse Zukunft am Beispiel des Luftverkehrs*, Dt. Univ.-Verlag, Wiesbaden.

Rothwell, R. (1992) Successful Industrial Innovation: Critical Factors for the 1990s, *R&D Management*, 22(3):221–240.

Roveda C. and Vecchiato R. (2006) Foresight in the Context of Industrial Clusters: The Case of Italian Districts. Presented at the Second International Seville Seminar on Future-Oriented Technology Analysis: Impact of FTA Approaches on Policy and Decision-Making, Seville, Spain, September 2006.

Ruff F. (2006) Corporate Foresight: Integrating the Future Business Environment into Innovation and Strategy, *International Journal of Technology Management*, 34(3,4):278–295.

Saffo, P. (2007) Six rules for effective forecasting, *Harvard Business Review*, 85(7–8):122–131.

Schmenner R. (1988) The Merit of Making Things Fast, *MIT Sloan Management Review*, 30(1):11.

Schumpeter J. (1994) [1942]. *Capitalism, Socialism and Democracy*, Routledge, London, pp. 82-83.

Schwarz J.O. (1991) *The Future of Futures Studies: A Delphi Study with a German Perspective*, Shaker Verlag, Aachen.

Schwarz J.O. (2005) Pitfalls in Implementing a Strategic Early Warning System, *Foresight* 7(4):22–30.

Schwarz J.O. (2008) Assessing the Future of Futures Studies in Management, *Futures*, 40(3):237–246.

Scifo G. (2002) *Complessità e caos nel marketing*, Seminari AISM 2001/2002.

Segerstahl B. and Kroemer G. (1989) Policy Responses to Large Accidents, *Proceedings of the Conference on Policy Responses to Large Accidents, IIASA*, 16–17 January 1989.

Shrivastava P. and Grant R. (1985) Empirically Derived Models of Strategic Decision-Making Processes, *Strategic Management Journal*, 6(2):97–113.

Sifonis J. and Goldberg B. (1996) *Corporation on a Tightrope: Balancing Leadership, Governance and Technology in an Age of Complexity*, Oxford University Press, New York.

Sinatra A. (1989) *Impresa e sistema competitive: strategie di innovazione e strategie di consolidamento*, UTET, Torino.

Slaughter R.A. (1996a) Foresight Beyond Strategy: Social Initiatives by Business and Government, *Long Range Planning*, 29(2):156–163.

Slaughter R.A. (1996b) Futures Studies – From Individual to Social Capacity, *Futures*, 28(8):751–762.

Slaughter R.A. (2004) *Futures Beyond Dystopia – Creating Social Foresight*, RoutledgeFalmer, London.

Smart, J. (2005) How to be a Tech Futurist. Presentation given to University of Advancing Technology. Retrieved from http://accelerating.org/presentations/Tech-Futurist(6.05).ppt.

Stacey R.D. (1992) *Managing the Unknowable: Strategic Boundaries Between Order and Chaos in Organizations*, Jossey-Bass, San Francisco.

Stadler C. (2011) *Enduring Success*, Stanford University Press, Stanford.

Stalk G., Evans P. and Schulman L.E. (1992) Competing on Capabilities: The New Rules of Corporate Strategy, *Harvard Business Review*, 70(2):57–70.

Stalk J. (1988) Time – The Next Source of Competitive Advantage, Harvard Business Case Services, 11 pages.

Steinle C., Ahlers F. and Rutter C. (2000) Zukunftsforschung und Strategieentwicklung in Finanzdienstleistungsunternehmungen: Konzept, empirisches Schlaglicht und Gestaltungsoptionen, *Kredit und Kapital*, 4:571–604.

Stevens G.A. and Burley J. (2003) Piloting the Rocket of Radical Innovation, *Research Technology Management*, 46(2):16–25.

St. Augustine (398) *The Confessions.*

Taleb N. (2008) *The Black Swan: The Impact of the Highly Improbable*, Random House, New York.

Tapscott D. (2008) *Grown Up Digital: How the Net Generation Is Changing Your World*, McGraw-Hill, New York.

Taylor R.P., Spehar B., Donkelaar P. and Hagerhall C.M. (2011) Perceptual and Physiological Responses to Jackson Pollock's Fractals, *Frontiers of Human Neuroscience*, 5:60.

Thamhain H.J. (2003) Managing Innovative R&D Teams, *R&D Management*, 33:297–311.

Tidd J., Bessant J. and Pavitt K. (1997) *Managing Innovation: Integrating Technological, Market and Organizational Change*, John Wiley & Sons, Chichester.

Tornatzky L. and Fleischer M. (1990) *The Process of Technology Innovation*, Lexington Books, Lexington, MA.

Tsoukas H. and Shepherd J. (2004) *Managing the Future: Foresight in the Knowledge Economy*, Blackwell, Malden MA.

Tuschman M.L. and O'Reilly C.A. (1996) Ambidextrous Organizations: Managing Evolutionary and Revolutionary Change, *California Management Review*, 38(4):8–30.

Tuschman M.L., Virany B. and Romanelli E. (1985) Executive Succession, Strategic Reorientations, and Organization Evolution – The Minicomputer Industry as a Case in Point, *Technology Society*, 7(2–3):297–313.

UNIDO (1995) Report on Technology Foresight.

Upton D. (1994) The Management of Manufacturing Flexibility, *California Management Review*, 36(2):72–89.

Utterback J.M., (1994) *Mastering the Dynamics of Innovation*, Harvard Business School Press, Boston.

Van der Duin P.A. (2006) *Qualitative Futures Research for Innovation*, Eburon, Delft.

Van der Heijden K. (2004) Can Internally Generated Futures Accelerate Organizational Learning? *Foresight* 36(2):145–159.

Van der Steen M., Van Twist M., van der Vlist M. and Demkes R. (2010) Integrating Futures Studies with Organizational Development: Design Options for the Scenario Project RWS2020, *Futures*, in press.

van Nierop O.A., Blankendaal A.C.M. and Overbeeke C.J. (1997) The Evolution of the Bicycle: A Dynamic Systems Approach, *Journal of Design History*, 3:253–267.

van Notten, P.W.F., Sleegers, A.M. and van Asselt, M.B.A. (2005) The Future Shocks: On the Role of Discontinuity in Scenario Development, *Technological Forecasting and Social Change*, 72:175–194.

Vecchiato R. and Roveda C. (2010) Strategic Foresight in Corporate Organizations: Handling the Effect and Response Uncertainty of Technology and Social Drivers of Change, *Technological Forecasting and Social Change*.

Veen W. (2002) *Celebrating Homo Zappiens: Adapting to New Ways of Learning Using ICT*, Delft University of Technology, the Netherlands.

Venkatraman N. (1989) The Concept of Fit in Strategy Research: Toward Verbal and Statistical Correspondence, *Academy of Management Review*, 14:423–444.

Vicari S. (1998) *La creatività dell'impresa: tra caso e necessità*, Etas.

Virilio P. (1999) La velocità assoluta. Interview on *Mediamente* (Italian TV programme).

Volberda H.W. (1998) *Building the Flexible Firm: How to Remain Competitive*, Oxford University Press, Oxford.

Von der Gracht H.A., Vennemann C. and Darkow I.L. (2010) Corporate Foresight and Innovation Management: A Portfolio-Approach in Evaluating Organizational Development, *Futures*, 42(4):380–393.

Von Zedtwitz, M., Gassmann, O. and Boutellier, R. (2004) Organizing Global R&D: Challenges and Dilemmas, *Journal of International Management*, 10(1):21–49.

Wack P. (1985) Scenarios: Shooting the Rapids, *Harvard Business Review*, Nov.–Dec., 139–150.

Weick K.E. (1979) *The Social Psychology of Organizing*, Addison-Wesley, Reading MA.

Weick K.E. and Sutcliffe K.M. (2001) *Managing the Unexpected – Assuring High Performance in an Age of Complexity*, Jossey-Bass, San Francisco.

Weick K. and Sutcliffe K. (2007) *Managing the Unexpected: Resilient Performance in an Age of Uncertainty*, Jossey Bass, San Francisco.

Weiser M. (1991) The Computer for the 21st Century, *Scientific American*, 265(9):66–75.

Whatmore J. (2002) What Will Research and Development/Innovation Be Like in Five Years Time?, *Foresight*, 4(2):7–9.

Wheatley M. (1994) *Leadership and the New Science: Learning about Organisation from a Disorderly Universe*, Berrett-Koehler, San Francisco.

Whitehead A.N. (1933) *Adventures of Ideas*, The Macmillan Company, New York.

Wilkinson A. (2014) OECD, presentation given at School of International Futures.

Wolff M.F. (1992) Scouting for Technology, *Research Technology Management*, 35(2):10–12.

Zahra S.A. and George G. (2002) Absorptive Capacity: A Review, *Reconceptualization, and Extension, Academy of Management Review*, 27:185–203.

Zander I. (1999) How Do You Mean "Global"? An Empirical Investigation of Innovation Networks in Multinational Corporations, *Research Policy*, 28(2–3):195–213.

Index

Printed in the United States
By Bookmasters